JEWISH TERRORISM IN ISRAEL

COLUMBIA STUDIES IN **TERRORISM AND IRREGULAR WARFARE**

COLUMBIA STUDIES IN **TERRORISM AND IRREGULAR WARFARE**
Bruce Hoffman, Series Editor

This series seeks to fill a conspicuous gap in the burgeoning literature on terrorism, guerrilla warfare, and insurgency. The series adheres to the highest standards of scholarship and discourse and publishes books that elucidate the strategy, operations, means, motivations, and effects posed by terrorist, guerrilla, and insurgent organizations and movements. It thereby provides a solid and increasingly expanding foundation of knowledge on these subjects for students, established scholars, and informed reading audiences alike.

Ami Pedahzur, *The Israeli Secret Services and the Struggle Against Terrorism*

AMI PEDAHZUR & ARIE PERLIGER **JEWISH**
TERRORISM IN ISRAEL

COLUMBIA UNIVERSITY PRESS   NEW YORK

COLUMBIA UNIVERSITY PRESS
Publishers Since 1893

NEW YORK   CHICHESTER, WEST SUSSEX

COPYRIGHT © 2009 COLUMBIA UNIVERSITY PRESS

Library of Congress Cataloging-in-Publication Data

Pedahzur, Ami.

Jewish terrorism in Israel / Ami Pedahzur and Arie Perliger.

p.   cm.—(Columbia studies in terrorism and irregular warfare)

Includes bibliographical references and index.

ISBN 978-0-231-15446-8 (cloth : alk. paper)—ISBN 978-0-231-52075-1 (ebook)

1. Terrorism—Palestine—History—20th century. 2. Terrorism—Palestine—History. 3. Violence—Political aspects—Israel. 4. Political violence—Religious aspects—Judaism. 5. Jews—Palestine—Political activity. 6. Jews—Israel—Political activity. 7. Arab-Israeli conflict—Influence. I. Perliger, Arie. II. Title. III. Series.

HV6433.I75P473 2009

363.325095694—dc22   2009011597

PRINTED IN THE UNITED STATES OF AMERICA

C 10 9 8 7 6 5 4 3 2 1
P 10 9 8 7 6 5 4 3 2 1

BOOK DESIGN BY **MARTIN N. HINZE**

CONTENTS

PREFACE ix

Life in the Counterculture
The Catastrophic Event
The Dynamic and Causes of Radicalization
Method
Book Structure

ONE **ANCIENT AND MODERN HISTORY** 1
The Founding Myths

Hasmoneans
Terrorism in Jerusalem
Jewish Political Activism in the Nineteenth
and Twentieth Centuries

TWO **EARLY AND MID-TWENTIETH CENTURY** 10
Ethno-Religious Terrorism

The Split Between the Etzel and the Lehi
The Assassination of Lord Moyne
From the Season to the United Resistance Movement
The Partition Plan
The Assassination of Israel Kastner
Kingdom of Israel (the Tzrifin Underground)
Brit Hakanaim (Covenant of the Zealots)

THREE **THE CAMP DAVID ACCORDS** 38
The Struggle over the Promised Land

The Attack on the Mayors
The Crisis of the Camp David Accords

The Jewish Underground
The Founding Clique
Vengeance
Removing the Abomination
The Massacre at the Islamic College
The Exposure of the Network and Conclusions

FOUR MEIR KAHANE AND THE KACH MOVEMENT 69
Jews Against Israelis

Hebron Then and Now
From Jewish Defense League to Kahanist Counterculture
Early Days
Yoel Lerner
The Modern Hasmonean Revolt
The Struggle in Sinai
TNT
The Committee for the Safety of the Roads
The Disciples
God of Vengeance

FIVE THE ASSASSINATION OF YITZHAK RABIN 98

The Vengeance Underground
The Yigal Amir Group
The Plot
Formation of the Network

SIX THE SECOND INTIFADA 111
Vengeance

The Hilltop Youth
The Bat Ayin Group
The Withdrawal from Gaza
Gush Katif
Sa Nur
Kfar Tapuach
Amona

SEVEN **ECCENTRIC CULTS, VENGEANCES, AND LONE WOLVES** 138

Uzi Meshulam Cult

The Jerusalem Groups: The Ein Kerem Group and the Lifta Gang

Spontaneous Vengeance

Interim Summary: The Exceptional Groups

Mental Health and External Events

Vengeance, Counterculture, and Mental Disturbances

The Lone Avengers

The Mindset of the Lone Wolves

EIGHT **IN THE NAME OF GOD, THE PEOPLE, AND THE LAND** 159
Reassessment of the Causes of Jewish Terrorism

Comparing Jewish Terrorism with Other Manifestations
of Religious Terrorism

Concluding Remarks: Looking Ahead

GLOSSARY 171

CHRONOLOGY OF ATTACKS AND EVENTS RELATED TO JEWISH
TERRORISM 175

NOTES 193

INDEX 227

The fact that many of those responsible for the pervasive wave of terrorism in recent decades have acted in the name of religion has generated an academic debate, which has focused on the direct responsibility of religions in general and Islam in particular in the perpetration of political violence.[1] The primordial approach, recently also called the cultural approach,[2] has been presented in works that have claimed that the very differences between religions, and the intolerant and exclusive nature of religious frameworks, have led them to a course of violent conflict.[3] Theological studies that have adopted this approach and explored the justifications for violence in the Old and New Testaments, the Koran, and other religious texts[4] have been met with wide-ranging criticism.[5] As a result, an alternative approach has evolved, based on the premise that the real conditions for terrorism are to be found in the struggle for resources, territory, or political influence and that religion in itself is not the most prominent cause of violence. According to this approach, terrorism is initiated by hierarchical organizations whose leaders carry out cost–benefit analyses and use violence as long as it helps them achieve the goals of their struggle.[6]

Both approaches offer some very important insights. However, over the years they have become somewhat dogmatic and lost a large amount of their explanatory power. The claims of the first can be discounted by the fact that religious terrorist groups have always been in the minority and, indeed, have made up less than 15 percent of all terrorist groups active in the twentieth century.[7] Furthermore, a great part of religious terrorism derives from intrareligious struggles, not from intercommunity conflicts.[8] The many cases in which different religious communities exist under the same political framework in the absence of violent conflict also highlights the incompatibility of the primordial approach. The assertions of the second approach, which is heavily based on theories of rational choice, stand on shaky ground. A large proportion of the groups that have carried out the last wave of terrorism cannot be characterized as hierarchical, and they correspond more closely to the definition of horizontal social networks.[9] In addition, attempts to empirically prove that terrorists have used violence in a calculated manner with the aim of freeing occupied territory or promoting other such political objectives have not received full support.[10] Furthermore, researchers have often interpreted the motivations of the terrorists in direct contradiction to the declarations and intentions of the terrorists themselves;[11] in other cases, they have been forced to admit that they were not able to identify the motives behind the use of terrorism except for the religious one.[12]

Given the inability of the approaches presented here to exclusively define the relationship between religion and political violence in general and fundamentalist terrorism in particular, we will offer an alternative framework for explaining the phenomenon. This framework focuses on the analysis of the sociological and cultural conditions that contribute to the radicalization of communities and the socialization processes among peers that eventually lead to the formation of terrorist cells.

LIFE IN THE COUNTERCULTURE

Totalistic ideologies are based on an absolute division of humanity into dual categories such as saved versus damned, godly versus demonic, and dark forces versus light forces. The psychology of totalism features the impulse to validate an absolute worldview by confronting demonized exemplars of evil as contrasting symbols.[13] Ideologies possessing a religious strain in particular provide the infrastructure for the development of a counterculture.[14] Subcultures, including religious ones, which accept the dominant culture in a given society, perhaps adding to it a series of beliefs and rituals that are shared by a community of believers, most often pose no threat to the cultural pillars of the society. However, a counterculture encapsulates the values and behavioral norms of a group that run counter to those of the current social mainstream.[15] On the whole, people committed to a certain worldview that stands in opposition to other cultures tend to join closed communities or social groups where they can live according to their chosen way of life with minimal and controlled exposure to outside influences.[16] Sharing a common physical space intensifies the effect of the counterculture on members of the community and their children. Ongoing ceremonial communication between them strengthens their belief in the righteousness of their path, their social cohesion, and their willingness to sacrifice personal resources for the collective and their faith.[17]

THE CATASTROPHIC EVENT

The mere existence of a counterculture community whose behaviors and norms represent a clear break from mainstream practices will not necessarily lead to terrorism. Crossing the line from objection to the values and ways of other cultures to an attempt to inflict harm on them involves two stages. The first is the occurrence of an external event that poses a potential threat to the community or its most cherished values. The second is community leaders framing the event as catastrophic.

Countercultures with members who hold totalistic worldviews are led by intermediaries, in many cases clerics, who are most often charismatic leaders.[18] Ordinarily these leaders are entrusted with translating the abstract ideals found in the holy texts of the community into concrete commands and disseminating them among its members. The intermediaries provide community members with all-encompassing answers to questions that occupy all people, from personal quandaries about existential matters to practical dilemmas having to do with everyday affairs. The determination that characterizes a totalistic ideology and those responsible for its interpretation leaves little space for critical thinking.[19] Any hesitation is taken for heresy, and competing worldviews are demonized and framed as endeavoring to deliberately destroy the culture that is following the "path of righteousness."[20] Accordingly, any threat to members of the community or its way of life will be perceived by its members as a potential catastrophic event. In situations like these, the importance of their leaders only increases, and if leaders magnify the perception of threat and call for a war "between the forces of light and the forces of darkness," the slide into violence by some community members will be unavoidable.[21]

THE DYNAMIC AND CAUSES OF RADICALIZATION

Who are the members of the counterculture who have crossed the line and taken the path of terrorism? First, we are speaking of people who have extremely high levels of identification with the community and commitment to its values. For them aggression, or even the threat of aggression, against the community's values or against one of its adherents is justification for a violent struggle. This total commitment is a result of an intensive interaction that takes place within primordial social groups that evolve mostly at workplaces, educational frameworks, or places of residence.[22] The group dynamic deepens the level of mutual obligation among its members. The same socialization process is also used as a catalyst for increasing the alienation of group members toward the laws and values of the mainstream culture and for further demonizing the enemy to the point where violence becomes almost unavoidable.[23] In addition, group members learn about the practical aspects of carrying out violent actions.[24] Second, people must enjoy a high level of biographical availability in order to take part in terrorist attacks.[25] Weak commitment to other frameworks allows them to spend more time with their comrades, increasing the intensity of their radicalism and internalization of violent practices. Third, in most cases, not all members of a radicalized social network will actually take part in a terrorist attack. Many reasons that prompt people to partake in terrorism have been documented. We broadly categorize these as crises. Crises include personal loss of loved ones or close peers in the community, a loss of status in the community or peer group, and a crisis stemming from a perceived assault on the person's or community's beliefs and way of life. This category excludes causes such as psychological disorders. Although we accept the fact that there are cases in which people engaged in political violence because of a mental disorder, we believe that they represent a small minority and that the same violent behavior would have eventually manifested in other areas.

METHOD

Because the subject of this book is terrorism, and because we did not want to extend the scope of this research to other manifestations of political protest and violence, the selection of the groups and acts of terrorism that are the focus of this book requires a clear and concise definition of Jewish terrorism. It is well known that one feature of the academic study of the field of terrorism is the great difficulty in drawing its boundaries. Nevertheless, in order to determine which cases should be included in this study, we have relied on four prominent distinctions that appear in the majority of conventional definitions of terrorism.[26] First, terrorism involves the use of violence. Second, there is a political motive that activates the violence. Third, there is an intention to strike fear among the victims and their community. Finally, the victims of terrorism are civilians or noncombatants.

This also includes victims who may belong to the security forces but are not on duty or engaged in formal operational activity.

Terrorism is a problematic field to study. It is hard to interview terrorists in a neutral environment that enables free discussion. Furthermore, most documents that are released either by the terrorists or by the governments that fight them are biased and often serve as tools in the psychological war between these adversaries. Therefore most scholars tend to rely on secondary sources. The case of Jewish terrorism in Israel enables us to overcome some of these methodological obstacles. We have been researching Jewish terrorism for more than ten years, during which we have gathered thousands of official documents, mostly court protocols,[27] interviewed twenty-five former terrorists, politicians, and spiritual leaders as well as law enforcement officials,[28] and conducted six comprehensive surveys of the communities where terrorist groups originated, which included more than 4,800 respondents.[29] Based on the information compiled from the documents, interviews, secondary sources, and surveys, we have been able to put together a historical mosaic of Jewish terrorism in Palestine and later in the State of Israel.

To test our main hypotheses we created three databases. The first includes detailed information on each of the 309 Jewish terrorist attacks perpetrated in Palestine and the State of Israel between 1932 and 2008.[30] The second is a biographical dataset of the 224 people who have taken part in the terrorist attacks,[31] and the third describes the type of ties between the members of each of the Jewish terrorist networks.

The importance of the latter dataset is that it enabled us to perform a social network analysis. We will analyze the types of ties inside the networks, how they are constructed and maintained, and how they influence recruitment into groups. Moreover, we will try to understand how the structure of the network has a direct effect on its activities. For example, we will examine how the existence or nonexistence of different subgroups in the network affects its ability to survive and its target selection, whether there is competition between subgroups, and how this affects network activity. We also will try to expose the network by detecting its main actors and uncovering their motives—the main motivation beyond Jewish terrorism networks. Finally, we will try to understand the networks' relationship with the surrounding environment by examining whether networks need collective support for their long-term survival, as some sociological theories claim.[32] Sociological convention argues that this type of support transforms membership in the network into a source of status, identity, cohesion, and self-esteem and provides a sense of belonging for members.[33]

Therefore, unlike the two first datasets, which were instrumental in the description and aggregate analysis of the attributes of those events or actors who make up the research population, the network analysis enabled us to map out and analyze the system of ties between the various actors and the ways in which these ties affected their activities.[34]

We argue that religious terrorism is not a one-faith phenomenon. In fact, identical patterns of radicalization and the uses of terrorism can be traced to any counterculture that adheres to a totalistic ideology, be it religious or secular. The wealth of information we have gathered and the in-depth look into processes that take place in countercultures, groups, and even on the individual level in the case of Jewish terrorism in Israel allow us to shed light on similar processes in other radicalized communities around the world that so far have been a puzzle to researchers and public alike.

BOOK STRUCTURE

The book is structured around two axes: analytical and chronological. Considering that any discussion about current Jewish terrorism cannot be complete without historical perspectives about the origins of Jewish violence, Chapters 1 and 2 present a review of political violence in Jewish history before the establishment of the State of Israel and in the early years of its existence. Chapters 3 and 4 address the cases of terrorist groups that have branched off from the two streams of the Israeli religious right and were active in the same period after the Six Day War in 1967 but nevertheless remained ideologically distinct. Specifically, these were the Gush Emunim stream, which engendered the Jewish Underground, and the Kahanist stream, which produced groups such as the TNT network. Chapter 5 investigates the manner in which Jewish terrorist groups that were active in the 1990s integrated elements from previous streams. We introduce the network that was responsible for the assassination of Prime Minister Yitzhak Rabin after the signing of the Oslo Accords. Chapter 6 presents the period of the second Palestinian intifada. Here, we give special attention to the groups that emerged from a new counterculture, that of the hilltop youth. This chapter, which is based on field research we conducted among the settlers of the occupied territories in the summer of 2005, also describes the events before and after the withdrawal from the settlements in Gaza and the West Bank at that time. Chapter 7 tells the stories of groups and lone wolves whose actions fell beyond the boundaries of the theoretical framework presented here. We try to investigate the motives behind these actions and why the perpetrators decided to take an individual path, differing from that of the more common manifestations of Jewish terrorism. In the concluding chapter we offer a comparison between Jewish terrorism and other manifestations of religious terrorism and test the power of our theory beyond the Israeli case.

███████████████

IN CONTEMPORARY DISCUSSIONS of insurgencies and terrorism, very few mention the fact that one of the first manifestations of terrorism can be traced back to the second century B.C.E. It occurred during Hellenistic rule in ancient Israel, which began in 332 B.C.E. with the occupation of the country by Alexander the Great and continued under his Hellenist successors, the Ptolemies and Seleucids, until 160 B.C.E. Those who often refer to this historical period are contemporary Jewish terrorists who admire the heroism of the ancient Jewish militants and aspire to follow their example.

HASMONEANS

The most prominent Jewish group to use organized violence in the Second Temple era was the Hashmonai (Hasmonean) family. For the sake of historical justice, it is important to note that the Hashmonaim conducted an ongoing campaign of guerrilla warfare against Hellenistic rule in Israel, and terrorism was only a small part of their arsenal of strategies. The foremost incident of terrorism to be carried out by the Hashmonaim was the murder of Apelles, a Hellenistic envoy. He had been sent to their town, Modi'in, in order to ensure that the assimilation policy of Antiochus IV (Epiphanes), who sought to impose a Hellenistic lifestyle on the Jews, was carried out according to the letter of the law.[1]

Despite the great historical gulf between the Hashmonai revolt and contemporary Jewish terrorism, it is hard not to be impressed by the similarity of the factors responsible for the violence and the fashion in which it developed. The murder of Apelles and his aides by Mattityahu (Mattathias) the Hashmonai did not occur in a vacuum. It was preceded by a major crisis that threatened the resources most highly valued by the Hashmonaim and many other Jews. Until the advent of Hellenistic rule, the Jews in Israel enjoyed extensive autonomy, although they were not sovereigns of their country. One of the central aspects of this autonomy was its religious and cultural freedom. The limited involvement of the various empires in the Jewish lifestyle helped make it feasible for the city of Jerusalem to prosper and for the Temple to become a spiritual and social center for the Jewish inhabitants of Israel.[2] In 218 B.C.E., Israel was taken from the Ptolemies by Antiochus III of the Seleucid dynasty. During his rule, the status quo was essentially maintained; however, his successors, Seleucus IV and especially Antiochus IV (Epiphanes), were more devoted to the ideal of Hellenistic cultural uniformity among the peoples under the empire's sovereignty. Among other efforts, the Seleucids strove to remodel Jerusalem into a Greek polis.[3]

In addition to the desecration of the Jews' cardinal spiritual symbol, this policy also had far-reaching social implications. The urban and more established Jewish classes found the Hellenistic way of life and novel cultural richness to their liking.[4] The fact that many of them willingly assimilated these cultural distinctions brought them into closer political favor with the authorities and turned them into an elite with unique privileges. In this fashion, a new empire-sponsored Jewish aristocracy came into being that sought to instate a series of reforms in the lifestyle of all Jews in Israel, and the support of this aristocracy for a polis-like Jerusalem weakened its status as the heart of the Jewish experience.[5]

The new social structure led to great frustration among rural Jews, who were alienated by the Hellenistic practices and felt that the new elites had brought about forced changes in their way of life, including a decline in Orthodox Judaism. However, these collective feelings of deprivation and frustration remained latent until the actual implementation of reforms in the taxation system in Israel. In contrast to the prior method of collecting taxes, which was based on a uniform poll tax for the whole population, the Seleucids granted significant tax concessions to the urban elites and assigned them the role of collecting taxes from the rural Jews.[6] After filling the tax quotas that they were required to hand over to the authorities, these same elites were permitted to pocket the balance, a fact that encouraged a particularly effective tax collection. This divide-and-conquer policy only heightened the tension between the different Jewish groups.[7]

However, the tax reforms were not the only reason for the outbreak of violence. The Jewish periphery was aware that the Seleucid international status was not particularly robust. The defeat of Antiochus III at the hands of the Roman legions in the Battle of Magnesia transformed the Roman Empire into a main actor in the Middle East. Among the Jewish farmer families, there was a widespread feeling that the days of the Hellenistic Empire were numbered, and siding with the Romans would reverse the division of power between the different groups of Jewish society.[8]

Mattityahu and his five sons held political and spiritual status among the rural Jews. They hailed from a family of priests from the Levi tribe that dwelled in the city of Modi'in. Mattityahu's distinction as a priest, his charisma, and that of his sons made them natural leaders of the periphery. His cry after slaying Apelles, "Those for God, come with me," became deeply etched in the Jewish collective memory and remains a slogan of Israeli independence and rectitude.[9] However, despite the myths woven around him, Mattityahu's days as commander of the rebellion were numbered. He died in 165 B.C.E., one year after the fighting broke out, and his son Yehudah (Judah) assumed the role of leader. In Mattityahu's days, rebel actions focused mainly on killing Hellenized Jews and attacks on Jewish population centers where the Hellenistic culture had been assimilated. However, under the command of Yehudah, the rebels also developed guerrilla warfare capabilities. They specialized in clandestine nighttime raids on army camps and, using this method, struck hard at the Seleucid forces.[10] Yehudah was also blessed with political acumen; he was able to establish close ties with the Roman Empire and promote its interests in the region.

By means of his military accomplishments, and together with the political backing of the Roman Empire, Yehudah was able to secure partial religious autonomy for the Jews and even restore the status of the Temple in Jerusalem as the Jewish ritual center.[11] Yehudah was killed in Elasa in the year 160 B.C.E. as a result of a tactical error in a battle against a superior Seleucid force. Particularly important to our contention that the violence was the product of a social network is the fact that the command of the rebellion after his death was taken up by Yehudah's brothers Yonatan (Jonathan) Apphus and Shimon (Simon) Thassi. Although he was younger than Shimon, Yonatan displayed political skills similar to those of his deceased brother. He strengthened the Hashmonaim's ties with different groups in the Seleucid camp but not at the expense of the alliance with the Romans.[12] He made diplomatic advances toward Ptolemy VI in Egypt and even made contact with the Spartans in southern Greece. Yonatan's diplomatic skills accorded him unprecedented political clout that was manifested principally in the expansion of the Hashmonai sovereignty to extensive parts of ancient Israel. Yonatan's rule lasted nearly seventeen years, until he was arrested by Trifon, who sought to take control of the Seleucid kingdom and feared Yonatan's power. After Yonatan died, his elder brother Shimon took over the helm. Under his command, Judea became a near-sovereign entity; a monarchial dynasty was subsequently established and assumed control of Judea for more than 100 years.[13] The story of the Hashmonaim became a founding myth of the Jewish nation throughout history and ultimately became one of the cultural cornerstones of the renewed Zionist movement.

TERRORISM IN JERUSALEM

A little more than 100 years after the fall of the Hashmonai kingdom, relations between the Jewish residents of Israel and the sovereign Romans and non-Jewish residents in Israel reached an unprecedented low point. Once again, differences on the matter of both Jewish cultural autonomy and tax rates led to the collapse of relations. A wave of violence broke out in 66 C.E. in the city of Caesarea. Gessius Florus, the Roman procurator in Judea, was furious at the urban Jews for protesting against the taxes and decided to revoke their civilian status. This decision laid the groundwork for the eruption of street fights between the city's Jewish and non-Jewish residents, and unrest quickly spread to other mixed cities. The gradually mounting violence led many Jews to flee their cities of residence and seek refuge within the walls of Jerusalem; however, the bloodshed also breached the walls of the city. Whereas the more moderate Jewish streams, such as the Sadducees and the Pharisees,[14] sought to tone down the violence, groups of zealots viewed the events as an opportunity to whip up the flames of the rebellion against the Roman authorities. Florus's policy played straight into the hands of the zealots. In order to signal to the Jews that he would no longer tolerate their provocations, the Roman procurator dispatched army units to Jerusalem to help collect the Temple taxes.[15] The refusal of the Temple priests to accept the dictates of the Roman legions resulted in the massacre of 3,000 of the city's Jewish residents. The subsequent Jewish response took Florus by surprise. While one group of guerrilla fighters scaled Roman outposts on the mountain of Masada and slaughtered the legion soldiers stationed there, another group, led by the son of the high priest, Elazar Ben-Hananiah, attacked the legions positioned in Jerusalem and recaptured the Temple Mount and Lower City.[16] In the following months, Jewish insurgents were also active in the central and northern parts of the country, but their militias ultimately could not withstand the superiority of the Roman military might. In 73 C.E., the forces of the Roman emperor, Titus Flavius Vespasianus, were able to suppress the rebellion, and in this manner the era of the Second Temple reached its conclusion.[17]

Israeli students are taught in Jewish history lessons that the Second Temple was destroyed because of blind hatred (or causeless hatred, *sin'at khinam* in Hebrew). However, very few of these students know that behind this time-worn phrase lies the story of a fierce political dispute that led to the most dramatic episode of political terrorism in early Jewish history. The tempestuous period that preceded the rebellion provided a fertile breeding ground for extreme political groups in Jewish towns and villages that were based on social networks and had their roots in extended families. Each of these groups had its own distinct features. The zealots in the Jerusalem region, who were led by Elazar Ben Shimon and Zechariah Ben Avkulos, did not merely settle for a fight against the Roman legions but also directed their arrows at the priests who upheld the oligarchic rule. Therefore their decision to join forces with Yochanan of Gush Halav, who left the Galilee for Jerusalem with the intention of taking over the city, was not surprising.[18] The fight for control of Jerusalem was particularly brutal. Eight thousand inhabitants of the city lost their lives in the battles before Yochanan was able to gain control. However, Yochanan's reign did not usher in a period of peace. Another group of zealots from the Judea Desert, headed by Shimon Bar Giora, was called to the aid of Yochanan's opponents and set off for Jerusalem. Bar Giora's band of fighters came from the weakest economic sectors; class ideology was a main distinction of his group. Before their assault on Jerusalem, they were involved primarily in robbing and pillaging the property of the local aristocracy.[19] The struggle between Shimon and Yochanan in Jerusalem ended in a status quo. While the people from the Galilee shored up their control of the Upper City and the Temple Mount, the Judean group took over the Lower City. Both groups eventually joined forces but only when the Romans attacked Jerusalem. By this stage, the Jewish soldiers were so exhausted from their internecine fighting that they did not have the strength to withstand the power of the Roman legions.[20]

However, the group most pertinent to our discussion is the Sicarians. According to documented Jewish history, this sect was the first group to systematically engage in terrorism. It appears that, at least initially, it consisted of a social network that evolved from the extended family of Menachem and Yehudah Galili (father and son). The origin of the name of the sect is still a source of dispute. One school claims that they were named after the dagger (*sicca*), which they used to kill their opponents. Another school asserts that the origins of the name come from the Latin word *sicarius,* which means killer–assassin.[21]

Although there is evidence of their activities as early as the Hashmonai rebellion, the Sicarians took shape as a group with a clear political agenda only after the death of Herod.[22] The Sicarian worldview can be discerned even in the ideological fundamentals of Jewish terrorist associations nearly 2,000 years after the disappearance of the original sect. The Sicarians aspired towards the autonomous existence of the Jewish people and unreservedly opposed foreign rule. For them, this was a religious principle of the highest degree. Their basic guideline was that noncapitulation to a foreign ruler was one of the three cardinal *yehareg ubal yaavor* commandments, that is, a person must be willing to sacrifice his or her life rather than violate one of these directives.[23] They also believed that the redemption of the people of Israel was approaching, and as long as the Romans continued to rule, its coming would be delayed. This ideology had its practical implications for the Sicarians. Their violent provocations against the Roman authorities were intended to aggravate the tension between the foreign rule and the Jewish populace and intensify the oppression of the Jewish residents of the country. In this way, they hoped to bring about a chain reaction that would ultimately lead to a large-scale Jewish uprising. They also did not refrain from terrorizing moderate Jews who sought to prevent the situation from deteriorating into a major confrontation.[24]

Like other groups of zealots, the Sicarians engaged in guerrilla warfare, but at the same time they also perfected operational methods that can be equated with those of modern-day terrorist groups. Their principal operational tactics were political assassinations and kidnappings as bargaining chips. Sicarian perpetrators of assassinations were known for their great daring. On many occasions, assassinations were carried out in Jerusalem on holidays, when the city was swarming with pilgrims. The assassins mingled with the crowds of celebrators and stabbed their victims with small daggers in broad daylight.[25] In this fashion, the Sicarians murdered the High Priest Yonatan, who had tried to prevent the rebellion against the Romans, and later, during the course of the rebellion, they took the lives of the priest Hanan Ben Hanan and his brother Hezekiah.[26] One of the more notorious kidnappings was carried out by the Sicarians in 63 C.E. Their target was the scribe (and personal secretary) of the high priest, Elazar Ben-Hananiah. In exchange, the abductors demanded the release of ten of their colleagues who had been arrested by the Romans. After an intense shuttling effort conducted by the high priest with Lucceius Albinus, the Roman procurator in Syria, the latter relented and the swap was effected.[27]

The legend of Masada, so deeply engraved in the Israeli collective conscious as the epitome of Jewish loyalty and rectitude in the face of a cruel enemy, is essentially a tragedy of political zeal for which the Sicarians were also responsible. In 66 C.E., a group of Sicarians were able to seize the Masada flat-top mountain (along the eastern periphery of the Judean Desert) from the Roman garrison. Located atop a precipitous crag, the great fortress was encircled by a 1,400-meter wall, and guard towers were positioned all along the wall.[28] Inside the fortress, there were many waterholes and food stores, which made it possible for the Sicarians, commanded by Elazar Ben Yair, to survive on the plateau for seven years. The fortress was used as an advantageous launching base for attacks against Jewish and Roman settlements.[29]

In 73 C.E., during the Great (Jewish) Revolt, the Roman procurator, Flavius Silva, lay siege to the Sicarians who were entrenched in Masada. After a number of months of blockade, Silva's legions were able to build a circumvallation wall and then a broad ramp on the western side of the fortress. This ramp allowed them to break into the Masada compound. As for the sight that greeted the legion soldiers after they penetrated the walls, there are differences of opinion. Most historians agree that the Sicarians set the buildings on fire in the compound.[30] However, whereas Josephus Flavius, on the basis of the testimonies of two survivors, described a mass suicide of 967 Sicarians who had realized that the battle was lost,[31] other historians argued that the Sicarians committed mass murder among themselves. According to the latter version, each man first killed all the members of his family and then ten men were assigned the task of slaying the rest of the inhabitants.[32]

The Great Revolt ended in a crushing defeat for the Jews. Roman legion soldiers destroyed the Temple, the symbol of Jewish sovereignty, and the Jews were banished from their country. The failure of the Great Revolt and the subsequent forced exile left deep scars in the Jewish collective memory. The fear that violence might lead to a similar tragedy remained so profound among the Jews that the Halacha (Jewish law) adopted a specific directive aimed at avoiding any future signs of rebellion that might again provoke the anger of the gentiles.[33] Indeed, over the course of nearly 2,000 years of Jewish Diaspora, descendants of these Jews have refrained almost entirely from engaging in terrorism. Although the scarcity of Jewish-instigated acts of political violence can be explained by the Jews' weakness facing the authorities in countries where they resided, this can also be regarded as a direct outcome of the Halachic decision. Therefore it is possible to assert that religion, which so often has been accused of inflaming violence and terrorism, can also play an entirely opposite role.

JEWISH POLITICAL ACTIVISM IN THE NINETEENTH AND TWENTIETH CENTURIES

The historical search for Jews who took part in acts of terrorism can be traced back to the nineteenth century. In view of the deeply influential proscription against violence and the long-standing conformity to its decree, it may also come as no surprise that these nineteenth-century activists could hardly be described as bona fide Jewish terrorists. They were mainly educated young people who had long since abandoned the Jewish faith in order to become part of the leftist avant-garde in Europe whose main undertaking was to defy the ruling authorities. These Jews were particularly prominent in the Russian revolutionary movement, whose efforts included attempts to undermine the tsar's rule. One of the most famous insurgents was Dmitri Bogrov, who came from a Jewish family in Kiev. On September 14, 1911, Bogrov shot dead the tsar's prime minister, Pyotr Stolypin, while he was attending a performance at the Kiev Opera House. The killing took place in the presence of Tsar Nicholas II, who was sitting close to the prime minister, and it was designed to incite political instability and ultimately inspire revolutionary fervor in Russia. Bogrov was tried in a military tribunal and was executed just ten days after the assassination.[34] Several decades later, on the other side of the Atlantic Ocean, the Weatherman underground movement took shape, and among its other aspirations, it sought to bring an end to American involvement in Vietnam. Members of the movement, many of them Jews, did not hesitate in engaging in classic terrorist tactics such as planting explosive charges and committing arson in order to advance their ideological goals.[35] The Jewish terrorists who operated in tsarist Russia and those in Nixon-era America shared the fact that they were young men and women with a developed sense of political awareness and were wholly committed to the political concerns that plagued their compatriots. In addition, their Jewish descent had no discernible relevance to the course of action they chose.

One exception worth mentioning is the Bund movement, which was established in Vilna in 1897 and was active primarily in Eastern Europe. Similar to other political movements at the time, the Bund also operated in the name of an antitsarist socialist ideology.[36] The uniqueness of the organization resided in the fact that along with its universal socialist perspective, Bundists did not hesitate in extolling the virtues and furthering the particular interests of Jewish laborers. In fact, they regarded the struggle for their rights as an essential part of their activities.

It would be somewhat of an exaggeration to describe the Bund as a terrorist network. It was basically a labor organization and political party that for a long time opposed the use of violence.[37] Nonetheless, there were isolated incidents in which the leaders of the organization endorsed attacks on symbols of capitalist exploitation such as industrialists and government officials. They justified these actions by claiming revenge for the harm done to their people or the need for self-defense. For example, after the Russian governor of Vilna, Von Wahl, gave the order to flog twenty Jewish laborers, he was shot and killed by a Bund activist, Hirsh Lekert.[38] Members of the central committee of the organization expressed their support for the act and declared, "Honor and glory to the avenger, who sacrificed himself for his brothers!"[39]

However, despite the occasional use of violence to further the status of Jewish workers, to a great degree the Bund was exceptional in terms of Jewish political aggression. The most severe manifestations of Jewish terrorism took place only with the resurgence of the Jewish settlement project in modern-day Eretz Israel (Land of Israel).

███████████████

AS JEWISH SETTLEMENT in Palestine bur-
geoned toward the end of the nineteenth century, it also gave birth to renewed manifestations of political violence. Although for the most part this
was a nationally rather than religiously motivated struggle, we have chosen
to review this period in light of the fact that the terrorist activities of some
of the groups active during this time will serve as a link between the historical era of Jewish terrorism and modern-day Jewish terrorism. Many
later perpetrators of terrorism were inspired by the Jewish struggle at the
turn of the twentieth century and in fact refer to it.

Near the end of the Ottoman rule, these acts of violence were carried
out primarily in self-defense by militias led by the Bar-Giora[1] and Hashomer[2]
organizations. In view of the authorities' lassitude in defending Jewish
settlements from the attacks of their Arab neighbors, these groups decided
to resort to arms and take into their own hands the task of protecting their
communities.[3] However, despite the determination of these groups, the
option of engaging in systematic terrorism was not viable. These actions
were an early indication of the differential attitudes of the various Jewish
ideological streams to the use of violence. The leaders of the political left
who enjoyed a dominant status at that time believed that violence should
be exercised in an orderly fashion. This was the combat doctrine that they
bequeathed to the Haganah organization and its military arm, the Palmach. Despite the informal nature of the relationships between members
of the Palmach, which in due course became myth and later served as an
example for many Israel Defense Forces (IDF) units, the organization assumed a paramilitary structure that was designed to form the blueprint for
the future army of the sovereign Jewish state. The forces were divided according to military corps, including air force, marine, intelligence units
and regional commands. The organization's higher ranks developed structured warfare doctrines intended to be of use in the struggle against the

violent Palestinian groups at the time.[4] The Palestinian groups were based in and operated from the villages and were dubbed gangs by leaders of the Yishuv (the Jewish community in Palestine). In any event, although many of the Palmach operations can be described as guerrilla raids, it is difficult to pin down occasions in which the organization actually mounted campaigns of terrorism.

Among the right-wing movements, however, this was not the case. The Etzel (also known as the Irgun) and the Lehi (also known as the Stern Gang), formerly active as one group, drew their ideology from the Revisionist perspective of Ze'ev Jabotinsky.[5] This Zionist ideologue believed that a Judaized Land of Israel should include both banks of the Jordan River, and as early as the 1920s he had already demanded that the Zionist movement lead the campaign against the British Mandate authorities with a forceful hand.[6] The Etzel was founded in Jerusalem in April 1931 and steadfastly reflected the ideas of Jabotinsky, who regarded political violence solely as a means of achieving the goal of establishing a sovereign and democratic Jewish state.[7] On the other hand, the people of Lehi, which splintered off from the Etzel in June 1940, considered the use of violence and terrorism a crucial component in the evolution of the Jewish nation. Its objective was to enable the Jewish people to liberate themselves from the defeatist disposition that typified Jewish communities in the Diaspora.[8] Although the majority of the members of these two groups were secular, their ideology gave prominence to the affinity between religion and nationalism. Leaders of the groups tended to embrace Jewish mythology and to draw a direct line between the stories from the Bible and their own struggle for Jewish independence. Whereas the leaders of the Etzel resolved that the struggle against the British Mandate authorities was a holy war of duty against enemies of the Jewish people,[9] the Lehi faction went one step further. This group's teachings, which were influenced to no small degree by European fascism, also incorporated messianic elements. The "Essentials of Revival," Lehi's public platform, gave preeminence to the aspiration of building a Third Temple. Lehi leaders even declared themselves the successors to the Jewish zealots from the Second Temple era.[10] It therefore comes as no surprise that the doctrine of the Lehi organization—the smallest among the active underground groups in the pre–State of Israel era—became one of the principal sources of inspiration for future national–religious terrorist groups in Israel in the following decades.

Despite the essential differences in the reasons that led to the emergence of Jewish terrorism (and the features of the groups that committed this terrorism) during the British Mandate, it is possible to point out some similarities to the groups that operated after the founding of the state. The withdrawal of Avraham Tehomi and his colleagues from the Haganah organization in order to establish the Etzel on April 10, 1931, had an obvious political motivation. Tehomi and his people belonged to the Revisionist stream and found it difficult to accept the absolute authority of the leftist movements from the Haganah leadership. However, this was not the sole deliberation or main reason in their decision to break away.[11] The members of the founding core group of the Etzel were categorically opposed to the Haganah's post-1929 official policy. After the events of that year—the destruction of the Jewish settlement in Hebron—the Haganah chose a passive policy of self-restraint with the intention of demonstrating to the British Mandate authorities that the Jewish Yishuv had no interest in fueling the tensions with the Palestinian national movement.[12] Tehomi and his Jerusalemite associates concluded that it was no longer possible to continue to belong to a group whose worldview differed so greatly from theirs.[13] Moreover, the structure of the Jerusalem group apparently had a role in the dynamics that led to their departure. The group led by Tehomi was a very condensed social network whose members saw themselves as belonging to one family that was exclusively responsible for the Jews' security in Jerusalem, and they devoted nearly all their time to this purpose. Most of them were veteran members who had known each other before immigrating to Eretz Israel from their connections in Odessa. Sometimes they were even called the Odessa Group. The tight bonds between members of the group prevented internal disputes or confrontations regarding the idea of splitting off from the Haganah. At the same time, they also fed an escalating internal dynamic within the group; its members would stir each other up in their resentment toward the policy of the Haganah organization.[14]

Directly after the declaration of their departure, members of the Jerusalem group made overtures to the Betar Movement and other political bodies of the civilian and religious right. In addition, by exploiting family and friendship ties, they were successful in recruiting additional youths and extending the reaches of their network.[15] The first five years of the Etzel's activities were devoted to shaping the network into an underground with paramilitary features and heightening the ideological differences between them and the Haganah. Etzel activities focused primarily on the struggle against restrictions imposed by the British Mandate authorities on the immigration of Jews to Eretz Israel. Its members smuggled immigrants into the country by evading the coastal blockade and helping them blend in among the veteran population.[16]

The Great Arab Revolt (also known as the Great Uprising),[17] the most significant event up to that point in the crystallization of the Palestinian national movement, was the key factor that prompted the heads of the Etzel to adopt terrorist tactics as a strategy. While the Haganah leadership still clung to the policy of restraint,[18] as far as the Etzel were concerned, the only way to deal with attacks perpetrated by Palestinian terrorist networks against the Jewish population was to pay them back in kind. This meant that they would terrorize Palestinian citizens in the attempt to sow fear in their communities and weaken their support for the Arab Revolt.[19] The Etzel's first act of terrorism was the murder of two Palestinian workers in a banana grove in the Sharon[20] region on April 20, 1936.[21] Between 1936 and 1939, there was a noticeable escalation in the degree of sophistication and cruelty of both the Palestinian groups and the Etzel as they carried out actions aimed at harming large numbers of civilians. Subsequently, the number of victims increased on both sides. By the time the Arab Revolt began to flag in 1939, Etzel had become highly skilled in executing acts of terrorism. Over three years, the group carried out sixty operations that took the lives of more than 120 Palestinians and injured hundreds more.[22]

Despite the temporary lull in the violent struggle with the Palestinian national movement, Etzel activists did not remain idle. Irgun commanders directed the substantial experience their men had accumulated in guerrilla actions and terrorism toward a new target: the British Mandate authorities. The immediate basis for this was a new series of immigration and land acquisition restrictions imposed by Mandate authorities on the Jewish Yishuv.[23] Whereas terrorist acts against Palestinians focused mainly on civilians, attacks on the British aimed at targets with more symbolic significance. One reason was that the British presence in Eretz Israel was chiefly military and administrative, so civilians were not included in the circle of potential victims. Yet this was not the only motive. For the Etzel, it was also important to build up prestige among the Jewish public.[24] Among the more prominent operations of the Etzel at that time were attacks on income tax bureaus and the Central Post Office in Jerusalem. However, the most notorious incident was the attack on the British Government Broadcasting House in the Melisende neighborhood in Jerusalem. After deciding to strike at this institution, the Etzel considered a forceful break-in but ruled out this option after discovering that the building was under continuous surveillance by British Army patrols. Therefore, it decided to plant an undercover agent disguised as a worker at the broadcasting station. In the early morning on August 2, 1939, the agent, whose code name was "Meir,"[25] made his way to the Royal Broadcasting House carrying three packages loaded with mines. The packages had been provided to him by his Etzel operators and were labeled "On His Majesty's Service." He also wore a jacket especially tailored for him containing a mine rigged to a stopwatch. After gaining entrance to the building with no particular difficulty, he hung his jacket on a coat hanger in the control room and placed the packages in the studio rooms. At 5:20 P.M., the mine in the control room exploded, killing a technician who was working there. Immediately afterwards, the packages in the studios blew up and one of the station's employees, May Weisenberg, who was broadcasting a youth program in English, was seriously injured and later died of her wounds. The building was severely damaged, and broadcasts were discontinued and relocated to the British broadcasting station in Ramallah.[26]

Etzel also targeted British police and army men known for their tough attitudes toward Jewish prisoners. The group's intention was to create a balance of terror with the Mandate authorities and force members of the police to reconsider their methods of interrogating Jewish detainees.[27] In particular, the assassination of Ralph Carnes by Etzel militants received wide publicity. Carnes was the head of the Jewish Division of the Palestine Police Force's Criminal Investigation Department (CID) and, according to the Etzel, tortured detainees apprehended by the British police. Because the CID continued to ignore the demands of the Etzel leadership to halt the abuse of Jewish detainees, the Etzel command issued a death sentence on Carnes's head.[28] Directly after the decree, members of the Etzel began shadowing the officer. They discovered that he lived in the peaceful Gan Rehavia quarter of Jerusalem and that a dirt path of some 110 yards, flanked by buildings in different stages of construction, had to be crossed in order to reach his home. With this information, the Etzel people concluded that the path leading to Carnes's house was an ideal location for carrying out the assassination. The date set for the operation was August 26, 1939. On the night before the operation, members of the Etzel planted a high-powered electric mine on the path leading to Carnes's house. They made a small hole in the ground marking the exact location of the mine, and an electric wire was stretched from the mine to the foundations of an unfinished house nearby. In this empty building, Etzel member Haim Corfu hid on the day of the assassination. He was disguised as a police officer and was responsible for detonating the mine at the right moment by means of a battery connected to the electric wire. When Carnes and a colleague, Ronald Barker, head of the Arab Division of the CID, returned home in the evening, they did not notice an innocent-looking couple, Matti Gross and Tikvah Yisraeli, who stood at the entrance to the path. After Carnes walked past them, Matti removed his cap from his head. This was the sign for Corfu that Carnes was in fact the person walking along the path. When Carnes and Barker reached the area where the mine had been planted, Corfu connected the battery to the wire using a special push-button switch and the mine exploded, killing the two officers on the spot.[29]

After the incident, the British Army commander in Jerusalem ordered the immediate closure of all Jewish cafés and movie theaters in Jerusalem until further notice. In response, the Etzel headquarters issued a warning that "any detective who dares abuse a Jewish prisoner will be put to death."[30]

THE SPLIT BETWEEN THE ETZEL AND THE LEHI

World War II posed a tough challenge for the Etzel. While Mandate authorities in Palestine continued their heavy-handed policy toward the Jewish Yishuv, the British Army was also at the forefront of the struggle against Nazi Germany. The Irgun's decision was to suspend their campaign against the Mandate authorities as long as the British were engaged in the attempt to defeat the Nazi enemy.[31] High-ranking members of the Etzel even volunteered to join the British Army, and on May 20, 1941, David Raziel, commander of the Etzel, was killed in the line of duty. He was hit directly by a bomb dropped by a German fighter plane while leading a small unit of Irgun members on an intelligence mission near Fallujah in Iraq. Raziel's Etzel cell had been on assignment for the British Army.[32] The willingness of high-ranking Etzel members to join forces with the

Mandate authorities was a thorn in the side of some members of the Etzel, headed by Avraham (Yair) Stern. In June 1940, the dispute reached the stage where it became a personal crisis between Raziel and Stern.[33] The latter decided to leave the Etzel and to form a new group: the "Etzel in Eretz Israel," which in due course became known as the Lehi (the Hebrew acronym for "Fighters for the Freedom of Israel").

Despite its collaboration with the British, the Etzel was not idle. The group's leaders took advantage of the World War II period to further establish its institutions. Similar to the Palmach, it set up a general headquarters, which was to be in charge of operational commands situated according to geographic jurisdiction. In addition, staff units were founded. During these years, the Etzel developed the warfare doctrine that was to become its trademark: deploying small units specializing in urban warfare and surprise attacks.[34]

The home front of the struggle against the British was not neglected. The Lehi moved in to fill the vacuum left behind by the Etzel. However, Stern's plans and his people were not as productive. In the Lehi's early days, the organization consisted of a small group of militants who lacked operational experience.[35] Their initial actions were mostly failed attempts at robbing banks in order to finance their struggle. The inadvertent killing of two Jewish bystanders during one of these failed robberies in January 1942 led to a substantial fall in the group's morale.[36] To make matters worse, three police were killed—two of them Jewish—during an attempt to assassinate the commander of the CID in the Lod region on January 20 of that same year.[37] This incident evoked rage across the board in the Jewish Yishuv and led to a collaboration between the British authorities and the Jewish Agency in the effort to subdue the various Jewish undergrounds.[38]

By the end of January 1942, many Lehi militants had been caught and detained. One month later, Stern was also shot dead.[39] In the wake of these events, members of the group scattered in all directions, and the organization became almost completely inoperative. Eight months later, the group reorganized after two of its main activists, Yitzhak Shamir and Eliyahu Giladi, escaped from detention. Shamir and Giladi began to reestablish connections between members and prepare them for action.[40] In November 1943, Natan Yellin-Mor and Yisrael Eldad (Scheib) also fled from jail, a development that breathed new life into the group.[41] While Yellin-Mor helped his associates in their efforts to restore the operational capabilities of the Lehi, Eldad devoted his time to authoring and circulating articles that were called cornerstones. Eldad's writings relied heavily on the mythology of the Jewish zealots and at the same time raised objections to socialist Zionism. They were adopted by Lehi members as their ideological doctrine and turned out to be quite effective in recruiting public support.[42] In due course, these writings became the unifying ideological base for the different Jewish terrorist groups in the sovereign State of Israel.

In February 1944, the Lehi made its comeback to the cycle of terrorism. However, once again, members of the group proved to be amateurs in comparison to their Etzel counterparts. The gunfire attacks they initiated against British soldiers in the streets of Tel Aviv and Jerusalem[43] led to another wave of arrests of Lehi members.[44] In early August 1944, the Lehi higher ranks sought to upgrade the level of their actions by carrying out a high-profile political assassination they hoped would make waves far and wide. The chosen target was British High Commissioner Harold Mac-Michael, whom the Lehi considered the main culprit responsible for what they perceived as the British government's ongoing abuse of the Jews and their rights.[45] However, this time they were unsuccessful; no less than seven attempts on MacMichael's life ended in failure.[46] Their first attempt consisted of planting a mine in a sewage pipe near the side exit of the church where MacMichael prayed every Sunday. However, despite the remote control mechanism installed the night before, on the day of the planned detonation, the mine simply refused to explode. It turned out that the wires connecting the mine to the detonating mechanism were faulty.[47] On another occasion, Lehi militants tried to shoot the commissioner near the government publishing house. They conducted numerous stakeouts of the location in order to gather intelligence about his routine. However, after raising the suspicions of some nuns who also interfered with the preparations, the Lehi leaders decided to call off the operation.[48] Additional plots were to attack MacMichael while he was taking the train or visiting a movie theater in Jerusalem; however, the capture of Lehi members several days before the appointed operation dates led to their cancellation in the fear that knowledge of the plans might reach the British.[49] After several more failed attempts, at last they resolved to attack the commissioner on the way to his farewell party that was to take place in Yaffo (Jaffa). The Lehi group decided that the ideal location for carrying out the assassination was on the road from Jerusalem to Yaffo. They planned to position a small group of observers at the third mile on the highway from Jerusalem to Tel Aviv, where the road curved and cars had to slow down. This small group would signal to another cell of their members disguised as surveyors on the side of the road to put up a roadblock made of rocks. As the convoy slowed down, mines would be detonated and Lehi guerrillas would storm the convoy with automatic fire and hand grenades. If the commissioner still remained unharmed by this ambush, a third unit would spring into action a few hundred yards down the road from the first ambush.[50] However, on the morning of the target day, problems already began to crop up. The wires connecting the mines to the detonators at the side of the road got entangled and the Lehi people were not able to unravel them, so they decided to give up the idea of the mines. Then, at 4 P.M., an Arab laborer arrived at the scene and began to remove the pile of rocks prepared in advance for the roadblock. Instead of the roadblock idea, the Lehi people decided to launch smoke grenades in order to slow down the convoy. When the procession of vehicles finally appeared at 4:10 P.M., the militants threw smoke grenades and charged the vehicles. Several minutes later, the commanding officer of the operation, Yehoshua Cohen, gave the order to withdraw because he was sure they had been successful in their mission. It turned out that Commissioner MacMichael had suffered only light injuries thanks to his driver's initiative. The moment that the driver became aware of the smoke grenades, he diverted the car to the side of the road and escaped by driving down a dirt lane along the side of the mountain.[51] Only in late 1944, when Lord Moyne was assassinated, did the Lehi finally gain the public recognition it so keenly sought.

THE ASSASSINATION OF LORD MOYNE

Cairo is a sweaty, colorful, and noisy city and a stark contrast from gray, rainy London. Therefore it was not surprising that British emissaries in the Egyptian capital in the 1930s and 1940s longed for an island of peace that would help them forget their placement in the Middle East. The Zamalek neighborhood, a posh suburb of Cairo, provided them with the quiet they sought. On the afternoon of November 6, 1944, the peace and quiet was sharply disturbed. A volley of gunshots tore into the midday calm of the drowsy neighborhood. A car belonging to Walter Edward Guinness, minister resident in the Middle East on behalf of the British Empire, who was also known by his royal title, Lord Moyne, halted in front of his house.

Inside the car, Lord Moyne was engaged in conversation with his adjutant and his personal secretary and did not spot the figure quickly approaching his car.[52] At his side, the adjutant noticed something was amiss and instinctively lay across the back seat and shielded his superior with his body. In this way, he sealed his own fate. He was the first one to succumb to the shots from the gun of the assassin who opened the back door of the car.[53] However, the assassin did not intend to leave the vicinity until he had completed his mission. The second volley of shots was aimed directly at Moyne's body. After confirming the British minister's death, the assassin retreated and joined his partner, who was waiting for him at the entrance to the house. The two then mounted their bikes and quickly took flight in the direction of the Bollack Bridge.[54] An Egyptian traffic officer who was stationed not far from the site of the murder heard the sudden commotion. The two youths riding fast on their bikes raised his suspicions, and he called them to halt. They ignored his shouts and rode even faster, but the officer did not lose his head. He drew his gun, aimed it at the retreating figures, and began to shoot. A bullet penetrated the back of one of the riders and cut short his flight. The second rider, who was unharmed and heard the cries of his accomplice, came back and tried to help him. Several officers summoned to the scene apprehended the both of them.[55]

In the investigation that followed, the perpetrators identified themselves as nineteen-year-old Eliahu Hakim, a Jew from Haifa, and Eliahu Beit-Tsouri, a twenty-two-year-old resident of Tel Aviv. Already in the first stage of the investigation, the two affirmed their membership in the Lehi and immediately confessed to the murder. The trial of Hakim and Beit-Tsouri was conducted in Cairo in the second week of January 1945 and captured the attention of the world media. Among other things, this was because the two stated peremptorily that they were not criminals and that the murder of Lord Moyne was a political action. Its aim was to censure the British authorities for breaking their promise to aid the Jewish people in establishing a sovereign entity in "Eretz Israel."[56]

The target of Lord Moyne was not chosen at random. The notion of assassinating a high-profile British figure in the Middle East had already been conceived by Avraham (Yair) Stern, leader of the Lehi, as far back as 1941 and three years before Moyne had even assumed his duties in this role. Its implementation was delayed because Richard Casey, Moyne's predecessor, was an Australian and Stern was keen on striking at an unmistakable and distinctive symbol of the United Kingdom.[57] Lord Moyne was the embodiment of exactly what Stern and his Lehi associates despised. In his previous position as secretary of state for the colonies, he exhibited a persistent pro-Arab inclination and took great care in adhering to the policy of restrictions on Jewish immigration to Palestine.[58] As far as the Lehi were concerned, Lord Moyne's actions reflected his fundamental anti-Semitic leanings. The much-disputed actions of the British police in the winter of 1942 greatly increased the already existing hostility felt toward him.

In February 1942, British police forces broke into a small residential apartment on 8 Mizrahi Street in the Florentine quarter of Tel Aviv. According to police information, a woman by the name of Tova Svorai rented an apartment that was used as a hiding place for Stern.[59] During this operation, the Lehi chief was found hiding in a closet in the apartment. After confirming his identity, the police shot the unarmed Stern and killed him. A short while later, they smuggled his body out of the apartment and forced Stern's family to bury him on the same day.[60] The British police claimed that Stern had resisted arrest, and they had had no alternative but to shoot him. Although this version was not corroborated, the intelligence officers who propounded it were backed by high-ranking officials of the British Empire. One of the most prominent voices to praise the police's actions was that of the colonial secretary.[61] For the Lehi leaders, the die was cast. They decided to launch the operation in Cairo, Lord Moyne's home base, and not on one of his visits to Palestine because they believed it essential to send a signal to the British authorities that officials of the British Empire were not safe anywhere in the Middle East.

The operation in Egypt required an intelligence and logistic infrastructure. To this end, the Lehi relied on a network of Jewish collaborators who operated in Egypt from within the ranks of the British Army. The key figure of the network was Benjamin Gafner, ex-member of the Etzel who volunteered to serve in the British Army and was posted in Egypt. Gafner was able to lay the foundations of an intricate network of connections consisting of Jewish soldiers who ideologically identified with the Lehi. In its early days, the network's primary function was to distribute *The Hazit* (*The Front*), the Lehi organ, in Egypt.[62] In addition, members made efforts to steal weapons from British Army depots and dispense them to activists in the underground. In the first half of 1943, network activity was slowed down because Gafner, the life and soul of the group, was assigned to a special unit of the British Army whose task was to rescue pilots who landed in German-controlled territories. Gafner's unit rescued more than 500 soldiers of the Allied forces from behind enemy lines, and he received a medal of distinction.[63] In June 1944, Gafner returned from Europe and met with Yitzhak Shamir, one of the Lehi commanders. Shamir informed him of the plan in progress to assassinate Moyne and asked him to recruit a network of activists in Egypt for this purpose. Gafner gladly agreed to this mission and, upon his return to Egypt, began to make preparations. To his chagrin, a short while later he was instructed by his officers in the British Army to rejoin his unit in Europe. Having no other choice, Gafner transferred authority of the network to one of his closest friends, Yosef Sitner, of the British Royal Air Force who was serving in Egypt at the time as a bulldozer operator. Sitner made good on the trust put in him. He assigned members of the network to different cells while concealing the nature of the planned operation from most of the activists; he even made sure that the cells had no knowledge of each other. The main role of the network was to conduct a constant surveillance of Moyne's daily routine and relay information to the assassination plotters in order to help them establish the most opportune place and time for carrying out the operation.[64]

Late in the summer of 1944, Eliahu Hakim arrived in Cairo. Natan Yellin-Mor, Shamir's associate in the underground leadership, was responsible for assigning the mission to Hakim. Yellin-Mor had been impressed by Hakim's marksman skills and also assumed that because of his Lebanese origins and command of Arabic, he would find it easier to blend into the Egyptian milieu.[65] Hakim introduced himself to Sitner using the alias Yitzhak Cohen and was promptly incorporated into the Moyne stakeout assignment. In order to help him find his way around the streets of Cairo and at the same time remove any sign of suspicion, he was joined by a handsome woman introduced to him as "Yaffa." The two of them began to stroll the streets of the Egyptian capital, and to a typical bystander they appeared to be nothing other than a couple in love.[66]

The decision to carry out the assassination close to Lord Moyne's residence was Hakim's idea because he was apprehensive about the heightened military presence around the minister's office. On October 18, 1944, Beit-Tsouri joined Hakim. The Lehi leaders assumed that in order to complete the operation, more than one assassin would be necessary. Despite his youth, Beit-Tsouri had earned the respect of both the Etzel and Lehi organizations.

He had established his reputation in one of the Etzel operations before the split between the two undergrounds. In this operation, Beit-Tsouri, who had impressive technical skills, had noticed that one of the mines carried by his commander had been assembled incorrectly and was about to explode. He warned his commander, deactivated the mine, and saved several of his colleagues from death.[67] The Lehi leaders decided that the capable and cool-headed youth would be an ideal partner for Hakim.

On his way to Cairo, Beit-Tsouri received news that was a source of significant concern. Sitner and other key figures of the network had suddenly been taken into custody by the British authorities, and the assassination planners feared the detentions were caused by an information leak about the operation.[68] Several days later, it turned out that the arrests had been a preemptive measure in anticipation of the upcoming convention of the first Arab summit, which was to take place in Egypt. Despite the collapse of their supporting network, Hakim and Beit-Tsouri decided to continue with the operation on their own.[69]

The trial of the two perpetrators began on January 10, 1945, and quickly developed into a gripping drama. Hakim and Beit-Tsouri, who confessed to the assassination, turned the hearings into a platform for slamming British imperialism and were even successful in winning the sympathy of Egyptian public opinion.[70] Unfortunately for them, this success was not of much help as far as their verdict was concerned. On January 18, the two were found guilty and sentenced to death. However, this still did not signify the end of their struggle. Despite the custom of carrying out the verdict within three weeks of the day of its reading, political pressure was applied both within Cairo and outside to commute their sentence. Winston Churchill himself put an end to the whole affair. Churchill, who had been close to Lord Moyne, delivered a speech on February 27 before the British Parliament in which he emphatically demanded "that the implementation of the verdict that was issued in regard to people who were found guilty of political murder—be quick and exemplary."[71] Less than a month later, on March 22, Hakim and Beit-Tsouri were executed by hanging.

FROM THE SEASON TO THE UNITED RESISTANCE MOVEMENT

The assassination turned out to be a double-edged sword. For the British and the Haganah, this episode was a catalyst for strengthening operational ties intended to bring about the dissolution of the right-wing undergrounds.[72] This period, also known as the Hunting Season, or Season for short, left a deep scar in the Israeli collective memory for many years. Haganah members not only desisted from granting refuge to people from the Lehi and Etzel, they gathered intelligence about them and in several cases even handed them over to the Mandate authorities.[73] Furthermore, Palmach fighters took part in the abductions and interrogations of members of right-wing undergrounds.[74] Members of the Lehi were the first to break under the pressure; they halted their activities a short while after the initiation of the Season.[75] The Etzel, on the other hand, continued its operations against the British until late February 1945. Menachem Begin, head of the underground who was forced to go into hiding, encouraged his people not to lay down their arms, but at the same time he instructed them not to aim their guns at the Yishuv leaders for fear of a causing a rift among the Jewish public that would never heal.[76]

By the winter of 1945, both sides were battle-weary. The Etzel had suffered blows that made it almost impossible to pursue its activities, and the Jewish Agency came under heavy public pressure and was accused of persecuting its political rivals.[77] Several months later, as the dimensions of the Holocaust of European Jewry began to unfold, together with the disappointment in the newly elected Labor government's decision to persist in the Mandate authorities' heavy-handed Jewish refugee immigration policy, the United Resistance Movement was established.[78] This was an umbrella movement that coordinated the actions of the Haganah, Etzel, and Lehi. Despite the rivalry between the different organizations, the Yishuv leadership realized that collaboration between all the factions would give the Zionist movement much greater leverage in the face of British and world opinion. With this in mind, leaders of the Haganah began to initiate negotiations between the different factions in August 1945, and in October of that year, the alliance was signed.[79]

Each of the underground groups sent a representative to the United Resistance Movement whose primary role was to approve actions devised by the different groups and to ensure that they conformed with the interests of the Jewish community in general. On June 29, 1946, 17,000 British soldiers raided Jewish settlements and arrested more than 2,700 members of the different undergrounds on what became known as the Black Sabbath.[80] The unprecedented wave of arrests and unearthing of weapon caches were a critical blow for the operative capacities of the Jewish undergrounds, especially the Haganah.[81] Heads of the United Resistance Movement tasked the Etzel with the responsibility for a reprisal. The disastrous results of this operation ultimately led to the dismantling of the underground alliance. About one month after the Black Sabbath, on July 26, members of an Etzel cell disguised as Arabs infiltrated the kitchen of the Café La Regence at the lavish King David Hotel in Jerusalem. The hotel had originally opened its doors in 1931 and seven years later was transformed into the nerve center of the British Mandate authorities in Palestine. Members of the cell placed milk containers full of explosives in the southern wing of the hotel and then quickly left the vicinity. Despite the fact that the Etzel gave warning of the explosives, the hotel management was not able to evacuate all its occupants. The ensuing explosion caused the collapse of the southern wing of the hotel; and 91 Britons, Arabs, and Jews were buried under the ruins, and 476 more were injured. The leaders of the Haganah were shocked at the results of the operation and strongly condemned the Etzel.[82]

They equally frowned on Lehi organization activities, although these did not include an active part in the attack on the hotel. Several months earlier, however, leaders of the Haganah had already voiced a strong protest against the Lehi attack on the British Army base on Yarkon Street in Tel Aviv because British soldiers had been killed in their sleep. The attack had been carried out against the soldiers of the British 6th Airborne Division, who were also popularly called Kalaniot (Hebrew for "anemones") because of their red caps, and they were infamous for their strong-arm tactics.[83] They were sleeping in their tents when Lehi fighters set upon them with gunfire and grenades.[84] In their defense, the Lehi people argued that the soldiers had not been sleeping and that seven of their own members had been killed during the course of the gunfight. A British armored vehicle arrived at the scene several minutes later with reinforcements so that, in any event, the Lehi militants were forced to retreat in the direction of the Kerem Hateimanim (Yemenite Vineyard) neighborhood in Tel Aviv.[85] Condemnation of the Lehi operation was widespread, principally regarding the immoral disregard for "purity of arms" (the Hebrew expression for the reasonable or justifiable use of weapons). This incident increased the feelings among the United Resistance leaders that they were losing control over the amount of violence perpetrated by the undergrounds.[86] Finally, in the summer of 1946, and mostly because of the differences of opinion in the United Resistance Movement, the short era of collusion between the assorted undergrounds came to an end.[87]

Not long after the United Resistance Movement disbanded, the Haganah and the British reached a ceasefire agreement. Nevertheless, the Etzel and the Lehi continued their activities with a vengeance. Among the more prominent operations of the Etzel in those months was the attempt to prevent the execution of three organization members, Meir Nakar, Avshalom Haviv, and Yaakov Weiss, by kidnapping two British sergeants.[88] The Etzel higher command hoped to force the Mandate authorities to reduce the verdict of the three in exchange for the release of the British abductees. After the Mandate authorities rejected the ultimatum and executed the three prisoners, the Etzel retaliated by hanging the two sergeants in a grove near Netanya.[89] Another major Etzel operation at that time was the raid of the Akko (Acre) prison on May 4, 1947. On that day, a convoy consisting of an army truck, two army vans in British camouflage colors, and two civilian vans set out for Akko. When they arrived at the port city, the truck and the two army vans made their way to the local market, not far from the ancient Ottoman fortress where the prison was located. The Etzel operatives were disguised as members of a British engineering army unit who had come to fix the telephone lines. They began to scale the ladders they brought with them and were able to climb onto the roof of the building next to the fortress. From this vantage point, using large hooks and ropes, they mounted explosive charges on the wall of the fortress. At the same time, another unit in one of the civilian vans took up position at the northern entrance to Akko. At 4:22 P.M., after the charges affixed to the wall had been detonated, this unit began to bombard the adjoining army complex with mortar fire. After the wall collapsed, there was a mass scramble of prisoners for freedom, and Etzel operatives collected their colleagues into waiting trucks and vans. Although twenty-seven members of the Etzel and Lehi succeeded in escaping, the incident claimed the lives of nine Etzel operatives.[90] More than 180 Arab prisoners took advantage of the operation to make their escape.[91]

THE PARTITION PLAN

The United Nations General Assembly Resolution on November 29, 1947, authorizing the partitioning of Eretz Israel and the establishment of two states, was warmly received by most of the Yishuv. The Lehi, on the other hand, perceived it as a British conspiracy intended to shore up control over the Middle East.[92] The organization responded to the partition plan with a series of terrorist attacks, which included the bombing of the offices of the British shipping company in Haifa, shooting attacks on police in Jerusalem, and a brazen attack on the Astoria Café in Haifa. In the latter incident, which targeted British soldiers and police who frequented the café, three Lehi members equipped with machine guns and grenades stormed into the restaurant, began spraying gunfire in all directions, and then made their getaway in a car waiting outside for them.[93]

The British Army's preparations for the end of the military presence in Palestine and the Yishuv leaders' fear of a fresh outbreak of fighting with the Arabs once the Mandate was terminated prompted the underground movements to reconcile their differences. They decided once more to collaborate, this time within a military framework that in May 1948 became the IDF.[94] However, relations between the various groups again turned sour. In the case of Etzel, this was caused by the *Altalena* incident, in which the weapons ship bearing this name was sunk by the newly founded Israeli army on June 22, 1948, during the first break in the battles of the War of Independence.[95] To this day there are differences of opinion regarding the motives of the Israeli government in its decision to sink the ship. In addition to the Etzel members on the *Altalena,* the ship also carried weapons direly needed by the fledgling Israeli army, which was engaged in a tough war. At any rate, there is agreement about the way the events took place.[96] The ship and the weapons onboard had been purchased by the Etzel before the declaration establishing the state and integrating the Irgun into the IDF. When Prime Minister David Ben-Gurion realized that the ship was making its way to Israel, he demanded that Menachem Begin consign the weapons onboard to the army. Begin did not turn down the request but stipulated that when the armaments were divided, preference would be granted to the Jerusalem battalion, which consisted of members of his organization and other army units with a larger Etzel representation. Both sides dug in their heels while the ship continued its trip across the Mediterranean Sea. When the *Altalena* finally berthed off the Kfar Vitkin coastline, waiting Etzel operatives started unloading its weapons. Ben-Gurion insisted that they halt the unloading at once. In the meanwhile, Begin had arrived at the site, and the standoff between his Etzel militants and the soldiers of the Alexandroni Brigade who were surrounding them rapidly deteriorated into an exchange of gunfire. At the end of this battle, six Etzel and two brigade members had been killed.[97] The ensuing ceasefire reached by both sides made it possible for Menachem Begin to board the ship at the head of a small force of Etzel members. He then set sail for the Tel Aviv shoreline, where he hoped to receive aid from his supporters. At the same time, Ben-Gurion would not agree to any compromise. Yigal Yadin, then chief of operations of the Israeli army, was put in charge of overpowering the group onboard the ship. IDF and Palmach units deployed along the Tel Aviv beach were given the order to open fire on the ship. Finally, in light of Begin's resolve not to surrender, Ben-Gurion gave the command to sink the *Altalena* with artillery fire. Begin and others abandoned the ship, which sank a short while later with ten Etzel members on board. In consequence, Begin ordered his people to refrain from violent confrontation with army forces, at any price. However, this did not stop Ben-Gurion from conducting a widespread wave of arrests of Etzel members and from dismantling all the organization units still operating in the army ranks.[98]

The Lehi was disarmed several months later in the wake of the assassination of the mediator on behalf of the United Nations Security Council, Swedish Count Folke Bernadotte.[99] The Swedish count was dispatched to the Middle East on July 24, 1948, with the aim of bringing the confrontation between the emergent State of Israel and the Arab armies to an end. His mediating efforts for both sides and his proposal to divide up the country and declare its ports as international sovereign areas was deemed by the Lehi as another imperialistic scheme designed to bolster the involvement of foreign powers in the region.[100] On Saturday, September 17, 1948, Lehi activists set up a roadblock of barrels and bricks on the street leading from Katamon and Talbia to the Rehavia neighborhood in order to block Bernadotte's motorcade. When the motorcade reached the barricade and was forced to stop, a white jeep (which had been stolen several days earlier from the United Nations forces) appeared with four young men with submachine guns.[101] Three of them got off the jeep and approached the first of the three cars in the motorcade. When they were unable to find Bernadotte, they proceeded to the second car, where two of them began to shoot at the count sitting inside. The third youth began firing in the air to deter passengers in the other cars from trying to prevent the assassination. After realizing they had killed the count, the perpetrators fled the scene.[102] In the attack, Bernadotte suffered fatal wounds and later died of his injuries. The French United Nations observer who was sitting next to him, Colonel Serot, was also hit by the gunfire and died immediately.[103]

Despite the fact that an unknown organization called the Homeland Front took responsibility for the operation, security officials assumed it was the work of the Lehi.[104] The authorities' retaliation was severe. At first, the interim State Council drafted legislation that made it possible to apply force against terrorist organizations attempting to subvert the State of Israel (the Prevention of Terrorism Ordinance).[105] Promptly afterwards, the Israeli government invoked the ordinance to declare the Lehi a terrorist organization, and in the weeks after Bernadotte's assassination, more than 200 Lehi members were held in administrative detention, including those who had already been conscripted to the Israeli army.[106] The Lehi leaders were arraigned and convicted of activity and membership in a terrorist organization, and the court established that only a terrorist organization with the experience, intelligence, and operative capacities of Lehi could have carried out the Bernadotte assassination.

However, several months later, just before the appointed date of the first official elections in the State of Israel, the government of Israel decided to grant amnesty to all Lehi prisoners on the basis of a state general order of pardon and the desire to embark on a new course with all civilians. In effect, all Lehi activists who had been arrested and imprisoned after the Bernadotte assassination were set free.[107] Yet the picture that evolved in the first years of the State of Israel showed clearly that this objective had not been met. A series of Jewish-instigated terrorist events made it clear that this type of terrorism was still alive and active.

THE ASSASSINATION OF ISRAEL KASTNER

In December 1949, an attempt was made to commit the first political assassination in the State of Israel. Avraham Zfati, a young Jew who was later found to be mentally ill, burst into the Kessem Cinema in Tel Aviv where the Knesset was convening, pulled out a gun he had hidden in his clothes, and aimed it at the government plenum. But at the last moment, the ushers prevented him from carrying out his intention. Almost eight years later, on October 29, 1957, another young man suffering from mental problems, Moshe Dueik, tried to perform a similar deed. He threw a hand grenade at the government seats while the Knesset was in the midst of a debate and caused minor injuries to David Ben-Gurion and a number of other ministers.[108] But these events were exceptions. Most Jewish terrorist incidents that took place after the establishment of the State of Israel were the work of social networks consisting of former Lehi members who rejected the social democratic characteristics of the new state and adhered to a combination of religious and nationalistic views. They argued for the predominance of Jewish religious and nationalistic values over universal democratic, social, and humanistic values. Some even promoted the idea of restoring the historic Kingdom of Israel. These people were alienated from the dominant political culture of the new state and were accustomed to an underground life of violent actions. They had difficulty abandoning their old ways and adjusting to the new reality, and this facilitated their slide into violent acts such as the assassination of Dr. Israel Kastner.

On Saturday night, March 3, 1957, Dr. Israel (Rudolf) Kastner returned to his home on Emanuel Avenue in northern Tel Aviv. He had finished another day's work as editor of the Israeli Hungarian-language newspaper *Uykelet* and parked his car in front of his house. When he got out of his car, a tall young man in a gray suit approached and asked him, "Are you Dr. Kastner?" When he answered in the affirmative, the young man suddenly drew a pistol and pulled the trigger. The gun made an empty metallic sound but did not shoot. Kastner came to his senses and tried to take advantage of the misfire by fleeing down the sidewalk. In the meanwhile, the young man pulled the trigger again. This time the pistol fired, but the bullet missed its target and hit Kastner's car. The third bullet hit Kastner, penetrated his right hip, continued through the abdomen, and came to a stop in his left hip. Kastner collapsed only 12 feet from the entrance to his house. The assassin then ran to a jeep that was waiting for him at the street corner and was able to escape. The stunned neighbors who found Dr. Kastner lying on the ground immediately called for medical help, but this turned out to be futile. Despite a number of surgical procedures in the next two weeks, Israel Kastner died.[109]

More than any other event of the time, Kastner's murder exposed the deep ideological rift between the different sectors of Israeli society in those years. Almost a decade after the undergrounds had been dismantled and after all major institutions and political factions had been grouped together under the sovereign framework of the State of Israel, political violence, which was based on the traditional dispute between the nationalist right wing and socialist–Zionist left wing, continued to take its toll. Isser Harel, who at that time headed the Mossad and was chief of the Israeli intelligence community, pointed out that Kastner's murder was the peak of political terrorism in Israel in the 1950s.[110]

Dr. Kastner was a wartime leader of Hungarian Jewry, and in 1944 he conducted secret negotiations with Adolf Eichmann to save Jews in his country. After the war, in the early 1950s, accusations were raised against Kastner for helping mainly his acquaintances and relatives and for hiding details of the "Final Solution" from the Hungarian Jews. The allegations were that by behaving as he did, he had prevented the possible rescue of many other Jews. The affair gained momentum between 1953 and 1955 in light of a series of political developments and a stepped-up criticism of Kastner, mainly by right-wing intellectuals.[111] The matter reached its peak when a slander suit was brought against Malchiel Greenwald, a member of the Mizrahi movement, after he distributed a pamphlet in Jerusalem in which he accused Kastner of treason against the Jewish people and collaboration with the Nazis.[112]

In a short while, the Greenwald slander trial transformed into severe accusations against the Zionist establishment and Hungarian Jewish leaders. With the help of a charismatic lawyer, Shmuel Tamir, the Kastner trial evolved into a public debate dealing with sensitive issues, such as the helplessness of European Jewish and Yishuv leaders during the war.[113] But above all, the legal arena served as an instrument for the Israeli right wing in butting the socialist political establishment, most of which had been part of the Yishuv leadership during the war. This changed the trial from a legal instrument that was supposed to determine whether Greenwald had relied on solid proof and conducted a systematic examination of his claims before putting them in writing into a legal debate over Kastner's guilt. After nine months of discussion that stirred up the emotions of a large part of the Israeli public, the court established that Malchiel Greenwald was not guilty of slander against Kastner. By so doing, the court actually adopted most of the allegations made against Kastner; as Judge Dr. Benjamin Halevy put it, "By accepting the 'gift' of the train [to freedom for those privileged enough to pay] . . . from the Nazis, Kastner sold his soul to the devil."[114] The outcome of the trial aroused a public storm and a hate campaign against Kastner, who was condemned as a traitor by factions of the Israeli right wing.[115] From this condemnation to the actual assassination, the road was not long.

On the night of the murder, the Shin Bet (General Security Service) had already been able to determine that the assassins were Revisionists, former members of the Lehi. But the more interesting fact was the revelation that the assassination mastermind, Joseph Menkes, who had recruited Ze'ev Eckstein, the gunman, and Dan Shemer, the accomplice who had been waiting in the getaway car,[116] belonged to an underground group called the Kingdom of Israel. Five years earlier, this group had engaged in terrorism and had been known among the Israeli public by its more popular name, the Tzrifin Underground.[117]

KINGDOM OF ISRAEL (THE TZRIFIN UNDERGROUND)

The rainstorm that poured down on Tel Aviv on February 9, 1953, did not drown out the deafening explosion near the eastern wall of the Soviet Embassy building in Tel Aviv. The explosive charge contained more than 70 pounds of standard explosive material and caused great damage to the embassy and the adjacent buildings. The embassy housecleaner was severely wounded, and two of the embassy's employees, one of whom was the ambassador's wife, were lightly wounded.[118] The police inquiry found that unknown people had been able to get through the embassy fence and plant a bomb in the yard. On the same night, Isser Harel convened the higher ranks of the Shin Bet. After it became clear to him that they had no information about the identity of the people behind the incident, he asked them to investigate whether these people had formerly belonged to the Lehi. Harel assumed that only members of the Lehi had the operational experience to execute such a complex act of terrorism.[119] This had been witnessed four months earlier when a Lehi operative, Dov Shilansky, smuggled a bomb into the Jerusalem offices of the Foreign Affairs Ministry in protest against the reparations agreement with Germany. Shilansky was arrested at the last minute when alert police officers asked him to present an identifying badge and reveal the contents of the bag he was carrying.[120] However, despite intense efforts, Shin Bet people failed to track down the plotters of the operation, and the investigation came to a dead end.

Only four months later, Shin Bet investigators chanced upon a breakthrough that enabled them to get to the bottom of the affair. Near midnight on May 26, police officers guarding the building of the Romanian Church in Jerusalem, where the Israeli Ministry of Education was located, noticed two young Orthodox men who aroused their suspicions. The officers secretly followed them and let them get close to the building. When it seemed that the two men were about to climb over the fence surrounding the church, the officers approached them and asked them to identify themselves. The two gave their names as Mordechai Freund and David Bloy. In a quick search of their belongings, the officers discovered explosives; more important, they found detailed lists of names and functionaries in the organization to which they belonged.[121] When the Shin Bet people went over the documents, they were able to identify the people named there. Almost all of them had been active in the Lehi at one time or another. On that night, arrests were carried out in Tel Aviv and Jerusalem on the basis of these lists, and soon an underground network was exposed.[122] It was called the Kingdom of Israel by its members but became known to the public as the Tzrifin Underground.[123] This network had initiated a series of attacks against diplomatic institutions from Eastern European countries and a number of sporadic shootings against outposts of the Jordanian Legion along the border in Jerusalem.

The head of the network was a former Lehi man, Ya'akov Heruti. Together with two other Lehi people, Shimon Bachar and Yeshayahu Shar'abi, they concluded that, in light of the lack of response of the Israeli government to the increasing oppression of Jews in the Communist Bloc countries, it was necessary to take organized action against these countries in order to deter them from persecuting Jews. In a conversation we conducted with Heruti at his office, he told us that he and his colleagues had been deeply affected by the persecution of the Jews in Eastern Europe.[124] They were furious about the exclusion of Jews from public life in the Communist Bloc countries, which included barring them from cultural life, politics, society, and the academy.[125] An example of the latter was explicitly manifested in the physicians' trial in Moscow[126] and in the Prague trials (the Klementis–Slansky trial).[127] In more theoretical terms, Heruti's people perceived these developments as a direct attack against members of both their community (in the broad sense of the term) and their faith. In retrospect, this does not seem very different from European Muslims who identify with the suffering of Muslims in places such as Palestine, Iraq, and Afghanistan and are willing under some conditions to resort to violent and radical actions.

Soon after the decision to embark on the campaign, Heruti engaged other members who had served with him in the Lehi. In addition, he recruited a group of sixteen- to eighteen-year-olds who had been raised in Revisionist homes and from a young age had identified with the heroic stories they heard from their parents about Lehi fighters. These young members admired Heruti and his associates and helped them mainly with intelligence gathering and logistics. At the same time, one member of the group, Ya'akov Blumenthal, had organized another clique of activists in Jerusalem, most of whom were Orthodox Jews. Two activists from this clique, who were working on their own, were the ones who were caught in the planned attack against the Ministry of Education. They wanted to protest the role of the Ministry of Education in the indoctrination and secularization of large numbers of religious Jewish immigrants from North African countries after they arrived in Israel.[128] Like many in their community, the two perceived this secularization process as a direct assault on the religious Jews' way of life and as an existential threat to the ultra-Orthodox community in Israel.

The fact that the Kingdom of Israel Underground was a social network of youths with a common background rather than a disciplined underground movement—as was the case with the Lehi and Etzel—demonstrates the essential change that had taken place in the structure and nature of the activities of Jewish groups engaging in terrorism. As we shall see, the network structure became the distinctive feature of most Jewish terrorist groups that were active after the establishment of the State of Israel. At the same time, these new groups abandoned the paramilitary organizational structure. The condensed network structure of the Kingdom of Israel demonstrated another fact that was manifested in future Jewish terrorist groups. It illustrated how radicalization processes concentrated in a small group can lead to violence, especially when there is imminent perception of an existential threat among group members and they also have suitable resources to execute their actions.[129]

BRIT HAKANAIM (COVENANT OF THE ZEALOTS)

The change in the structure of Jewish terrorist groups can be observed in another violent group that was operational in the first years after Israel's establishment: the Brit Hakanaim (Covenant of the Zealots). The emergence of the Brit Hakanaim underground can be traced to April 10, 1950, when a number of yeshiva students from the Porat Yosef Yeshiva in Jerusalem, including Rabbi Shlomo Lorentz (who later became a member of Knesset), and Rabbi Mordechai Eliyahu (later on, the chief rabbi of Israel),[130] decided to establish a group on the basis of their religious beliefs.

The aims of their group were to struggle violently for the absorption of religious principles into everyday life in Israel and to fight against what they perceived as discrimination against the Orthodox community in Eretz Israel. They started recruiting other yeshiva students, whom they had known and anticipated would agree to join the group. At its prime, the group consisted of more than thirty-five yeshiva students.

To a great extent, the social impetus for the growth of Brit Hakanaim was the shock experienced by the ultra-Orthodox public after the establishment of a secular state in Eretz Israel. The new state promoted a principled and ideological framework that did not come from the original Hebraic sources of Israel. Members of the ultra-Orthodox public felt that only a Messiah who is a descendant of King David could be the founder of the Jewish sovereign state and the Third Temple, and therefore they regarded the nascent state as the desecration of a long-lasting Jewish tradition.[131]

A number of additional and central issues increased the polarization between the secular Jewish population and the religious one, motivating the members of Brit Hakanaim to act violently. First of all, as mentioned earlier, in the case of the Orthodox clique of the Kingdom of Israel group, there was the unpopular Israeli government policy insisting that the children of mostly religious or traditional Jewish immigrants who arrived after Israel's establishment were to study in the secular national education system. This provoked great anger among the religious and ultra-Orthodox public. Members of Brit Hakanaim perceived this as the initial stage in a culture war intended to put an end to the Orthodox world and therefore felt an obligation to fight against it.[132] According to Rabbi Mordechai Eliyahu, "We had started to receive bits of information about what was going on in the immigrant camps where it was forbidden to cover one's head and study the Torah. . . . I could not tolerate this kind of anarchy. . . . I believed that through the underground, I would be able to impose the life of the Torah in the country."[133]

In addition to the educational conflict, there was also the issue of the Sabbath, which increased tension between secular and religious people. Although the Orthodox public sometimes engaged in violent demonstrations in order to stop all public activity during the Sabbath,[134] there were also other violent secular counteractivities. For example, anonymous secular people attacked the Minster of Transportation, David Pinkas, in response to the Sabbath regulations he imposed (as a result of an oil shortage, the government established that for two days a week there would be no traffic, and one of them was Sabbath).[135] Another matter that worsened the tension between the two publics was the issue of recruiting girls to the army. In the days before the establishment of Israel, an agreement had been reached between Ben-Gurion and the religious public leaders to the effect that every young girl whose religiousness had been confirmed would be exempt from army service. But when the IDF was established, the leaders of the country worked tirelessly to dissolve the agreement. Mordechai Eliyahu stated that "a few days after . . . the Knesset was about to discuss an amendment to the security service law. . . . I understood that we had to respond . . . that talking wouldn't help; we had to do more drastic things. The aim was that it be known in the Knesset that there are circles who object to the law."[136]

The issues outlined here created a feeling among many people in the ultra-Orthodox counterculture that in order to prevent the devastating secularization of the Jewish people, and primarily in order to maintain the nature of the ultra-Orthodox community, it was necessary to establish an alternative Jewish sovereign framework of a Halacha state (based on Jewish law). This revolutionary state of mind was accompanied by much agitation, especially among the youth of the ultra-Orthodox community, and led to the emergence of Brit Hakanaim, whose members believed that these religious issues were crucial principles. In order to uphold the character of the Jewish people, according to their beliefs, the only possible response was to take violent measures. In the documents displayed during the trial of its members, the underground raised two pretentious goals based on this viewpoint: "the establishment of an Orthodox regime, based on the principle of God's justice, a dictatorial regime with no democracy,"[137] and "imposing that all citizens live according to the Torah by influencing the existing governing system."[138]

Despite the attempt to devise a covert underground group, the Brit Hakanaim's weak point was its inability to convert the ideological principles that inspired its members into a revolutionary operative framework. To a large extent, this stemmed from the character of the members and social framework of the group. Although it maintained a sophisticated, illegal political culture whose roots came from life in the Diaspora, ultra-Orthodox society at the time did not aspire to conduct a violent struggle against the government. This is what existed in the Diaspora, and this was the situation in Israel. Therefore, without an external supporting counterculture that would provide assistance to the group, its prospects of realizing its goals were low to begin with. In addition, group members and leaders suffered from a lack of experience in all things related to violent and clandestine activities.[139]

Brit Hakanaim initiated its violent actions in January 1951, aiming "to wipe out the desecrations."[140] On January 18, the group carried out a two-pronged action of setting fire to several private cars in north Jerusalem (because their owners drove on Sabbath) and putting bags soaked with oil in Egged's (the bus cooperative) garage in Jerusalem to protest public transportation on the Sabbath. Later on, in February and March 1951, twelve cars and taxicabs and a nonkosher butchery were set on fire,[141] in addition to a bomb attack on a restaurant that was open on the Sabbath.[142]

The group's most ambitious terrorist attack was supposed to be a bilateral action: planting a bomb in the Knesset on the day of the debate over the army recruitment of girls (the "Bride Operation") and setting on fire and destroying the archives of the recruitment office of the Ministry of Defense in Jerusalem (the "Watermelon Operation"). However, the group's leaders feared that such a drastic action would provoke a severe response by the state and put many human lives in danger.[143] It was decided nonetheless to launch the operation but with a minor change: a scare bomb, which would not cause loss of life.[144] After an early closure of the Knesset meeting, and before they had time to implement their plan, the group members were arrested by the Shin Bet, which had managed to infiltrate two agents into the underground network.[145] After extended investigations, most of the group members who had been arrested were gradually released, and only four central leaders were arraigned and prosecuted: Yehuda Rieder, Mordechai Eliyahu, Eliyahu Raful-Rafael, and Noah Wermesser. All of them received sentences ranging from six months to a year in prison.[146]

Similar to the Kingdom of Israel, evidence demonstrated that this group was not an established organization. During the trial, Brit Hakanaim turned out to be a social network of friends and acquaintances, and the fact that they spent much time together had radicalized their attitudes. Moreover, they felt that their cherished resources were in danger, and this also led them to undertake violent measures.

These episodes of Jewish terrorism in the first years of the State of Israel can be regarded as birth pangs. Certain groups suffering in the past from severe exclusion had difficulties liberating themselves from the old, illegal patterns of thinking that had been imprinted in them during the pre-state period. Indeed, after several years of adjustment, Jewish terrorism disappeared from Israeli politics and society. It raised its head again only after the Yom Kippur War in the form of two new movements: the Gush Emunim and Kahanist movements. Both belonged to the religious right side of the political map in Israel, although there were significant differences between them. The next two chapters are devoted to the Jewish terrorist groups that emerged from these two movements.

The Struggle over the Promised Land

████████████████

IT WAS TWILIGHT ON A SUMMER DAY in late July 2005 as we drove to a meeting with Yehuda Etzion at the settlement of Ofra in the West Bank. Etzion warmly welcomed us at the entrance to his office. It was hard to imagine that this same bearded, smiling man, who was engaged in diligently editing seven volumes of the writings of Shabtai Ben-Dov,[1] had thirty years before plotted to destroy the holy mosques on the Temple Mount and had not been far from carrying out this action. From Etzion's perspective, it should have been the crowning achievement of the group then dubbed by the Israeli media as the Jewish Underground.

Approximately two hours before we met with Etzion, we visited the Temple Mount to assess the possible implications of an explosion on the mosques and surrounding compound. Because of the tension prevailing in Jerusalem since the outbreak of the Al-Aqsa Intifada, permission to enter the Temple Mount is granted only to small groups and at certain hours. The Temple Mount compound and the mosques are under the exclusive control of the Jordanian Waqf;[2] Israeli police and soldiers are nowhere to be seen. A visitor who is admitted to the compound encounters wary glances from the many people praying there. Entrance to the mosques themselves, which according to Etzion are anathema, is strictly forbidden to non-Muslim visitors.

A conversation with a tour guide who approached us on his own initiative was very instructive in regard to the great sensitivity of the site. Muslims consider the Temple Mount to be the third most religious site after the cities of Mecca and Medina in Saudi Arabia, and according to Islamic tradition, the Al-Aqsa Mosque was built by the very first human being. Its great religious significance is rooted in the belief that the prophet Mohammed rode up this mountain on his magnificent horse and from this summit made his ascent to the heavens. By contrast, the Jews believe that the whole world was built around the watering stone located on the mountain and that Abraham's binding of Isaac took place there. According to Jewish tradition, the Temple Mount is also the site of the First and Second Temples, and the prayers of Jews everywhere in the world should be extended in this direction.

In modern Jewish thought, predominant convention prohibits ascending and praying on the Temple Mount for fear that worshippers who do not know the exact location of the center of the Temple, the holy of the holies, will defile it by their very presence. It is therefore the custom of the majority of Jews to pray at the foot of the Temple Mount and face the wall that, according to tradition, is the western wall of the original ramparts encircling the mountain. However, in recent years a growing number of Jewish believers have assembled into groups that, to a great degree, share the beliefs of Etzion, namely that it is a Jew's obligation to climb the Temple Mount and pray at this location in order to expedite the Jewish redemption process.[3]

Unlike the majority of messianic groups, which are busy in prayer and preparations for the "day of redemption" and, at most, engage in occasional provocation at the gates to the Temple Mount, Etzion believed that sabotaging the mosques was the only way to hasten the coming of the redemption. In this chapter we describe the formation and the actions of the highly sophisticated Jewish terrorist network that operated since the establishment of the State of Israel and launched its first operation on the night of June 2, 1980.

THE ATTACK ON THE MAYORS

It was a typical hot and humid summer night on the West Bank. In the light of the nearly full moon, small, silent groups of people made their way through the byways of the towns of Ramallah, Hebron, Nablus, El Bira, and East Jerusalem. Each cell consisted of three members, who kept conversation to a minimum. Some of them had been introduced to each other only several hours earlier. However, each knew his part perfectly well. When they arrived at their destinations, they worked in clockwork coordination with each other, their actions taking a matter of minutes. Immediately after finishing their work, the dark figures crept out to the vehicles awaiting them and were swallowed up by the night.

At 6:15 A.M., just after the morning light began to glimmer, there was a first sign of the impending events. A hand grenade connected to an explosive charge exploded in the kasbah of Hebron and injured seven local residents,

some of them traders in the market who had opened their stores in anticipation of the dawning business day.[4] Precisely one and a half hours later, it
became apparent to the Palestinian residents and Israeli security forces that
the event in Hebron was not an accident.

As was his custom each morning, the mayor of Ramallah, Karim
Khalaf, left his house to set out for the municipal offices. A few seconds
after he turned the key in the ignition of his luxury Cadillac parked near
his house, there was a huge blast. Switching on the car's ignition had detonated an explosive charge planted in his car. Khalaf, who was moderately
wounded, was rescued by members of his family and rushed to the local
hospital. For more than three hours, medical teams worked hard to save
his right leg; however, in the end they were left with no option but to amputate it.[5] About forty-five minutes later, the same scenario was repeated
with frightening precision. This time the attack was in the city of Nablus,
some 20 miles north of Ramallah. Bassam Shaka, the mayor of Nablus,
was readying himself for a workday at the town hall. Seconds after he turned
on his Opel 199 automobile, the front of the car exploded. His wife, Aya,
rushed out of the house and saw her husband in the damaged car with the
lower part of his body severely mangled. The doctors did all they could to
save Shaka's legs, but after six hours in the operating room they were
forced to amputate both of them.[6]

Three additional attacks planned for the same morning ended in failure. In the wake of the explosions that took place in those early morning
hours, the commander of the Israel Defense Forces (IDF) in the West
Bank, Brigadier-General Binyamin Ben-Eliezer, ordered inspections on
the cars of all West Bank mayors to check whether any of them were
booby-trapped. This cautionary measure saved the mayor of El-Bira, Ibrahim Tawil, from possible severe injury. Immediately after Karim Khalaf's
car exploded, Tawil sped to the hospital in Ramallah to visit his wounded
colleague. To his great fortune, one of the El-Bira council members gave
him a ride in his private car. While at the hospital, Tawil was summoned
back to his house by the military administration, which had decided to
examine his car. He told them that he generally parked his Peugeot 504 at
a garage that belonged to one of his neighbors and was located 120 yards
from his house. A bomb disposal expert of the Israel Police, Suleiman Hirbawi, was dispatched to the scene. When the sapper attempted to enter the
garage, an explosive device connected to the lock exploded, and Hirbawi

was moderately injured in the head and chest. However, after he was rushed to Hadassah Hospital in Jerusalem, the doctors established that he had lost his sight. Additional sappers were sent to the site, and after the garage gate was broken down, it turned out that the car itself had not been wired for explosives.[7]

In the other two instances, the terrorists themselves had second thoughts and for similar reasons decided not to install the explosives. The cell that was sent to the city of Bethlehem in order to booby-trap the car of Dr. Ahmed Hamzi Natshe, a member of the National Steering Committee,[8] decided to cut short the operation because it could not locate his car. Members of the cell who were sent out to strike at Ibrahim Dakkak, another member of the National Steering Committee who lived in East Jerusalem, discovered to their disappointment that his car was not parked in its regular place. It turned out that Dakkak had left his house the day before and had flown to Jordan.[9]

In retrospect, the multipronged attack on the West Bank mayors probably was the most sophisticated act of terrorism committed by Jews since the founding of the State of Israel. Evidence of the complexity of the operation was demonstrated not only by the capability to strike simultaneously at targets in different Palestinian cities but also by the fact that only a carefully measured amount of explosive was planted both in Khalaf's and Shaka's cars, thus leading to a severe injury of the lower limbs but not to the deaths of the mayors.[10]

What were the reasons and circumstances leading to the attacks on the mayors? How did the group that carried out these operations evolve? We will try to offer some answers to these questions in this chapter by using the theoretical framework presented in the Preface. But first, it is necessary to provide some essentials of the political context surrounding the emergence of the Jewish Underground.

THE CRISIS OF THE CAMP DAVID ACCORDS

The core group of the Jewish Underground began to crystallize immediately after the signing of the peace agreements between Israel and Egypt in 1979. Their actions were the most extreme expression of the rupture that plagued the settler movement after the Israeli government's decision to accept the principle of peace with Arab countries in exchange for the return of the occupied territories. The range of issues threshed out in the Camp

David Accords included the question of the return of the Sinai Peninsula to Egypt and the evacuation of Jewish settlements in this region. Egypt, which had fought hard to preserve its status as leader of the Arab world, also sought to represent the interests of the Palestinian people in the talks with Israel and succeeded in including the notion of Palestinian autonomy in the West Bank and Gaza Strip in the agreements.

Prima facie, the people of Gush Emunim did not seem to have a genuine reason to fear the agreements; the State of Israel was not intent on withdrawing from territories in the West Bank. Prime Minister Menachem Begin guaranteed the settlers an unprecedented building campaign in the region and delivered on this promise.[11] To elucidate the reasons for the crisis undergone by certain members of the movement, the Gush Emunim ideology must be examined in comparison to other political movements that endorsed the settlement project.

Secular elements in the Israeli political system that supported the settlements, including the Herut Movement and smaller groups of political activists, such as the Ein Vered Circle, which matured under the influence of the Labor movement activist ideology,[12] regarded the settlement project on the West Bank as the subsequent phase of the Zionist settlement enterprise. In their view, this was the consummation of the historical process of the conquest of the Promised Land and an important strategic maneuver. Relying on the precedent of the pre-state Zionist settlement of Eretz Israel, which asserted that constructing settlements in the border or frontier areas was the first stage in attaining Jewish sovereignty over these areas and would also bolster the security of Jews living in central Israel, secular supporters of the settlements believed that Jewish settlements in the West Bank would help expand the state's borders and reinforce its strategic status.

For Gush Emunim followers, the settlement initiative had other significance. As they saw it, the establishment of the State of Israel followed by the 1967 Six-Day War were fundamental milestones in the redemption of the people of Israel. The Six-Day War was particularly significant because it involved the "liberation" of some of the most holy places for the Jewish people and foremost, the Western Wall in Jerusalem and the Cave of the Patriarchs in Hebron. They called these historical events Hatkhalata De'Geula ("beginning" or "dawn of the redemption").[13] For many of them, the final outcome of the redemption would be the establishment of the

Kingdom of Israel. This meant that Jewish sovereignty would be reinstated in all parts of the biblical Land of Israel and that the land would be governed according to the laws of the Halakha.[14] Settlement of biblical Eretz Israel was therefore the harbinger of an all-inclusive revolution of faith, and therefore any territorial secession constituted an existential threat to their worldview.[15]

In addition to the ideology of the Gush Emunim settlers, the practical aspect of life in the West Bank must also be noted. In contrast to members of secular movements who supported the settlement of the West Bank—mainly on the pages of newspapers—the people of Gush Emunim actually put into practice the edict of settling the land. The attitude of the governments of Israel in the occupied territories created a propitious breeding ground for the development of a frontier culture[16] for settlers who saw themselves appointed on behalf of the state and in charge of protecting Jewish interests in these areas.[17] Because of the shortage of manpower and in light of the settlers' keen desire to establish authority in their residential areas, the State of Israel had granted them extensive authority in regard to law enforcement.[18] This situation led to a lack of distinction between the security forces and the settlers, so that the latter became part of the legislative, judicial, and executive bodies in the areas conquered by Israel.

The government license granted to the settlers along with the authorities' clemency toward (and tacit agreement with) illegal acts committed by them,[19] in particular with regard to the haphazard establishment of the settlements and the harm caused to their Palestinian neighbors,[20] encouraged the perpetuation of the frontier culture. This unwritten policy reinforced the belief of the Gush Emunim people that they were faithfully fulfilling a mission imparted to them by the State of Israel.[21]

They considered the government's decision to discuss the evacuation of Sinai and the notion of Palestinian autonomy in the West Bank illegitimate.[22] However, the Gush Emunim leaders did not confer the same degree of importance to the Sinai settlements destined to be evacuated (and the settlements in the Golan Heights) as they did to the settlements in the West Bank, whose evacuation was not on the agenda. The reason for this was that the majority of the settlements in Sinai and the Golan Heights were built by secular settlement movements, and the sites where they were established had only limited theological significance, if any. Yet it was the Gush Emunim youths who became key activists and stood at the forefront of the Movement to Halt the Retreat in Sinai and led the struggle against the dismantling of the largest Jewish settlement constructed there: Yamit. They were also the same activists who holed up on the roofs of the city and engaged in violent confrontation with the IDF soldiers who were sent to evacuate them.[23]

The aim of the Gush Emunim leaders, who had encouraged these youths, was to make the government of Israel pay a particularly high price for the evacuation of the less significant Sinai settlements in order to deter the heads of state from considering a future uprooting of West Bank settlements.[24] In order to mobilize their young followers to the struggle, the spiritual leaders of Gush Emunim emphasized that the upcoming evacuation was an existential threat to the settler movement and their way of life. Above all, they stressed to their supporters, it imperiled the notion of the greater Land of Israel and hence the feasibility of the redemption process. For example, the most important spiritual leader of Gush Emunim, Rabbi Zvi Yehuda Hacohen Kook, indicated the severity of the situation by declaring to his students at the Merkaz Harav Yeshiva that the evacuation of the settlements was "no less than an act of treason by the government against the idea of the Greater Land of Israel"[25] and that the agreements had no moral validation because they contradicted the basic principle of the Jewish faith. In another instance, groups of Gush Emunim rabbis published a manifesto declaring that "the evacuation contradicts the Jewish faith, the Law of the Torah, and presents a massive setback to the idea of the Greater Land of Israel."[26]

The fact that Menachem Begin—leader of the Herut Movement, which had inscribed on its banner the concept of the Greater Land of Israel and whose ideology and supporting leadership were wind in the sails of the Gush Emunim settlement movement—was the one who signed the peace agreements with Egypt led to another crisis. The settler leaders failed to grasp the factors responsible for the radical change in Begin's attitudes.[27] Furthermore, it was clear to them that such an action put forward and led by the largest hawkish political party in Israel would bring in parliamentary support from both center and left-wing parties, and therefore the chances of blocking this initiative in Parliament were slim.[28] Therefore, even in the early stages of the peace negotiations between Israel and Egypt, it was evident that the most important battle would be fought in the streets. The majority of the leaders of the settlers and their supporters sought to muster Israeli public opinion in order to indicate to the government that despite across-the-board support in Knesset, this was not a legitimate move.[29] Rabbi Haim Druckman explained at a press conference of Gush Emunim leaders a few weeks before the evacuation, "We should not lose hope; the support of the general public for our just demand could influence the government not to carry out the immoral act of evacuation."[30] In their speeches to the general public, the settler leaders emphasized different issues and not the ones they usually did when addressing their own followers. The security risks of the evacuation of the Sinai Peninsula and especially the inability to trust the Egyptian nondemocratic regime were the points they highlighted.

At any rate, although at some point 60 percent of the Israeli public opposed the evacuation, the more radical elements of Gush Emunim believed that the extraparliamentary struggle had to be carried out in more extreme ways. Among these more radical elements were members of the Jewish Underground.

THE JEWISH UNDERGROUND

Despite the impressive title coined by the media, the "Jewish Underground," for the group that mounted the attacks against the city mayors, the perpetrators did not make up an institutionalized faction. Like most other Jewish terrorist groups that emerged after the establishment of the State of Israel, this one consisted of a social network that was active for limited periods of time and recruited members on a friend-brings-a-friend basis from family, friendships and neighbors. The network included a number of cliques of settlers from the West Bank and Golan Heights, some of them officers and combatants in the reserves' elite IDF fighting units. The connections between the cliques were weak, and in effect they operated at different times and independent of each other. The terrorists themselves, except for network hubs,[31] were not acquainted with most of the other activists in the network and were similarly not aware of the range of the planned operations. One of the participants in the attack against the city mayors, Natan Natanzon, expressed it well:

> Underground? A load of rubbish. We went to the Supreme [Court] in order to put an end to that detestable name. People went out, did some work, sometimes took a risk and came home. This one came

from working with a calf, and that one from working with a horse, and another, from working on a tractor and they got together for a short-term operation. Take a man like me. I took part because I had to locate where Shaka lived. The whole operation took three weeks. But there were those who were involved in it for three days, three hours, that's all. Why did they make such an issue out of it?[32]

The loose structure of the network enabled different members who were elected or recruited to take part or not take part in a specific operation according to the degree of correspondence between the nature of the operation and their personal beliefs. For example, some members of the group who participated in the attacks against the mayors did not play a part in the planning of the attack on the Temple Mount and vice versa. Judge Zvi Cohen, who stood at the head of the panel that sentenced the members of the Jewish Underground,[33] succinctly called attention to the nuances of the goals of the different activists:

The evidence provides support for three motives, not necessarily shared by all the defendants. The first motive, at the heart of the Temple Mount conspiracy, is religious. The second motive—the security of the settlers in the West Bank. This was revealed in other offenses. . . . A less prominent motive is that of relations among friends.[34]

Justice Cohen's statement not only describes the various goals of members of the Jewish Underground but also, to a great degree, provides an indication of the group's structure. The Jewish Underground consisted of a

FIGURE 3.1 **THE JEWISH UNDERGROUND**

K-Core Analysis

A *k*-core is a maximal group of actors, all of whom are connected to a number (*k*) of other members of the group. The *k*-core approach allows actors to join the group if they are connected to *k* members, regardless of how many other members they are not connected to. For additional information, see *Introduction to Social Network Methods*, http://faculty.ucr.edu/~hanneman/nettext/C11_Cliques.html; Robert A. Hanneman and Mark Riddle. *Introduction to Social Network Methods*. Riverside: University of California, Riverside, 2005) (published in digital form at http://faculty.ucr.edu/~hanneman/).

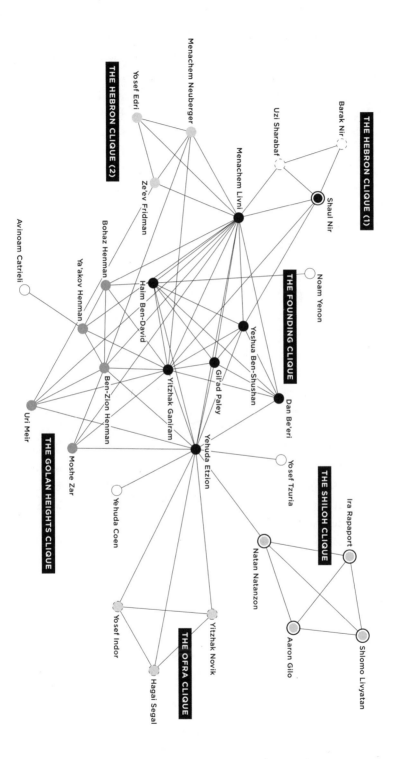

THE HEBRON CLIQUE (1)

Barak Nir

Uzi Sharabaf

Shaul Nir

Menachem Livni

Noam Yenon

THE FOUNDING CLIQUE

Yeshua Ben-Shushan

Dan Be'eri

Yosef Tzuria

THE SHILOH CLIQUE

Ira Rapaport

Natan Natanzon

Shlomo Livyatan

Aaron Gilo

Yosef Edri

THE HEBRON CLIQUE (2)

Menachem Neuberger

Ze'ev Fridman

Bohaz Henman

Haim Ben-David

Ya'akov Henman

Ben-Zion Henman

Yitzhak Ganiram

Gil'ad Paley

Avinoam Catrieli

Uri Meir

Moshe Zar

THE GOLAN HEIGHTS CLIQUE

Yehuda Etzion

Yehuda Coen

Yosef Indor

Yitzhak Novik

THE OFRA CLIQUE

Hagai Segal

central clique that included members of the founding nucleus: Menachem Livni, Yehuda Etzion, Yeshua Ben-Shushan, and Dan Be'eri. Directly below it, there were four central subgroups or cliques. Each one of these included members from a certain geographic area. Figure 3.1 demonstrates that the majority of the activists were recruited to underground activities by members of the founding clique who functioned as hubs and tied together all the elements of the network.

We can now more easily understand Justice Cohen's argument. He stated that whereas the Jewish Underground founding clique promoted sabotage of the mosques on the Temple Mount as the most important goal of the group, the aim of most activists in the other cliques was to harm Palestinians and defend Jewish settlements in the West Bank.

In the beginning, the Jewish Underground consisted of a small group of settlers from the Samaria area who met at social gatherings. They shared their hard feelings in the wake of the peace negotiations between Israel and Egypt, which reached their climax in the signing of the peace accords on March 26, 1979.

THE FOUNDING CLIQUE

The founding clique of the Jewish Underground included four members: Yehuda Etzion, Menachem Livni, Yeshua Ben-Shushan, and Dan Be'eri. Ben-Shushan and Be'eri became acquainted in 1974 while studying Kabbalah together with Rabbi Mordechai Atiah in Jerusalem.[35] Despite their different backgrounds—Be'eri is a French Christian who converted to Judaism and immigrated to Israel in 1968, and Ben-Shushan is a sabra and native of Jerusalem—they found a common language, and a strong friendship formed between the two.[36] Both of them lamented the fact that the Temple Mount, the Jews' most revered site, was in the hands of strangers, and they believed that as long as this situation continued, the redemption of the Jewish nation would be put off. Their conclusion was that the settlement of Jews in the West Bank was pointless unless control of the Temple Mount was restored to the people of Israel.[37]

As negotiations between Israel and Egypt began to move forward, the talks between the two friends about the future of the Temple Mount assumed a more concrete nature. Apart from the fact that the Israeli takeover of the Temple Mount would lead to a major spiritual transition among the Israeli people, they also believed that exploding the mosques could prevent the evacuation of the Sinai settlements in the wake of the rift that would ensue between the State of Israel and the Muslim world.[38]

In 1978, the pair of friends presented their ideas to Menachem Livni, a resident of Kiryat Arba. Livni, who was a battalion commander (reserves) and an expert in sabotage materials, was a prominent figure in the settler community and had known the two since the days of the struggle for the annexation of Givat Harsina to Kiryat Arba.[39] He quickly realized that Ben-Shushan and Be'eri's scheming in regard to the mosques on the Temple Mount was identical to the ideas proposed by another close friend, Yehuda Etzion, from the Ofra settlement. Etzion was the intellectual among the lot,[40] a learned man who was significantly inspired by the beliefs of Shabtai Ben-Dov and who had sought to devise a plan for the redemption movement in which he would sow the seeds of the restoration of the Sanhedrin.[41] He believed with all his heart that the removal of the mosques was "the only way for the State of Israel to ultimately become the true, worthy and promised Kingdom of Israel."[42]

After Livni introduced Etzion to Ben-Shushan and Be'eri, the group began meeting every Thursday at Ben-Shushan's house for "empowerment" meetings. The objective of these meetings was to discuss the practical ways of implementing the plan to blow up the mosques.[43] In the next few weeks, Etzion engaged in efforts to expand the network. He understood that in order to carry out a terrorist attack at the heavily guarded Temple Mount, a broad infrastructure of activists and collaborators was necessary.[44] Among the first ones invited to the meetings at Ben-Shushan's house was Gil'ad Paley, Etzion's cousin. Because Paley, a resident of the Golan Heights, did not have a driver's license, he co-opted another friend, Haim Ben-David, who drove him to Jerusalem, and in this way Ben-David also became an accomplice to the idea of attacking the mosques. At a later stage, Yitzhak Ganiram, another resident of the Golan Heights, also joined the group. Ganiram was already acquainted with Livni through his wife, who had been adopted by Livni and his family when she had performed her national service in Hebron,[45] but the person who persuaded him to join was in fact Ben-Shushan. In a chance meeting between the two, the latter described to him the intolerable situation of the Temple Mount. When the police interrogated Ganiram, he confessed that he had been very much impressed by Ben-Shushan's Halakhic knowledge:

He gave me a spiritually remarkable lecture on how humiliating the situation was. I didn't understand a large part of it because it involved elements from the kabbalah. I agreed that the situation was disgraceful and undesirable, and then he began to talk about the possibility that one day we Jews would have to do something and bring the Muslim places of worship down from there. Bring down— meaning, to blow them up. This did [not] seem logical to me because the State of Israel would be forced to rebuild them. He said that we shouldn't look at it from a realistic point of view, but rather in a way that would bring about a great change. I didn't understand all of his spiritual explanations on this matter.[46]

Although the other members of the group agreed that the mosques on the Temple Mount impeded the implementation of the goals of the people of Israel, at the beginning of 1980 they were still skeptical about their ability and even desire to blow them up. Yehuda Etzion described it this way: "This was still a time of doubts and questions [about] whether we were worthy of setting forth on this great course."[47]

VENGEANCE

While members of the group were pondering viable ways of carrying out their vision, a severe terrorist attack was executed in Hebron on Saturday, May 2, 1980. After praying at the Cave of the Patriarchs, six yeshiva students returning to Beit Hadassah were murdered by Fatah activists. Beit Hadassah was a building situated at the very center of the Arab part of Hebron. It had been purchased by Jews and eventually became a focal point of their activities in the city.[48] The killings shocked the group members, as Yehuda Etzion explained: "And then our youths were murdered at Beit Hadassah. . . . And therefore—although without including it in the general effort to bring about a redemption movement that would lead the country towards its true goals—we decided to respond affirmatively [to the idea of the attack against the city mayors]."[49]

They had already begun to discuss the need for a counteroperation at the funeral procession for the yeshiva boys.[50] The fact that they knew each other and were aware that none of them had inhibitions about engaging in terrorism made it easier for them to translate their thoughts into actions. The turmoil that plagued the spiritual leaders of the settlers and the radical articulations of some of them provided the moral footing for the decision to mount the counteroperation. In a forum including leaders of the Jewish settlement movement in Hebron, which convened after the murder of the six yeshiva youths, Rabbi Levinger and Rabbi Waldeman urged Livni and Etzion to respond to the incident in an "appropriate" manner and to commit an act "so that the Arabs would learn a lesson."[51] On the basis of Livni's testimony to his investigators, it is evident that the rabbis felt the same way as he did. They regarded terrorism as a tool that had the potential of deterring the Palestinian population and forcing the Israeli government to provide better security for the settlers. In fact, Livni testified that before the attack on the city mayors, Rabbi Waldeman approached and asked him whether he could take part in the operation.[52]

Immediately after the meeting with the rabbis, Livni got in touch with Etzion, and they began to discuss possible ways of taking revenge. The proposal that stood out among all the others was an attack on public officials of the Palestinian community in the West Bank. At first, Etzion had reservations. He was afraid that the attack would be detrimental to their prospective operation on the mosques, which in his mind was the group's main objective. However, in the end, he was persuaded that carrying out the operation would extend the group's network and help its members gain operational experience.[53]

Ten days after the Hebron killings, the group met once again, this time at the wedding of Rabbi Levinger's daughter. On this occasion, Etzion and Livni presented their proposal of retaliation to the rest of the members of the group. The event also proved to be an ideal opportunity for expanding the network. Members of the clique approached acquaintances who they thought would probably agree to take part in the counterattack. For example, in a conversation during the wedding that took place between Ganiram and Moshe Zar—one of the more prominent Jewish land agents in the West Bank, who at that time still lived in the Golan Heights—the latter did not need much coaxing and immediately agreed to take part in the operation.[54]

The decision to embark on the operation against the mayors is indeed corroboration of the importance of the vengeance motive.[55] However, the other factors that inspired the group's leaders were also of significant merit. In carrying out the attack, they had in mind three key objectives. The first was to facilitate a deterioration in the relations between Israel and the

Arab countries with the intention of preventing progress in the peace process with Egypt. For the most part, they hoped that this would halt the evacuation of the settlements in north Sinai.[56] The second objective was to create a balance of deterrence vis-à-vis the Palestinian organizations. Group members held leaders of the Palestinian public directly accountable for the increase in attacks against Jews in the West Bank, and by striking at them, they hoped to deter the Palestinians from future attacks. Menachem Livni explains,

> It is not possible to educate and judge a multitude of people who live in keep with defective moral criteria, according to another set of moral criteria belonging to a more ethical human system. . . . That is, at least in the first stage, it is necessary to take action against a hostile Arab population using a language that they understand.[57]

The third objective of the attacks was to signal to the government of Israel that if the settlers were not provided with adequate state protection, they would have no option but to protect themselves in any way they saw fit.[58]

After selecting the targets of their attacks and establishing the mode of operation, the founding clique continued to try to recruit new candidates in order to expand the network. The most outstanding recruiter was Yehuda Etzion. His rhetorical skills, broad education, and infectious enthusiasm were of great advantage. For example, he was successful in getting two of his neighbors in Ofra to join the group. These were Yitzhak Novik, who was a captain (reserves) of a combat unit, and Hagai Segal, a student at the Hebrew University who eventually became one of the more prominent media figures to emerge from the settler community. At a later stage, an additional expansion of the network took place on the basis of family and friendship ties. In this fashion, Etzion conscripted two more of his acquaintances, Yosef Indor and Natan Natanzon. The latter, a resident of the Shiloh settlement, helped sign on two additional friends from his own settlement. These were Ira Rapaport, a familiar figure among the settler community who was later appointed a Zionist Histadrut emissary to the United States, and Shlomo Livyatan, an officer of the IDF Civil Administration. Natanzon had become friendly with Livyatan when he was secretary of the Shiloh settlement. Later, Livyatan recruited his colleague from the Civil Administration, IDF officer Aaron Gilo.[59]

The other members in the founding clique also relied on personal ties in order to enlarge the circle of collaborators. Menachem Livni recruited two of his acquaintances, Menachem Neuberger and Ze'ev Fridman. He had met Neuberger through Rabbi Waldeman, who was his father-in-law and head of the yeshivat hesder (a yeshiva program combined with military service) in Kiryat Arba, the town where Livni lived. Livni had met Fridman when the latter was serving as head of the Kiryat Arba Council. Yitzhak Ganiram from the Golan Heights enlisted other members from settlements in his region, such as Uri Meir and Ben-Zion Henman. He had met these two while working with them at the Golan Heights Field School.[60]

Although recruitment proceeded according to the "friend-brings-a-friend" method, and it seemed that the decisive factor in approaching certain potential candidates was their degree of readiness to take part in violent actions, recruiters also took operative considerations into account. Some candidates were taken on because they had skills that could contribute to the operation's success. For example, Fridman's special status as head of the Kiryat Arba Council made it possible for the group to use the council's facilities in their preparations.[61] Natanzon was admitted because he was known for his connections with people from the Civil Administration and therefore was asked to get hold of information about the residence and daily routine of Bassam Shaka, the mayor of Nablus. For the same reason, Shlomo Livyatan was taken on. As an officer of the Civil Administration, he was able to gain access to highly valuable information on the residences and routines of the targeted figures. The role of Aaron Gilo, Civil Administration officer of Ramallah, was to make sure that Jews and IDF officers would not be harmed during the operation.[62] He was asked to notify his peers in advance if Israeli security forces were in the vicinity of the designated sites.

While Etzion was busy broadening the ranks, Livni began to work on the practical aspects of the operation: choosing the method of attack and weapons, preparing explosive devices, and training new recruits. They also divided between themselves responsibility for the cells. Livni assumed responsibility for the cells in Bethlehem and Jerusalem while Etzion attended to the cells in Ramallah/El Bira and Nablus. These two members also supervised intelligence gathering and were in charge of maintaining surveillance over the houses of the designated targets. They also established the procedures for obtaining and transferring explosives to the operators and trained them for the upcoming attacks on the targets. To a large degree, the two functioned as the network's hubs and were the motivating force behind the group.

The loose structure of the network, consisting of the founding clique core and subgroups at the periphery, had a significant effect on the manner in which the attacks were carried out. First, the cells were divided according to the original subgroups that formed the Jewish Underground. For example, the cell that operated in Jerusalem consisted of members of the clique from the Golan Heights, and the cell that executed the attacks in Ramallah was made up of the clique of members from Ofra. There were two reasons for this. The first was that members of a cell who were acquaintances would trust each other. Second, this mode of operation allowed a great degree of compartmentalization. Most of the participants did not have any information on the actual range of the operation or the identity of the members of the other cells. Some members specifically insisted on this anonymity. For example, Moshe Zar asked to receive no information other than the exclusive details of his designated job. Therefore, other than driving Natanzon and Rapaport to Nablus—where they planted the explosive device under Bassam Shaka's car—he was not aware of the other events of that same night.[63] Even the clique made up of the founders of the underground (i.e., Etzion, Livni, Be'eri, and Ben-Shushan, and to a certain degree also Paley and Henman) were not acquainted with all those who took part in the operation. Yehuda Etzion said that some of the members of the network became aware of the others only in jail, four years after carrying out the operation.[64] Livni described it in a very lucid fashion:

> There was no organizational structure in this operation [referring to the plan to blow up the mosque at the Temple Mount] as well as in the previous operations. The people committed themselves to this job on the basis of an idealistic identification with each respective operation, including the matter of the Temple Mount. There was no order or commanding structure that gave orders to be carried out and so on. And things were done out of a feeling of ideological participation in the affair.[65]

The loose structure of the group also made it easier to sever all connections between the different cliques immediately after the coordinated assaults. While the founding clique continued to plan for the truly important operation, the attack on the mosques of the Temple Mount, most members of the other cells returned to their daily routine. For nearly all of them, this was their last contact with the Jewish Underground. From the perspective of the group members, the unique network structure also had its less positive aspects. The fact that each cell separately prepared itself for the operation produced a differentiation in results. Whereas several cells succeeded in carrying out their assignments, others failed because of inadequate skills, ineffective planning, or flawed intelligence.

REMOVING THE ABOMINATION

In the wake of the attack on the mayors, a disagreement broke out between the members of the founding clique regarding the central goal of blowing up the mosques. Whereas Menachem Livni believed that the main benefit of this action would be in preventing the withdrawal from Sinai,[66] Etzion, and to a large extent also Ben-Shushan and Be'eri, regarded this as the first step in a long educational journey of the redemption movement toward conquering the heart of the whole nation.[67] These conceptual differences also gave rise to differences in the motivations of the conspirators. Although Etzion himself maintained that he was completely devoted, heart and soul, to the operation, Livni agreed to it but only if several external conditions were fulfilled:

And when this matter is made possible by a deeper and broader readiness of the Israeli public—including wider backing by the rabbis—the action will be taken. And if it doesn't become possible, the very fact that the group is working on it and preparing itself for it involves a greater action, that is: make me an opening the size of the eye of a needle, and I shall make you an opening the size of a hall. In other words, there are situations where the group acts and believes the deed will be accomplished in some way by the Holy One, Blessed Be He.[68]

With this attitude, Livni was effectively disavowing the worldview of Etzion, who believed the Jewish Underground was a kind of advance guard at the head of "the army" whose actions were destined to shape the history of the Jewish people in their land. For Livni, the role of the group was not only to lead "the army" but also to look back and see whether the public was responsive to their ideas. He was so preoccupied with public support for the underground that he followed the public opinion polls in the newspapers measuring the support for their terrorist attacks. During his trial, he said that he had learned from the polls that the public was sympathetic toward the actions taken against the Arabs; they allowed the Jews to hold their heads high. Still, he admitted that these same publications showed that the underground had failed to fully enlist the public's support, and subsequently he concluded that blowing up the mosques would not be received well.[69]

At this stage, the disagreement between Etzion and Livni was evident. Whereas members of the founding clique under the influence of Etzion regarded the sabotage of the mosques as a central and feasible objective— to the point of disparaging any other operation[70]—members of the other cliques who were aware of this secret matter leaned more toward Livni's point of view. Although they believed that the very presence of the mosques on the Temple Mount constituted a holy desecration, they did not view the operation as a goal that should be achieved at any price, and they feared the severe regional and international ramifications of such an act.

Despite the differences, plans for carrying out the Temple Mount operation were not neglected. This was mainly because, notwithstanding the different motives, most of the activists still believed it was necessary to remove the mosques and also because they assumed that when the time came to act, they could reexamine the conditions and determine whether they could muster enough public support for an act of this type. In any event, as illustrated by Livni's statement just quoted, great importance was put into the preparation and training of the people irrespective of the actual implementation of the attack on the mosques.

In the first stages of preparation, members of the founding clique devoted their time to recruiting new activists. For example, in the beginning of 1982, Livni approached Shaul Nir, a former marine commando whom he knew from their mutual work in the Association for the Advancement of Jewish Settlement in Hebron, and asked him whether he would be willing to participate in the operation. Nir agreed and convinced his brother Barak, who volunteered to survey the security arrangements on the Temple Mount, to join as well. In general, family connections appeared to be an effective channel for inducting new members into the underground. In this manner, Ben-Zion Henman, who was already at that time a key activist in the network, recruited his son Bohaz and his brother Ya'akov, a pilot in the Israeli air force.[71] The three of them lived in the village of Nov in the Golan Heights, where Henman and his brother settled after helping form Gush Etzion at the end of the 1960s as part of the founding nucleus of the Gush Emunim movement.

The main activity of the group at this junction focused on gathering intelligence, stocking up sabotage materials, and discussing the best tactics to destroy the mosques without causing serious damage to the Temple Mount and the Western Wall. Great responsibility was laid on the shoulders of Dan Be'eri. He took advantage of his past as a Christian believer; cloaking himself in a priest's robes and passing himself off as a man of faith, he would inspect the Temple Mount environs. Exploiting his ability to speak fluent French, he was able to convince the Waqf officials that he had come to the Temple Mount for research purposes. His real mission was to measure the distances between the columns that held up the Dome of the Rock in order to estimate the amount of explosives needed to effect its inward collapse. Be'eri took his role very seriously and was so persuasive that the people of the Waqf provided him with an assistant to help him with the tape measure.[72]

After collecting information on the architectural dimensions of the Dome of the Rock, the group went ahead with the preparation of the explosive charges. They planned to build containers with explosive devices placed in such a way that after detonation, the blast waves would be aimed at the columns, thus causing a controlled collapse of the dome.[73] Livni, who had once worked in an aircraft engine factory in Beit Shemesh,[74] knew where they built such containers. He located a metal factory in the city of Rishon LeZion,[75] gave the owner the exact specifications of the containers, and paid for them in advance. After their delivery, he concealed the explosives in the containers and stashed them away in Kfar Abraham, near Petah Tikva,[76] and in Ya'akov Henman's chicken coop in the village of Nov on the Golan. When the existence of the Jewish Underground was ultimately discovered, the containers were found fully intact, wrapped in polyethylene sheets and ready for detonation.[77]

At the next stage, members of the network concentrated on finding the most convenient way to access the Temple Mount. After long weeks of observation, they concluded that the most suitable place for infiltration was in the area of the Golden Gate (Sha'ar Harahamim), where the walls were low and security was lacking.[78] After the decision was made regarding the path of entry, members of the group began to practice scaling walls while carrying weighted containers to simulate a load of explosive charges. The sites chosen for the training were Radar Hill near Jerusalem and an area of cliffs on a Netanya beach. During one of the training exercises near Netanya, some Border Police soldiers on patrol asked them to explain their activities. Without hesitating, the conspirators responded that they were instructors in the youth movement, Bnei Akiva,[79] training for a route march of novice scouts.

The last remaining problem was how to neutralize the Waqf guards in charge of defending the mosques. The decision was made to eliminate them despite the fact that members of the network knew they were unarmed. They planned to carry out the killings using submachine guns equipped with silencers. Most members of the group already had Uzi submachine guns—provided to them by the IDF because they lived in the West Bank[80]—but getting hold of silencers was a much more complex matter. To this end, they mobilized Avinoam Catrieli, a combat means officer in the Katzkhar (a Hebrew acronym for Chief Paratroopers and Infantry Officer) headquarters,[81] who, in the course of his army job, regularly requisitioned special combat materials for IDF elite units. Catrieli, wearing the uniform of a paratrooper officer, and Ya'akov Henman, dressed as an air force pilot, proceeded to the Bnei Barak store that provided combat materials for the Ministry of Defense. The shop owner was not at all suspicious of a pilot and a paratrooper officer who bought silencers and paid for them in cash.[82]

The careful preparations of network members proved that, despite their differences of opinion about the timing and conditions for implementation of the operation, they did not back away from nearly carrying it out. This seemed to be the impression of judges Finkelman and Cohen when they rendered their verdict in the trial of the Jewish Underground:

> Just look at the long, hard road the defendants have traveled together, how much they have invested together, how far they went in their planning, collecting of combat materials, assembling special equipment for carrying out their mission, surveillance, etc. Only about one year before his arrest, Yehuda Etzion rented a storeroom apartment in Jerusalem for a period of two years. Add to all this the clear and crystallized worldview of each of the defendants, and you

cannot escape the conclusion of an extant resolve to conspire to commit the crime. It was only the actual execution that was postponed from time to time.[83]

The decision not to carry out the operation was eventually reached in April 1982, after preparations had been completed. Whereas the "messianic" activists in the founding clique, headed by Yehuda Etzion, stuck to their contention that the attack on the Temple Mount had to be executed without delay, the reservations of Menachem Livni, Gil'ad Paley, and Yitzhak Ganiram only increased. They feared that the action might lead to an all-out war between Israel and the Arab countries and to the isolation of Israel in the international arena. They also feared that the government of Israel would ultimately be forced by the international community to build new mosques on the ruins of the destroyed mosques. From a Halakhic perspective, rebuilding the mosques was a forbidden act, and therefore, in the final analysis, the operation had become a double-edged sword.[84]

Livni's reservations led him to hold theoretical discussions with various rabbis about whether it was permissible, from a Halakhic point of view, to initiate actions that would prevent the withdrawal from Sinai. Livni also asked whether they should, at the same time, attempt to regain Jewish control of the Temple Mount because, according to tradition, the Jews would be permitted to return and establish the new temple on the mount only after the Messiah's arrival. But not a single prominent theological figure would give his blessings for such an action.[85] For example, one of the rabbis, whose identity remains unknown, answered him with a well-known Talmudic passage: "The children of Israel were cautioned against three things: They were not to revolt against the nations of the world, and they were not to enter the Temple Mount, and they were not to force the coming of the Messiah."[86] Other members of the group also sought rabbinical endorsement, but they too returned empty-handed.[87] One of the more prominent objectors to the Jewish Underground's activities was Rabbi Shlomo Avinar, a Gush Emunim leader[88] who, during one of his lessons in his settlement, Keshet, was asked by an underground member, Haim Ben-David, his opinion on "taking the law into one's hands on the assumption that Jews had attacked Khalaf and Shaka." The rabbi answered that they had caused harm to the sovereignty of Israel in its present embodiment: "The principle of 'if anyone comes to kill you, kill him first' is widely known," he said, "all the more true when speaking of one who comes to kill many by incitement to murder. But the question of 'what should be done' rests in the hands of the state authority; even if there are breaches in the efficiency of the security system or if there is a general weakness of governmental directives, acts of personal, unorganized terrorism, are not worth the damage caused to the sovereignty of Israel. An attack on a government is an attack on the sovereignty at large."[89]

Avinar's response and that of other prominent rabbis, such as Yoel Ben-Nun, a Gush Emunim spiritual leader who categorically opposed the group's actions, had significant impact on the uncertainty of the majority of the collaborators who intended to blow up the Temple Mount mosques. Therefore, unable to obtain spiritual support for the operation, Menachem Neuberger from Kiryat Arba[90] and Gil'ad Paley and Haim Ben-David from the Golan Heights, who had taken part in the attack on the mayors, withdrew from the plot to attack the Temple Mount.[91] The failure to secure rabbinical authorization also reinforced Livni's earlier reservations about the operation and prompted him to pull out from it once and for all. In his confession, he explicitly mentioned this:

> It was decided, after consultations with rabbis, not to carry out the operation for the following reasons: a) the nation is not inclined towards such an act; b) there is the possibility of harm to Jews during the course of the operation due to heightened security measures on the mount in the wake of the attack by Goodman [an American Jew who opened fire on Palestinian worshippers in 1979] on the Temple Mount; c) the objections of the rabbis; d) the heavy sense of responsibility regarding the matter and its results.[92]

Therefore, even though rabbis from the immediate social networks of the Jewish Underground members would give their blessings to their actions, the fact that prominent rabbis from the religious Zionist stream refrained from granting their stamp of approval played a central role in the decision of many members not to take part in the operation.

Members of the founding clique, who saw their plans running aground, tried to counter the rabbis' objections by drawing on their own extensive religious education. In the attempt to offset the doubts that were gnawing away at their associates, they sought justification for attacking the Temple

Mount mosques in the teachings and adjudications of rabbis who were no longer living.[93] For example, Dan Be'eri scoured the writings of Rabbi Zvi Yehuda Kook for some reference to a possible endorsement of the plan for exploding the mosques. In Hagai Segal's words,

> Be'eri's position concerning the possible outcome of blowing up the Dome of the Rock is based, among other things, on a concept held by Rabbi Zvi Yehuda Kook which reduces the public's freedom of choice much more than that of the individual. . . . The acknowledgment of the greatness of these or any other rabbis does not oblige me to accept their opinion on matters of worldly importance, especially when speaking of matters far removed from their area of specialization, and which I, myself, have thoroughly investigated.[94]

Yehuda Etzion found what he felt was the true inspiration for the Jewish Underground's actions in the writings of Shabtai Ben-Dov. As far back as 1958, Ben-Dov wrote, "When indeed 'the Eternal One of Israel will not lie' . . . a supreme national awakening will rise forth among us . . . from the total revolution that stands before us, from the liberation of the Temple Mount from the predatory wolves of the entire world."[95] Yehuda Etzion, the Jewish Underground member most devoted to the Temple Mount operation, saw in these words justification for the operation.

These attempts to obtain some kind of religious validation for the Temple Mount operation did not persuade Livni, who, in the end, decided not to take part in blowing up the mosques. Livni's decision was the final nail in the coffin for the operation because he was the only one with the technical know-how needed to manage the detonation of the explosives. Aside from this practical consideration, Livni was also one of the dominant figures in the group. His decision led to the withdrawal of additional members, including Yeshua Ben-Shushan and Dan Be'eri, and weakened the social cohesion of the network.[96]

Only Yehuda Etzion remained faithful to the original plan. This fact demonstrates that, unlike his friends, he did not regard terrorism as a tool for achieving strategic objectives. For him, the group's actions were aimed exclusively at opening the way to redemption, and sabotaging the mosques was just one step toward that goal. As far as he was concerned, if the members of the underground were successful in their attack on the Temple

Mount but this action did *not* bring about the realization of his vision, the attack would still be nothing more than a common crime.[97] Even after serving two years of his seven-year prison sentence, Etzion showed no remorse concerning the plan, as demonstrated in his own words:

> Because the leadership of the state still denies and turns their back on redemption, we must establish the Movement of Redemption. We must build a new force that will develop, very slowly, while evolving with the aid of educational and social activity into a new leadership. Of course I cannot predict if the Dome of the Rock will be removed from the mount during the course of the efforts of this new entity or after it is already leading the nation, but one fact is certain, that the mount will be purified, because that is our duty and that is what God wants from us. All this will not happen in one year, nor in one generation, but a duty remains a duty, and so we must be prepared for it and endure patiently and courageously.[98]

Then again, it appears that the effects of time and maturity were greater than the penalty of imprisonment. In the summer of 2005, when we visited Etzion at his house in Ofra, we found a reconciled man who admitted to us that the idea of sabotaging the mosques was fundamentally wrong and in fact childish. He also said that, after so many years, it was clear to him that even if the operation had succeeded, it would not have brought the people of Israel any closer to the exalted goal to which he aspired.[99]

After retreating from the idea of blowing up the Temple Mount mosques, the Jewish Underground dissolved, and its members returned to their daily routine.[100] Nevertheless, the network structure of the underground later allowed it to assume a renewed form. Several members of the original group, not necessarily the main figures, felt there was still justification for a Jewish group that would act in response to Palestinian violence. In this fashion, the plan for the second terrorist attack of the Jewish Underground, which targeted the Islamic College in Hebron, was born.

THE MASSACRE AT THE ISLAMIC COLLEGE

Although the public associates the terrorist attack on the Islamic College in Hebron with the Jewish Underground, the terrorists who actually took part in it had no connection to the attack on the mayors. The motivating force behind the operation, Shaul Nir, who was twenty-nine at the time, devoted most of his time to purchasing houses on behalf of the Association for the Advancement of Jewish Settlement in Hebron, headed by Menachem Livni. In his search for abandoned houses in Hebron, Nir became very well acquainted with the city, a fact that greatly facilitated intelligence gathering in preparation for the attack on the Islamic College.

In this case as well, the direct motive behind it was the desire to avenge a recent terrorist attack. On July 1, 1983, Aharon Gross, a yeshiva student, was stabbed to death while passing the wholesale market in Hebron on his way to the Cave of the Patriarchs. Nir had known Gross personally for a long time and was enraged by what he considered the completely inadequate responses of the security forces to attacks against Jews. He felt that he could not bear the situation any longer and decided to take matters into his own hands. The natural person for him to turn to was Menachem Livni, who had enlisted him in the preparations for the attack on the Temple Mount. After a short period of indecision, Livni agreed to help:

After some doubts and out of a real sense of *pikuakh nefesh* [the dictate to save the life of another], I agreed to help in the attack on the Islamic College. . . . For the sake of the operation, I supplied a Kalachnikov that I had and also two grenades [stolen by Livni during his reserve duty]. Shaul Nir gathered intelligence on the target, and in light of this information proposed to carry out a shooting attack while the students were outside on their break. I was particularly concerned about the possibility of women being injured and asked my friends to take great care and avoid harming women. I was at my wife's parents' house in Rehovot at the time of the attack. The operation was carried out by Barak Nir—driver (I don't know him and I don't have any connection with him; he was recruited by Shaul Nir), Uzi Sharabaf—operations, Shaul Nir—operations. . . . Yitzhak Ganiram helped out with the vehicle for the mission; coordination with Akla was through me. . . . Yeshua only knew about the plan the morning before it was carried out. A report of the action was submitted to Yehuda [Etzion] shortly after its implementation and he informed me that he was opposed to it. . . . Yehuda Etzion was angry that no one had told him about it beforehand and he was in fact opposed to the operation.[101]

Livni's words once again illustrate the loose nature of the network. The initiative for the plan did not come from the founding clique. Moreover, Yehuda Etzion, who for years had been reputed to be the leader of the Jewish Underground, learned of the involvement of his associates in the attack only after it had been carried out.

After getting the green light from Livni, Nir began recruiting people for the operation. The first and most natural candidate was his brother Barak, who had previously helped him in the preparations for the Temple Mount mosques attack. The second person he approached was Uziahu (Uzi) Sharabaf, who was Rabbi Levinger's son-in-law and one of the leaders of the settlers in Kiryat Arba. Sharabaf had been a close friend of Aharon Gross, and therefore Nir imagined—and rightly so—that it would be easy to persuade him.[102]

Much like the attack on the mayors, this operation was also planned meticulously. Shaul Nir arrived at the southwest entrance to the Islamic College on July 26, 1983, at 11:50 A.M., when the streets of Hebron were swarming with people going about their daily business.[103] He drew his Kalachnikov and fired two bursts into the air.[104] This was to signal to his friends that the area was "clean" and that they could proceed with the attack. Seconds later, a Peugeot 504 stopped in front of the college entrance and Uzi Sharabaf jumped out. He and Nir ran into the courtyard and with their automatic rifles opened fire on the students there. At the same time, Barak Nir also got out of the car and started firing at students who had run to the upper floor windows of the college to see what was happening. Zohair El Anti, a teacher and Ramallah resident, was injured by a bullet that pierced his hand in the middle of class while he was writing on the blackboard.[105] Meanwhile, Nir and Sharabaf continued their automatic fire while making their way toward the main entrance to the building. When they got to the doorway, they tossed in a hand grenade, which rolled into the corridor where the student council happened to be in session. One of the council members described the moment: "We hit the floor and began to scream without understanding what was going on around us. We saw blood pouring from council member Walid Siam's hand. We realized that a massacre was taking place at the university."[106]

Many of the students went into shock, and several even jumped from the windows of the second and third floors. After lobbing the grenade, Nir and Sharabaf decided not to enter the building. They quickly retraced their footsteps, entered the waiting getaway car, and sped away, tires screech-ing.[107] When they reached the area of Beit Guvrin, 14 miles northwest of Hebron, they burned their firearms along with the clothes they were wearing and then drove to a gas station, where another car awaited them. Yizhak Ganiram arrived a little while later, started up the abandoned vehicle, and drove it to his house in the Golan Heights.[108] The results of the attack were grave. Three students were killed, and thirty-three were wounded.[109] In contrast to the attack on the mayors, the intention this time was not just to settle for serious injury but to kill as many Islamic College students as possible.[110]

THE EXPOSURE OF THE NETWORK AND CONCLUSIONS

The fact that the Islamic College attack took place without mishap and did not draw a harsh reaction from the security forces against the Jewish pop-ulation of Hebron spurred Nir's cell on to carry out further acts of terror-ism against the Palestinian population of the city. On December 10, 1983, a hand grenade was thrown at the Romano House, which was inhabited by several Hebron Jewish settlers.[111] Livni and Nir decided to strike back, and, once again, Uzi Sharabaf joined them. On the night of December 30, 1983, Nir and Sharabaf concealed booby-trapped fragmentation grenades—which Livni had stolen during his reserve duty—at the entrance to the Sheikh El Rashad mosque in Hebron.[112] The grenades were placed in a plastic bag and attached to the door of the mosque. In the morning, when guard Suliman El Zid arrived and tried to remove the bag, it exploded and he was wounded in the stomach and head.[113] On the following night, the two of them set out on another mission. This time they planted two gre-nades at the entrance to the Ali Baka mosque in such a way that they would explode when the door was opened. Events unfolded in a similar manner. The mosque guard, Schada Issa, arrived for morning prayer ac-companied by a group of worshippers. When he placed his hand on the door handle, the grenades exploded. Once again, the guard was the only one who sustained injuries from the blast.[114] During his investigation, Nir claimed that the actions were meant only to wound and not to kill, on the supposition that wounding Palestinians would suffice to deter them from future attacks against Jews: "The grenade was set in such a way that it would not cause death, in a deep crevasse between the mosque door and the street, in a different place, so that the side of the threshold would block the blast wave; and the second one was put in a raised area, so that the main force of the explosion would pass over whoever stood in its path."[115]

The actions in Hebron were minor in comparison to the final one planned by Nir and Livni. This attack was intended to be the most deadly of them all and was carried out less than two years after the attack on the Islamic College in Hebron. This time it also had a clear, strategic objective, as Nir explained: "the need to save the State of Israel from those who would destroy her from within, who are incapable of taking action against Arab terrorists."[116]

As in previous operations, this action also involved careful planning. After deciding that the target of the attack would be the buses of the Arab East Jerusalem Transportation Company, "Juliani," they approached Haim Ben-David and Bohaz Henman, who had helped in the attack on the mayors, and asked them to dismantle old mines and make bombs from the explosive material inside them. On the night of April 26, 1984, Shaul Nir and Sharabaf traveled from Hebron to Jerusalem, where Barak Nir awaited them. The three began to rig the buses,[117] which were parked for the night at various locations in northeast Jerusalem. In each of the four designated buses, they concealed a medium-size bomb weighing 7 pounds, which was connected to a timer, and two smaller secondary charges. The main devices were affixed under the engines of the buses or to the rear axles, and the secondary charges were placed in the front of the buses near the front axles. The aim of placing the charges at these locations was to cause maximum human injury; destroying the axles would lead to the driver's loss of control over the bus and a certain collision.[118] The timers on the bombs were set to go off at different times in each bus. The first bomb was set for 5:30 A.M., when the buses were packed with East Jerusalem Palestinian laborers on their way to work.[119]

However, in contrast to the group's previous operations, this attack was foiled by the General Security Service (GSS, formerly known as Shin Bet) before it was even launched. There are two versions of how this happened. The first, which was widely published in the media and accepted by most members of the underground, argued that after four years of clandestine activity, the GSS succeeded in recruiting one of the underground activists as an agent, apparently Shaul Nir.[120] Although information about the attack on the buses was relayed by Nir to his GSS operators nearly two months before its intended perpetration, it was decided that the best time to arrest the members would be in the middle of the act.[121] On the morning of the attack, after hiding the bombs in the buses, the agent made contact with the security forces. They then arrested the gang, without any resistance, on their way to Hebron. At the time of the arrests Nir, as prearranged, offered to defuse the bombs himself so that the sappers, who might not be familiar with the detonation devices, would not be harmed.[122]

The second version was presented to us by Yitzhak Pantik, who at the time was head of the operations branch of the Non-Arabic (Jewish) Department in the GSS. According to his version, after the Islamic College and other attacks in Hebron, the GSS succeeded in locating some of the group members by using advanced intelligence-gathering techniques, such as wiretapping and round-the-clock surveillance of suspects. In this way, the Jewish Department of the GSS succeeded in discovering the beginning of a trail that eventually led them to the conspirators.[123] Pantik's version maintained that members of the cell were under surveillance the night the explosives were planted, and immediately after their arrest the GSS and police defused them. Pantik categorically rejected the claim that there was a double agent working from within the ranks of the Jewish Underground.[124]

After the bombs were dismantled, the second stage of uncovering the network began. On that same day, a GSS and police dragnet was launched and, accompanied by Border Police soldiers, swept across the West Bank and the Golan Heights.[125] The security forces possessed extensive intelligence information on each of the members, including their current and previous addresses and other places where they might be located.[126] In addition, they performed exhaustive searches of all the detainees' homes in order to locate any combat or sabotage materials.[127] However, at the time of the arrests, the GSS did not know with certainty whether the detainees were connected to the attack on the mayors. Only after all the arrests were made and all the members of the network involved in the action except for Etzion were rounded up did the full extent of the group's activities become evident. In this manner, the network that had operated from 1980 to 1984 came to an end.

The case of the Jewish Underground includes all the respective elements in the theoretical framework presented in the Preface for explaining the emergence of religious terrorism. Radicalization within a specific counterculture, fostered by a threatening external event and portrayed by spiritual leaders as catastrophic for members of the counterculture and their beliefs, led a series of social networks connected by several hubs to resort to violence. Furthermore, the crucial role of the spiritual leaders was manifested in the abandoned attack on the mosques. The noncompliance of the spiritual leaders in regard to the destruction of the mosques led eventually to its cancellation, whereas direct support for the attack on the mayors led to its rapid implementation.

Additionally, the story of the Jewish Underground emphasizes the importance of intragroup socialization. The process of radicalization took place in small and informal groups in the various settlements. Thus, although the Jewish Underground network included a core and a periphery, during the course of its growth it was able to maintain its nonhierarchical and informal character. Members of the founding group who were the initiators engaged in very low levels of supervision of the subgroups that constituted the periphery. This is demonstrated by the fact that the later operations of the Jewish Underground were conducted by specific subgroups in the network. Finally, personal crises resulting from the loss of loved ones or close peers in the community were prominent and direct causes for initiating violence, emphasizing the importance of feelings of vengeance in the final steps in the slide to violence.

Jews Against Israelis

▬▬▬▬▬

HEBRON THEN AND NOW

The early morning hours of February in the city of Hebron, built on a summit in the West Bank hills, can be bone chilling. However, the frosty air does not deter either Jews or Muslims from leaving their homes before dawn and setting out toward the Cave of the Patriarchs to pray at the tombs of Abraham, Isaac, and Jacob, the forefathers of adherents to both religions.

The soldiers guarding the Cave of the Patriarchs on February 25, 1994, never imagined that Dr. Baruch Goldstein, a Kiryat Arba resident who arrived at the site dressed in his Israel Defense Forces Medical Corps officer's uniform, had anything else in mind other than to pray at the morning service as he did every morning.[1] At 5:00 A.M., Goldstein crossed the corridor separating the Hall of Abraham, where the Jews prayed, from the Hall of Isaac, where some 800 Muslim residents of Hebron were praying at the time. The worshippers, in supplication on their knees, did not notice the Jew who stood behind them and cocked the Galil assault rifle he was carrying. A few seconds later the hall was filled with a deafening sound. Goldstein had tossed a hand grenade into the center of the room and immediately opened fire on the worshippers. Everybody in the room was stricken with shock. The Palestinians did not understand where the barrage of automatic gunfire was coming from, so in the meantime Goldstein was able to reload and empty a number of magazines. After firing more than 100 bullets, the weapon jammed, and the gunfire finally stopped.[2] It was then that some of the worshippers identified the source of the gunfire and began to lay into the murderer with a fire extinguisher they found in the room. Several moments later, Goldstein was no longer breathing. A horrific sight greeted the rescue forces that arrived at the scene. The floor of the hall was covered with blood and strewn with dead and moaning bodies.

By the end of the day, it was made public that 29 worshippers had been murdered by the doctor from Kiryat Arba, and 125 more had been injured.

However, these were not the only casualties of Goldstein's terrorist attack. A few hours after the echoes of gunfire in the Cave of the Patriarchs died away, harsh confrontations erupted all over the West Bank between enraged Palestinians and Israel Defense Forces (IDF) soldiers. During these clashes, 20 more Palestinians were killed and 120 were injured.[3]

The State Commission of Inquiry, headed by Supreme Court president Meir Shamgar and appointed by the government to investigate the events of that day in the Cave of the Patriarchs, could not determine precisely what the reasons were for the worst act of Jewish terrorism in Israeli history.[4] Even so, testimonies presented at the commission hearings indicated that Goldstein suffered from deep distress and frustration at the implementation of the Oslo Accords. At that time the main Arab cities in the West Bank were being transferred to the control of the Palestinian National Authority (PNA). These procedures radically contradicted his beliefs and worldview, and he was also very upset at the continuing Palestinian violence against the settlers, which he saw as a direct result of the peace agreements and the Israeli surrender to Palestinian demands.[5] The commission also established that Goldstein had acted alone. This conclusion may be accurate in regard to the final event itself; however, the incident concealed a much more complex picture.

Goldstein was not a lone wolf. He was not a terrorist like Theodore Kaczynski, better known as the Unabomber, who for years sent letter bombs to professors and businessmen from his remote forest cabin near Lincoln, Montana. The truth is that Goldstein was the absolute opposite of Kaczynski. Not only was he one of the pillars of his community in Kiryat Arba, but for many years he was one of the central figures in the Kahane movement.

Baruch Kappel Goldstein was born in 1959 in New York, and he knew Rabbi Meir Kahane from his childhood days in Brooklyn. When Goldstein began his studies at the Yeshiva University, he was deeply impressed by Kahane's writings and joined the Jewish Defense League (JDL), founded by Kahane.[6] After completing his medical studies at the Albert Einstein College, Goldstein decided to put into practice his Zionist worldview and settled in Kiryat Arba. He was conscripted to the IDF and served as a doctor in the Regional Brigade.[7] In his role as a family physician in Kiryat Arba, during his military service, and even after his discharge, Goldstein often provided medical assistance to victims of terrorism in the Hebron area.

Aside from his work as a doctor, Goldstein continued to pursue his political endeavors. On the eve of the elections for the 11th Knesset in 1988, Kahane invited Goldstein to join his Kach party list of candidates. In the party's campaign ads, great emphasis was placed on the fact that Goldstein was a military doctor in order to increase the respectability of the list of the party's candidates, many of whom were known to the public for their violent pasts and racist remarks.[8] Nevertheless, the party was barred from competing in the elections in light of the members' brazen demands, calling for harm to the Arabs and the elimination of the democratic regime in Israel. The party's disqualification put an end to Goldstein's future as a parliamentarian. However, he did not give up and also ran in the Kiryat Arba City Council elections in the early 1990s and was in fact elected. As the years went by, and particularly after the signing of the Oslo Accords, Goldstein's views became more radical. Even among residents of Kiryat Arba and Hebron, who were the most radical of all settlers in the West Bank in those years, the doctor was a prominent figure, customarily wearing a yellow star bearing the word *JUDE* on his person. The message was clear: He likened Israeli democracy to the Nazi regime.

A few hours after the massacre at the Cave of the Patriarchs, Goldstein's Kahanist colleagues published the following announcement: "Members of 'Kahane Chai' mourn the death of the martyr Baruch Goldstein, who died this morning in Hebron in the sanctification of God's name."[9] Not only did Rabbi Kahane's followers view Goldstein as a faithful emissary of their movement; the Israeli government also indicated a direct link between Goldstein and the Kahanist political stream. In a rare procedure in Israeli politics, the Israeli government decided to apply the Prevention of Terrorism Ordinance to Kach and Kahane Chai.[10] During a speech to the Knesset on February 28, 1994, Prime Minister Yitzhak Rabin announced,

> This murderer emerged from a small political frame. He sprung up and grew in a swamp whose spiritual sources are here and across the ocean; they are foreign to Judaism, [they] are not ours. . . . To him and his ilk we say, you are not part of the community of Israel, you are not part of the national democratic camp in which we are all partners.[11]

More than eleven years after Rabin made his speech, we went to Hebron to observe at close hand the community to which Goldstein belonged.

When we arrived in Hebron late one morning, we were greeted by a ghost town. The streets were empty, apart from IDF soldiers stationed at improvised posts on the road leading from the Cave of the Patriarchs to the Jewish neighborhood of Avraham Avinu. The only place where we could find directions was at the snack bar near the Cave of the Patriarchs. The building, which was small and also housed a souvenir shop, served as a meeting place for people from the city's Jewish community who belong to a broad spectrum of religious Zionist streams.

Still, even at the entrance to the snack bar it was clear to us who owned this town. We were greeted by Baruch Marzel, for many years Rabbi Meir Kahane's right-hand man and since his death the acting leader of the Kach movement. He looked at us with a calculating gaze. Without saying a word to us, Marzel summoned the owner of the establishment. He too eyed us suspiciously and, after he seemed somewhat reassured, agreed to sell us a cold drink. We received our drinks and sat down not far from Marzel's table, trying to overhear their conversation. From the fragments of sentences that reached us, we understood that Marzel was involved in preparations for collecting youths from the Jewish settlement in Hebron and transporting them to protest activities throughout the country. While he was still giving out orders to the youths, Rabbi Moshe Levinger, a long-time member of the Gush Emunim movement and the first post-1967 Jewish settler in Hebron, appeared in the doorway.

Levinger and his followers were the ones who, in April 1968, less than a year after the occupation of Hebron, rented the city's Park Hotel[12] from its Palestinian owner, Faiz Kawasmeh,[13] in order to celebrate the Passover Seder there. At the end of the holiday, however, the Jews announced they had no intention of leaving the hotel and established the first settlement in the West Bank within its confines. This planted the seeds for the founding of Kiryat Arba,[14] the renewal of Jewish residency in Hebron, and the construction of dozens of settlements throughout the West Bank.

The meeting between Levinger and Marzel surprised us. Levinger was a legendary figure among Gush Emunim admirers and symbolized the political violence of the settlers, and he was even involved in violent acts committed against Palestinians.[15] He looked older and more tired than his years. Marzel, on the other hand, who had shed much of his excess weight in recent years, looked young and dynamic. From the snippets of conversation between the two, it was clear that almost forty years after Levinger had laid the foundations for the Jewish settlement in this city, the man who now set the tone was Baruch Marzel. This state of affairs is not to be taken lightly. Kach was never a settlement movement. Furthermore, the heads of Gush Emunim steered clear of Kahane and his followers, to the point of blocking the Kahanists' efforts to establish settlements in the spirit of Kahane's teachings.

During the short walk from the Cave of the Patriarchs to the Avraham Avinu neighborhood, we received a clearer picture of life in Hebron. In the past few decades, Kahane's disciples had managed to take over the city and additional settlements. The walk between the two sites takes no more than ten minutes, but the visitor can see how Kahane's ideology, which was denounced by many in Israel and around the world, has gained strength here. Although Meir Kahane believed in the Greater Land of Israel, this was merely a secondary issue for him. In his view, the main issue was the total separation of Jews and Arabs and the expulsion of the latter from the sovereign State of Israel and from the West Bank and the Gaza Strip. In Hebron, at least, his teachings had been transformed from vision into reality. The small minority of some 500 Jews had managed[16] to convince policymakers in Israel that the Palestinian residents were a danger to their security. In 2003 a military order was issued, forcing all Palestinian residents to move out of the area of the Cave of the Patriarchs and the Kasbah of Hebron's old city.[17]

The neglected look of the marketplace indicated the long period that had passed since it was used for commerce. Most of the stores were locked with heavy steel shutters and their facades sprayed with Hebrew graffiti: "Death to the Arabs," "Rabbi Kahane was right," "Sharon, Rabin is waiting for you," and the Star of David with the fist symbol of the Kach movement. The few Palestinians who maintained residence in the area are under curfew for most of the day.[18] They often watch the activities in the street through the windows of their homes, covered with iron grates that the army has installed in order to prevent them from throwing objects at Jews on their way to the Cave of the Patriarchs.

In this chapter we will devote our attention to the Kahanist counterculture. We will discuss its history and how it evolved, and the ways in which it fostered the emergence of religious Jewish terrorism. We will illustrate how these processes for the most part conform to the requisites of our theoretical framework.

FROM JEWISH DEFENSE LEAGUE TO
KAHANIST COUNTERCULTURE

Although the most palpable expressions of Kahanism in recent decades can be found in Hebron, the roots of this movement are in the JDL, founded by Meir Kahane in New York in 1968. Although Kahanist terrorism has so far received little coverage,[19] Kahane himself, the ideology he developed, and his political party in Israel have all been examined from many angles.[20]

Even though theoretically they belong to the national religious stream, Kahane and his followers were antithetical to the Gush Emunim movement from almost every perspective, and they can in fact be viewed as constituting a separate counterculture. From an ideological point of view, the top priority for Kach members was their xenophobic outlook and the obligation to take revenge on Israel's enemies. Kahane opined that harm to a Jew was considered a desecration of God's name, thus making vengeance against the gentiles a religious precept. Furthermore, unlike the religious Zionists, who aimed to combine the principles of the Halakha and democracy, or the ultra-Orthodox, who cloistered themselves in their communities and viewed the secular government in Israel as a temporary evil that would eventually pass, Kahane resolutely lashed out at the very idea of democracy. He repeatedly invoked the story of the Hashmonai (Hasmonean) Revolt with the Seleucid regime representing the Israeli democracy, which he defined as foreign and hostile to Judaism. It was therefore not surprising that he would call the secular Jews who denied his worldview "Hellenists." Kahane used more than ancient Jewish history as a foundation for his worldview. He was an avid admirer of the Etzel organization and its leader, Menachem Begin. Kahane's followers often reminisced over stories of the Lehi and wholeheartedly embraced veterans of the pre–State of Israel underground movements, who were happy to share tales of their escapades.

The peace accords between Israel and Egypt, which were signed by Begin, were a source of personal crisis for Kahane and generated a collective crisis for his movement. Kahane found it hard to believe that the fierce hawk who more than any other political leader represented the ideology of a Greater Land of Israel had changed his mind and agreed to concede parts of the homeland. Unlike that of the Jewish Underground, Kahane's supporters' adoption of terrorism was less strategic and more emotional.

For them, the Camp David Accords constituted the "final writ of divorce" from Israel, and they set up an imaginary border in their minds between the pragmatic, modern, secular Israel and the religious, conservative State of Judea, which in the future would be run according to the rules of the Halakha.[21] In other words, this was a major step in the transformation of the Kahanist stream from a subculture into a counterculture as it gradually estranged itself from Israeli mainstream culture and norms and began to advance a cultural and political alternative.

For Kahane, however, Begin represented something more. Ever since Israel's establishment, Begin had headed the Herut Movement, and Kahane had cut his political teeth in the New York branch of this organization. The left-wing parties that at that time held the reins of government in Israel related to Herut and its leader as untouchables. Kahane developed a deep solidarity with the feeling of humiliation that accompanied Begin and an even deeper loathing for the Israeli left. Like Begin, Kahane became a magnet that attracted the support of representatives of social groups in Israel who had been relegated to the periphery. While Begin, the grassroots leader, recruited the masses to support his party, Kahane made do with the marginal few and radicals who viewed the use of violence as a convenient platform for expressing their frustrations. However, Kahane's exclusion was twofold. He was rebuffed by both mainstream Israeli politics and the home to which he wanted to belong: the settlers' movement and religious Zionist camp. When he landed in Israel, Kahane expected religious Zionism to embrace him. To his surprise, the embrace was only lip service, and when he tried to fit into the existing political system, he was given the cold shoulder. As the years passed, hostility grew between Gush Emunim followers, who viewed the Kahanists as a bunch of uncouth hoodlums, and Kach members, who perceived the settler leadership as elitist and despicable.

The foreignness to and alienation from mainstream politics and society further fostered the consolidation of the Kahanist stream as a counterculture community. This was also reflected in the demographic makeup of the Kahanist terrorist groups. Kahane's followers closely resembled their rabbi. Like him, most of them were migrants who had not managed to don the image of the sabra—the native-born bona fide Israeli. In his early years in Israel, Kahane attracted mainly immigrants from the United States and the Soviet Union. These were joined by young Israelis, mostly second-generation immigrants from Middle Eastern and North African countries, who in the 1950s had been sidelined to the geographic, social, and economic periphery in Israel. The demographic characteristics of Kahane supporters were also clearly evident in the structure of Kach's terrorist networks. Whereas the Jewish Underground could be described as a broad, loose social network of mostly sabras, the Kahanist groups formed small, tight networks known in the professional literature as all-channel networks, with distinct social features: They consisted of immigrants from the United States, childhood friends and friends from the Kahanist youth movement.[22] Surprisingly, the characteristics of the Kahanist cells resembled, more than anything else, the global Salafi jihad[23] cells of current times. In both cases we are dealing with immigrants who failed to assimilate in their new countries and who created segregated communities that were alienated from the values of the majority culture. Over time, they gradually radicalized and began to spontaneously set up terrorist networks based on primordial or other close ties.[24]

Unlike the centralization and iron-fisted practices of Rabbi Kahane in the regular management of Kach,[25] when it came to the instigation of Kahanist terrorism, things were completely different. Very few operations were undertaken by Kahane and his close aides who formed the movement's leadership clique (see Figure 4.1 for an overview of the Kahane groups). The other operations were independently initiated by Kach members and admirers, and in certain cases even by people who simply identified with the movement's ideology and were inspired by it. This was also the case with respect to logistic ties with Kahane and his aides. Although a number of networks that contacted the rabbi were rewarded with his blessing and even his assistance, others received implied support at best.

From an operational perspective, even though engaging in terrorism was an integral part of Kahane's worldview, the overwhelming majority of the operations initiated by his close associates suffered from inadequate planning and in most cases ended in failure. Still, these activists were well known because of their displays of hooliganism. The semiperipheral networks, those that were not linked directly to the leadership clique, used terrorism more effectively. Even so, the most severe acts were the result of plotting by completely peripheral groups whose connection with Kach was limited to its ideological influence.

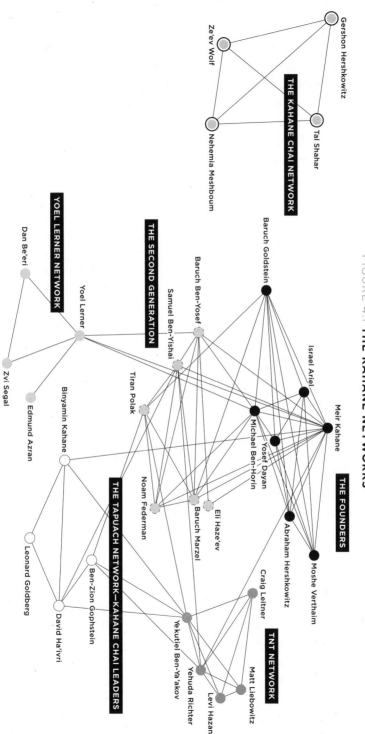

FIGURE 4.1 **THE KAHANE NETWORKS**

THE KAHANE CHAI NETWORK

Gershon Hershkowitz

Ze'ev Wolf

Tal Shahar

Nehemia Meshboum

YOEL LERNER NETWORK

Dan Be'eri

Zvi Segal

Yoel Lerner

Edmund Azran

THE SECOND GENERATION

Baruch Ben-Yosef

Samuel Ben-Yishai

Tiran Polak

THE FOUNDERS

Baruch Goldstein

Israel Ariel

Meir Kahane

Michael Ben-Horin

Yosef Dayan

Eli Haze'ev

Baruch Marzel

Moshe Verthaim

Abraham Hershkowitz

Noam Federman

Binyamin Kahane

Leonard Goldberg

David Ha'ivri

THE TAPUACH NETWORK–KAHANE CHAI LEADERS

Ben-Zion Gophstein

Yekutiel Ben-Ya'akov

Craig Leitner

TNT NETWORK

Matt Liebowitz

Yehuda Richter

Levi Hazan

EARLY DAYS

Hooliganism went hand in hand with Kahane from the early days of the JDL. The movement's motto was "Never Again,"[26] and its early actions were devoted mainly to protecting elderly Jews, residents of New York's poorer neighborhoods, from assault by young African Americans and Latin Americans, whom the activists despised. In late 1969, Kahane decided to expand the goals of the JDL and join in the struggle against Soviet authorities who prevented the immigration of Jews to Israel. This was also an opportunity to step up the movement's activities.

On December 29, 1969, the group's violent potential was first realized when at 1:00 P.M. three groups of JDL activists simultaneously attacked a number of Soviet targets in New York. The targets were the offices of TASS, the official Soviet news agency; the offices of Intourist, the Soviet travel agency; and a jet belonging to Aeroflot, the Soviet civilian airline. Four activists were involved in the attack on TASS, including Kahane. After storming the offices, they ordered all workers and visitors, including two Soviet journalists they had beaten, to be silent. Then, with buckets of blue paint they had prepared in advance, they began painting the walls with slogans such as "Am Yisrael Chai" ("People of Israel Live [Forever]") and "Let My People Go."

The Intourist offices were invaded by a group of JDL activists headed by Abraham Hershkowitz. After Hershkowitz announced that anyone who felt like it could leave, the activists locked the doors and began painting the office walls with slogans denouncing the Soviet regime and supporting the release of Jewish emigration refuseniks.[27] However, the most daring attack took place at New York's Kennedy International Airport. Six young JDL activists from the City University of New York managed to outmaneuver all the security mechanisms and gain entry to the planes' parking area. Their goal was to chain themselves to the wheels of a Soviet jet in order to protest the Soviet Union's policy toward Jewish emigration refuseniks.[28] The youths eventually came across a huge Ilyushin jet belonging to Aeroflot and split into two smaller groups. The first consisted of two activists who chained themselves to the wheels of the plane shouting "Am Yisrael Chai,"[29] while all four members of the other group began climbing the stairs to the passenger section. Soviet flight attendants who were preparing the plane for flight paled with fright when the youths burst into the plane and began painting slogans in Hebrew on its walls.[30] All six youths were ultimately arrested by airport security personnel, but they had succeeded in bringing the goals of their struggle to the public's attention.

Even though events such as these prompted the American legal authorities to direct their attention to Kahane and his adherents, the latter were not deterred from continuing their activities. Apparently Kahane's close ties with the Italian Mafia in New York and his connections with the Federal Bureau of Investigation[31] gave him a feeling that he had nothing to fear from the law enforcement systems. At 4:00 A.M. on January 8, 1971, a strong explosion rocked the Soviet cultural building on 18th Street in Washington, D.C., just a few buildings away from the Soviet Embassy. The explosion blasted the iron gate at the front of the building, hurling it 80 feet down the street, and shattered all the building's windows and some windows in nearby buildings as well. Luckily, the explosion occurred before office hours, so no one was hurt. The JDL never claimed responsibility for this action. However, about half an hour after the explosion, a woman phoned the Associated Press news agency and anonymously announced that this was an example of what was to come if emigration restrictions on Soviet Jewry were not lifted. She even used the JDL's motto, "Never Again."[32]

In retrospect, it is evident that Kahane's confidence was misplaced if he believed that the American legal authorities would take into consideration the fact that he had once collaborated with them. In May 1971 he was arrested, with six other JDL activists, on suspicion of purchasing a large quantity of weapons and conspiring to manufacture explosives.[33] The weapon purchases were exposed after the New York Police Department's Office of Special Investigations managed to plant a young agent, aged twenty-two, in the JDL ranks under the alias of Richard Rosenthal. Very soon, Rosenthal revealed to his operators that the JDL had managed to establish connections in Israel and was smuggling Israeli Uzi and Swedish Karl Gustav submachine guns from there. He also uncovered information about a discharged IDF soldier by the name of Dov who had come to the JDL camp in the Catskill Mountains to teach JDL activists how to assemble timer-activated bombs.[34]

After the discovery of the JDL's illegal activities, Kahane was given a five-year suspended sentence.[35] In the summer of 1971, he decided to immigrate to Israel. Despite his declared intentions to invest time in establishing educational projects in the country, within a short time Kahane instituted the Israeli branch of the JDL. Not long after, young immigrants from the United States and the Soviet Union could be seen in the city streets wearing yellow T-shirts emblazoned with the fist surrounded by a black Star of David.[36] The youths sought to intimidate Christian missionaries in Israel, members of the Black Hebrew sect that dwells in Dimona,[37] and of course the Arab citizens of Israel. Similar to their actions in the United States, in Israel most of their conduct did not go beyond acts of thuggery and hooliganism.[38]

All this changed after the murder of eleven Israeli athletes at the 1972 Munich Olympics, which marked the peak of the wave of Palestinian terrorist attacks against Israeli targets worldwide. Although the world remembers very well the Israeli Mossad's "Wrath of God" operation—the targeted assassinations of Palestine Liberation Organization activists in Europe and the Middle East—few people know that the JDL also engaged in efforts to retaliate. In August 1972, Kahane and two of his close associates in the JDL, Abraham Hershkowitz and Joseph Schneider,[39] decided to launch an attack against the Libyan Embassy in Rome. Via this location, weapons had been transferred to the athletes' murderers. The daring plan was to reach Rome and meet with another eleven JDL activists who were due to arrive there from the United States, take over the embassy using a diversion tactic,[40] and then demand that all those who collaborated with the Palestinian terrorists be transported to Israel to stand trial. If their terms were not met, Kahane and his men planned to execute the occupants of the embassy at timed intervals until their demands were fulfilled. They figured that at least half the occupants of the embassy would be executed before the authorities would comply with their conditions.[41]

In order to carry out their plan, in August 1972 the three approached Amichai Faglin, a former operations officer in the Etzel, for assistance in obtaining weapons. They knew that Faglin had several arms caches, consisting mainly of weapons confiscated from the enemy in the 1956 Sinai Campaign and Six-Day War in 1967. Faglin agreed to help, and when Schneider and Hershkovitz met with him in mid-September 1972, he supplied them with a wide variety of firearms and ammunition, including Karl Gustav submachine guns, two Beretta pistols, three IDF hand grenades, and dozens of bullets and detonators. Faglin hid all the armaments in a machine for making cookies, which fit into a crate. Hershkovitz was to send the crate to New York via the "Amit" Customs Clearing firm, and the crate was supposed to be picked up by the group of JDL activists who would participate in the attack on the embassy. Kahane and his men anticipated it would be easier to smuggle the arms into Italy from the United States. However, while the crate was in the El Al freight department, the company's security guards opened it and discovered the weapons.[42] Twenty-four hours later, Hershkovitz was arrested, and Kahane was arrested a week later. Kahane's co-conspirators in the United States were never found, but Hershkovitz later said that their leader was an Israeli émigré, a former officer in the IDF. Hershkovitz also said that a few days before his arrest, he heard rumors that their plans had been revealed. He later found out that it was Kahane himself who had disclosed the operation to security personnel because he suspected the Mossad was planning a similar operation. He contacted Mossad agents and warned them that the two attacks should be coordinated.[43]

Other than his plan to attack the Libyan Embassy in Rome, Kahane's early years in Israel involved mainly provocations that were aimed at attracting the media's attention. At the same time, he established a broad infrastructure of supporters who were drawn to his charismatic image and were captivated by his excellent rhetorical abilities.[44] Knowing that it would be difficult to find support among the liberal upper-class sections of Israeli society, he was inclined to hold party rallies and assemblies on the fringes of Israeli society, in villages and towns in the periphery, which were populated mostly by lower-class workers and immigrants. In the periphery, he was able to mobilize support and excite his listeners, rapidly becoming a symbol and a Messiah-like leader for his followers. They were drawn by his leadership qualities, combined with his radical but straightforward political agenda, which claimed that most of the ills of Israeli society originated in its Arab citizens and Western liberal elements, and dealing with these elements offered a remedy to all their social and security problems. Many of them were convinced that the true salvation of the Jewish people could be attained if Kahane became an important and influential political leader.

In those years, the backbone of the movement's leadership also came into existence. Among the prominent activists were Rabbi Israel Ariel, Dr. Baruch Goldstein, Yossi Dayan, Yehuda Richter, and Baruch Marzel. Kahane liked to surround himself with disciples who admired him and whom he did not consider a threat. In the rare cases in which someone challenged his decisions, Rabbi Kahane made sure to force him out of the more influential inner circle.[45] This explains the autonomous activities of Kahane's former friend, Yoel Lerner.

YOEL LERNER

American immigrants dominated the Kahanist movement in Israel from the very beginning. One of the more prominent figures who accompanied Kahane practically from the day he arrived in Israel was Yoel Lerner. Lerner was born in New York but had spent most of his childhood with his parents in South Africa. At the age of eighteen, Lerner returned to New York in order to study mathematics at the Massachusetts Institute of Technology. He remained there for a brief time but soon felt that his true place was in Israel. After immigrating, he became a religious Jew and completed his bachelor's degree studies at the Hebrew University of Jerusalem.[46] Like Kahane, Lerner also believed in the importance of a Torah-based education and even established and ran a religious school in Kiryat Shmona, a town near Israel's border with Lebanon.[47] At the same time, he began to take an interest in Israeli politics and quickly became disillusioned with the National Religious Party and its candidates, whom he regarded as moderates. He sought an ideological home that was more suited to his proactive worldview. Almost by chance, after finding their flyer in his mailbox, Lerner paid a visit to the Jerusalem offices of Kach.[48] Lerner and Kahane were deeply impressed by one another and soon became close friends. Their common background and the extensive education they shared, which evidently served as a strong foundation for their friendship, all the same did not bridge their differences of opinion. As strange as it sounds, Lerner was more radical than most Kach members. He believed in active terrorism and took a great interest in ways to blow up the mosques on the Temple Mount. He even plotted a popular uprising designed to lead to the overthrow of the Israeli government.[49]

Lerner acted on his beliefs. Shortly after the end of the battles of the Yom Kippur War (1973 war), while Israel was still picking up the pieces, Lerner found time in early 1974 to set fire to Christian institutions in Jerusalem. Among other places, he torched the Swedish Church and the Zion House. However, the prosecution was not able to connect him to those fires beyond a reasonable doubt. He was convicted of incitement after a search of his home uncovered detailed plans to launch a revolution in Israel, and he was sentenced to thirteen months in jail. During the long months in prison, his worldview did not change very much.[50]

After a visit from Rabbi Zvi Yehuda Kook, the Gush Emunim spiritual leader, Lerner developed a position quite similar to that of Yehuda Etzion, whose history was addressed in Chapter 3. Lerner believed that in order to establish a Halakhic state in Israel, the Third Temple had to be built, and the first prerequisite for the success of this task was the bombing of the Temple Mount mosques.[51]

Lerner did not waste much time. Upon his release from jail, he went to teach at the Netiv Meir Yeshiva in Jerusalem, which was affiliated with the Bnei Akiva youth movement,[52] and there he began to form the Gal (the Hebrew acronym for "Redemption for Israel") underground. Lerner was the connecting link of the three subgroups that made up this network. At the center of the network was a clique of yeshiva graduates, Lerner's colleagues, whose role was to make the strategic decisions. Lerner would not tell us the names of the group's members, but he did say that one of them joined on the basis of Rabbi Kook's explicit recommendation. The other two subgroups were composed of Lerner's students. One clique consisted of older teens who had already undergone some military and guerrilla training, and the other clique was made up of youngsters who were supposed to undergo a series of training sessions. The various groups were isolated from each other in order to prevent their possible discovery by the authorities.[53]

Members of the senior clique diligently met once every two weeks at a secret apartment in Jerusalem. During their meetings, they decided on a "Forty-Day Plan to Replace the Israeli Government." They wanted to create a revolutionary dynamic among the religious and right-wing publics in Israel by perpetrating thirteen operations, most of them violent, planned at set intervals. The final operation was supposed to have been the bombing of the Temple Mount mosques.[54]

The conspirators drafted precise plans of every aspect of each operation. Among other things, they prepared an infrastructure for establishing an improvised radio station that would break into the broadcast of the official Israeli stations' news bulletin. Gal members even built an improvised prison for government officials. The members of the various groups were told to keep track of the afternoon newspapers for a cryptic message. The signal for the onset of the revolution was a quote from the Book of Jonah: "Another forty days, and Nineveh shall be overthrown."[55]

There was a certain degree of inconsistency between the information we received from Lerner and the newspaper articles from that period. Lerner described a calculated process of preparations leading up to the operations. The weapons and explosives were supplied by Edmond Azran, a former IDF officer and one of Lerner's students. A few of the network's members were trained in gathering tactical intelligence, and others learned to prepare explosives. Training sessions were held in the fields near Beit Shemesh, a small town between Tel Aviv and Jerusalem.[56] The newspapers, on the other hand, depicted an amateurish group of hot-headed youngsters who did not follow Lerner's plans closely and who were interested mainly in engaging in violent actions.[57]

According to the newspaper reports, this was also the main reason for the discovery of the group. One of the network's members wanted to attack the Arab student dormitories at the Hebrew University with a hand grenade. Lerner objected to this because it was not part of his "Forty-Day Plan." Lerner's account made it obvious that the young man who planned the grenade strike, Misha Mishkan of Beit El, was collaborating with the General Security Service (GSS), because the day after his conversation with Lerner, the latter was summoned for a police interrogation and informed that the security forces were well aware of his plans. At the conclusion of the investigation into the Gal underground, indictments were filed against ten of its members, including Lerner and Azran. Whereas the youths were given prison sentences of a few months, Lerner was put behind bars for five years.[58] On this occasion as well, the time he spent in prison did not soften his stance. On the contrary, as soon as he was released from jail, he prepared for the establishment of a new underground.

THE MODERN HASMONEAN REVOLT

In 1937, Rabbi Moshe Zvi Segal,[59] who lived in Jerusalem and belonged to the religious Zionist camp, founded a youth movement called the Brit Hashmonaim ("Hasmonean Covenant"). This was a religious movement greatly influenced by the person and teachings of Lehi leader Yair Stern and was active during the years of the British Mandate in Israel. In 1981, more than thirty years after the movement was dismantled, and in the midst of the struggle against the Camp David Accords, Yoel Lerner approached the aging Segal and asked him to breathe life back into the youth movement. Segal, immensely troubled and heartbroken by the Israeli government's evacuation of Jewish settlements in the Sinai Peninsula and its intention to grant political autonomy for the Palestinians in the West Bank, was more than happy to comply. The two were soon able to put together a group of boys, residents of the Jewish Quarter of the Old City of Jerusalem, several of whom were Lerner's students from the Netiv Meir Yeshiva.[60]

The movement's ideology was greatly inspired by the Kahanist concept that modern Israeli society could be likened to Jewish society during the time of the Hashmonaim. Lerner and his youths assumed the role of the Maccabees and got ready to fight the Hellenistic Jews, who thronged after Western culture and neglected the path of the Torah.[61] In more general terms, they saw the movement as the young avant-garde of a counterculture that stood for a normative and cultural alternative to the majority culture, whose secular tendencies led it to promote unacceptable sinfulness such as the Camp David Accords. At the founding conference of the movement, it turned out that these ideas were a drawing card for people outside the circles of the Kahanist movements. Among those present at the event were Dan Be'eri, who later became a central figure of the Jewish Underground, and Yael Ben-Dov, the widow of Shabtai Ben-Dov, one of the prominent thinkers who influenced Yehuda Etzion, also a key member of the Jewish Underground.[62]

Although highly active in the struggle against the Camp David agreements, the Brit Hashmonaim group did not carry out any documented acts of terrorism. In fact, the only operation they planned was also the one that led to their discovery and landed Lerner in jail once again. In the winter of 1982, a few months before the evacuation of the Sinai settlements, one of Lerner's young followers presented him with a detailed plot for blowing up the Dome of the Rock mosque by means of an explosive charge detonated by a solar-powered photoelectric cell. At first, Lerner had reservations about the plan, mainly because he doubted the group's ability to execute it. Gradually, however, he became convinced and secretly proposed the idea to the other boys. The group then formulated an elaborate scheme based on the original idea.[63]

The boy who initiated the plan shouldered most of its implementation. He was supposed to enter the Temple Mount compound via the Mugrabi

Gate (the Dung Gate) in the late afternoon, cross the plaza to the east, and reach the far wall that forms the periphery of the Temple Mount. Then he would attach an almost invisible fishing line to the wall and drape it down outside.[64] On the same night, Lerner and the boy planned to return to the external side of the wall, tie a thick rope to the fishing line, and pull it up. The boy was then to climb up the rope with an explosive charge attached to his body. According to the plan, the bomb was to be planted at a certain point between the Dome of the Chain[65] and the Dome of the Rock. An additional person was to keep watch from the roof of the Kotel Yeshiva and whistle in warning to the boy if someone was coming.[66]

Lerner and his students intended to steal the explosives from a training area near the Shivta army base in the Negev, knowing that IDF units often left behind remnants of explosive materials in training areas. This was also the Achilles heel of the plan that led to its disclosure. Despite conducting an extensive and painstaking search, Lerner and his accomplices did not find any explosives and were therefore forced to postpone the implementation of their plan.[67] One of the female students, who was informed of the plan in confidence, told her parents at some point, and they passed on the information to a cousin who worked for the GSS.[68]

At his trial, Lerner took advantage of a line of defense similar to that presented by Kahane in 1972 when he attempted to explain his involvement in the attack on the Libyan consulate. Lerner claimed he had agreed to take part in the planning of the operation only for the sake of appearance—in effect, in order to be able to prevent it. When asked why he did not turn in the boy who had engineered the operation, Lerner quoted a statement by the eminent eleventh-century biblical exegete Rashi: "A man's student is as dear to him as his own self."[69]

THE STRUGGLE IN SINAI

The first incident in which Kahane's closest followers almost engaged in serious violence took place in Yamit in April 1982. Yamit was the urban center for the Jewish settlers of the Sinai Peninsula. It was also the focal point of the strongest opposition to the evacuation of Israeli settlers from Sinai, as stipulated by the terms of the peace agreement between Israel and Egypt. Gush Emunim activists and members of the Movement to Halt the Retreat in Sinai, accompanied by their rabbis and families, made their way to Yamit before the disengagement, intending to block the evacuation with their own bodies. In the last two weeks of the struggle, the confrontation between the army and the settlers who had barricaded themselves in the houses deteriorated into serious violence.[70] Despite their small numbers and the fact that they had no real role in the resistance movement, on Sunday, April 18, Kach members captured the headlines.[71]

On that day, ten young Kach members, all of them American citizens and former members of the JDL, including Baruch Goldstein's sister, Bat-Sheva, holed themselves up in a large bomb shelter located in the center of Yamit, near the local motel. They then announced their intentions to commit suicide one after the other the moment the army began to evacuate the town. Yehuda Richter, the group's leader and one of Kahane's closest aides, passed a note through the shelter ventilation opening with a list of the means at the group's disposal for executing their threat: weapons, cyanide pills, and gas cylinders. He claimed that the group had received rabbinical approbation for their action from Rabbi Israel Ariel,[72] another member of Rabbi Kahane's inner circle. Richter added that from the moment the evacuation started, they would start committing suicide in the bomb shelter, which they called the "Sanctification of God's Name Bunker," at the rate of one person every half hour.[73] In the first few hours after the delivery of this note, the security forces doubted the sincerity of the Kach members' intentions, but after they discovered that the walls of the bunker were booby-trapped with gas cylinders, the IDF changed their approach. Additional proof of the seriousness of their intentions was a note that a youth who was accidentally trapped with the group managed to smuggle out to his parents: "I became involved in this affair by accident. I was sleeping in the shelter when they entered, and they won't let me out. They have already passed out slips of paper and are waiting in line to die. I drew number six."[74]

Immediately after news of this situation broke out, there was an intense flurry of activity in the vicinity of the bunker. Rabbis, Kach followers, and frightened parents and friends arrived at the narrow opening to the bunker and tried to persuade the youngsters not to carry out their threat, but to no avail. At the same time, the IDF, now realizing that the people in the bunker had serious intentions, tried to locate Rabbi Kahane, who was in the United States at the time, in order to ask him to come to Yamit immediately.[75]

Two days from the beginning of the predicament, the political system was increasingly pressured to find a solution. After meeting with the parents of one of the girls in the bunker, Prime Minister Menachem Begin promised them that Yamit would not be evacuated before a resolution to the situation was found. He then asked Israel's Chief Ashkenazi Rabbi,[76] Shlomo Goren, to speak to the young people who were threatening suicide. Unfortunately, neither he nor Chief Sephardi Rabbi Ovadiah Yosef, who also arrived at the besieged town, was able to persuade the youths to come out of the bunker and put an end to the affair. It appeared as if Rabbi Kahane was the only hope to end the episode without bloodshed.

It therefore came as no surprise that the moment he landed in Israel on April 21, Kahane was flown to Yamit by order of the prime minister. Kahane immediately tried to persuade Richter to end the standoff, but the latter was not prepared to halt the affair without some kind of achievement. Kahane was furious and asked him, "Do you have a rabbi?"[77] With this question, Kahane was actually indicating himself, and Richter replied, "Yes." Then Kahane responded, "If so, then you have to listen to me." Immediately afterward, Kahane entered the bunker and began persuading all the other youngsters to back down from their suicide threats. Kahane, who understood that Richter was not willing to end the affair without some kind of public image achievement, came out of the bunker at 4:30 A.M. on April 22 and began negotiating with IDF deputy chief of staff Moshe Levy and Southern Region commander Haim Erez. The rabbi explained that he had persuaded the youngsters not to commit suicide, but he asked that the occupants of the bunker be allowed to remain until the day Sinai was handed over to Egyptian control and the Israeli forces left. Kahane also asked that a request be relayed to Begin to arrange with the Egyptians for some sort of Israeli presence in Sinai.[78] The IDF officers refused both these requests, and on the morning of April 23, the army's patience ran out. A unit of the special forces broke into the bunker and arrested all its occupants, including Kahane.[79]

Even though Kahane did not persuade his followers to leave the bunker, his efforts to bring a nonviolent end to the confrontation secured him the political legitimacy he had been yearning for. For a few days he was accepted by the political system, and two years later he gained public support when he was elected to the Eleventh Knesset in 1984. In fact, for the first time since immigrating to Israel, Kahane finally mustered enough votes to be eligible for a seat in the Israeli legislature.

TNT

Levi Hazan, Craig Leitner, Yehuda Richter, Matt Liebowitz, and Mike Guzovsky knew each other from the JDL summer camps held each year in the Catskill Mountains of the state of New York. At these camps, the youngsters absorbed Kahane's teachings and learned how to use a gun. Many of these young men immigrated to Israel in the 1980s, when they were already in their twenties. A few, such as Matt Liebowitz, left their native land for fear of being tried for JDL-related violent activities. Others, including Richter and Guzovsky, decided to take this dramatic step as a result of their desire to join Rabbi Kahane and serve in the IDF.[80]

After they settled in Israel, the transition to terrorism was gradual. Guzovsky, Leitner, and Richter, who chose to live in the Avraham Avinu neighborhood in Hebron, supported one another in coping with the hardships they encountered as immigrants and generally spent many hours together. In the summer of 1983, after numerous conversations that lasted until the small hours of the night, the three, who in the meantime had been joined by Liebowitz and Hazan, were still infuriated about the implementation of the Camp David agreements. They decided that the time had come to put into practice the values they had learned, the same values that were the incentives for their immigration.[81] The first of these principles was to take revenge on the Arabs, so in July of that year, the five embarked on their violent campaign. To begin with, they set fire to cars and buses owned by Palestinians and the offices of the East Jerusalem newspaper *Al-Fajr*.[82]

In the winter of 1984 they stepped up their operations. After the death of four Jews and the wounding of twenty-eight others in the December 6 attack by Palestinian terrorists on the No. 18 bus in Jerusalem, TNT members attacked houses in Jerusalem's Arab "Shuafat" neighborhood with Molotov cocktails, causing extensive damage to property but no injuries.[83] After that operation, Leitner spoke to Kach activist Baruch Gordon, a resident of the settlement of Beit El, and asked him to notify the media that the TNT (the Hebrew acronym for "Terrorism Against Terrorism") group claimed responsibility for the attack.[84] A few weeks later, Leitner, Richter, and Guzovsky embarked on another violent campaign. This time, they severely beat a number of Palestinians in Jerusalem, and then, in Hebron, they set fire to a large number of cars.[85] Despite the significant damage they caused, the group's members felt frustrated that Palestinian terrorists were not deterred from continuing to strike at Jewish targets. The TNT group therefore decided to switch the aim of their activities from damaging property to harming people, in the spirit of "an eye for an eye and a tooth for a tooth." Because of technical limitations and the need to find escape routes, they decided that the ideal operation for them would be to ambush a Palestinian bus while it was en route. After reconnoitering roads in the West Bank and searching for a convenient place to execute the attack, they decided on a side road near the village of Mazra'a e-Sharqiya, not far from Ramallah.[86]

On the night of March 15, 1984, a heavy fog covered the Ramallah region, but this did not put off Leitner, Liebowitz, and Richter. Leitner parked their car at the roadside while his friends went in search of a good place to ambush the designated target. A short while after positioning themselves on a mound of dirt beside the road, they saw the bus coming toward them. When they estimated that the bus was close enough, they opened fire with an M16 semiautomatic rifle that belonged to Guzovsky's father, injuring six Palestinians.[87] Seconds later, Liebowitz and Richter slipped away in the fog to where Leitner waited with the car.[88] Poor visibility made it difficult for them to find their way back to Jerusalem, but they eventually found themselves in the neighborhood of Ramot. Here, they stopped beside a dumpster and disposed of the ski masks and gloves they had used during the attack. They then proceeded to a public telephone and Leitner phoned one of the network's members, whose role was to notify the media of the operation. However, as Leitner's friends waited for him in the car, none of them noticed the police car approaching them. Within minutes, the police overpowered and arrested them. It later turned out that information of the operation had been leaked to the GSS. The GSS had in fact been trailing the conspirators but had lost them in the fog and so were unable to prevent the attack.[89]

THE COMMITTEE FOR THE SAFETY OF THE ROADS

On June 6, 1987, a bus transporting Jews was pelted with stones by a crowd of Arabs at the Beit Dagan Junction, just outside Jerusalem. One of the passengers, a resident of Kiryat Arba, was wounded and needed hospitalization.[90] This incident aroused the wrath of the residents of Kiryat Arba and the Jewish settlement in Hebron, and they began to pour into the streets. Prominent local Kach activists, headed by Samuel Ben-Yishai, who led a group calling itself the Committee for the Safety of the Roads, decided they had to take some kind of action. They felt that there must be retribution and that it was inconceivable that Jews should be harmed without an appropriate response.

With amazing swiftness the group's activists assembled their Kiryat Arba followers and joined those already awaiting them in the Jewish settlement in Hebron. After several hours of planning, seventy of them got into their cars and headed for the Deheishe refugee camp, near Bethlehem. Upon their arrival, they entered the camp with the clear intention of initiating a violent confrontation with the astonished local residents. They began firing in the air with their M16 rifles, aiming at windows and roof-mounted water tanks.[91] Very quickly the local residents began to surround the advancing group, and violent brawls erupted. Only about an hour after the beginning of the incident, IDF forces arrived at the camp to end the confrontation and were surprised when members of the Committee for the Safety of the Roads began lashing out at them as well, refusing to leave the site. The soldiers were finally forced to use tear gas to drive the activists out of the refugee camp.[92] Such incidents were the common mode of operation used by the Committee for the Safety of the Roads, but its members also operated covertly. For example, on January 15, 1988, after the hurling of two Molotov cocktails at Jews in Hebron, four activists of the group set out shortly after midnight, each armed with a simple kitchen knife. All through the night, they prowled the side streets of Hebron, slashing the tires of more than 400 cars.[93]

To a great extent, the group's violence was a direct result of the complicated situation facing the founding members of Kach in the wake of Kahane's election to the Knesset. On one hand, Kahane and his aides sought to maintain their wild image, which had gained them the seat in the Knesset in the first place. On the other hand, Israeli democracy was gearing up for a struggle against Kahanism and in 1987 amended the Basic Law: The Knesset in order to ban racist and antidemocratic parties from Israeli parliament.[94] Kahane supporters found a solution by engaging in low levels of violence, mainly with the intention of continuing to provide provocative footage for the television cameras. In this venture, the Kahanists were decidedly successful. In those years, Israel had only one television station, which was like the country's tribal campfire. One Friday night, the main edition of the news program broadcast a scene that became engraved in the collective memory. Baruch Marzel, Rabbi Kahane's parliamentary assistant, accompanied by a group of thugs and armed with an Uzi submachine gun, strode through the center of the Hebron market, striking and kicking the cars of startled Palestinians and overturning fruit and vegetable stands, while IDF soldiers stood by, unmoving.

Those were the "years of glory" for the Committee for the Safety of the Roads. This period also marked the rise of the second generation of Kach leaders, including Noam Federman, Mike Guzovsky (Yekutiel Ben-Ya'akov), Tiran Polak, and Samuel Ben-Yishai. These were men who had spent their youth in the Kach movement; they had been taken under the wing of Rabbi Kahane and become his faithful aides. This same group later became the backbone of the Kach leadership. The Committee for the Safety of the Roads was founded in defiance of the Israeli government and security forces, which Kahane felt did not provide the residents of the West Bank with sufficient protection from Palestinian attacks. As in previous instances, this defensive initiative, too, was more of a loose social network than an established organization. Kach members in Hebron, who by that time had become the center of the movement's activities, were the ones who mounted the first operations, serving as an example to their friends in other settlements.

Originally, members of the committee had planned to provide armed escorts to buses transporting settlers, but because this was not a real organization but rather a network of Kahane's most militant disciples, their activities quickly deviated from protecting Jews to violently attacking Palestinian property and terrorizing Arab residents. After the First Intifada erupted in December 1987, the committee's operations became much more offensive, frequent, and violent, and the group started to grow branches all over the West Bank and Jerusalem. In the late 1980s, for example, a subnetwork of the committee calling itself the "Judea Police" began operating in the Old City of Jerusalem, attacking Palestinian residents in East Jerusalem and even inside the Old City. Thus the Intifada brought about the reinforcement of the committee's status and its operational capabilities, allowing it to more easily mobilize support and recruits and rationalize its activity.

Kahane's provocative behavior in the Knesset, which included constant confrontation with left-wing and Arab Knesset members and the recurrent proposal of racist bills, outraged most Knesset parties and the media. At the same time, the riotous actions of his supporters, members of the Committee for the Safety of the Roads, helped Kach expand its circle of supporters.

This violence turned out to be a double-edged sword. On October 5, 1988, the Central Elections Committee determined that the Kach party could not run in the elections for the Twelfth Knesset because of its racist statements and its demands for the elimination of the democratic government in Israel. This resolution was ratified by the Supreme Court. Kahane's disciples, most of them members in the Committee for the Safety of the Roads, responded with their own decision to divorce themselves from the State of Israel. On December 27 of that year, at an impressive ceremony at the five-star Plaza Hotel in Jerusalem, Kach members declared the establishment of the State of Judea, designed to take over from the State of Israel if and when Israeli leaders opted to withdraw from the West Bank. Michael Ben-Horin, a veteran Kahanist, was appointed president of the State of Judea.[95]

The State of Judea movement's main goal was to preserve the organizational structure of Kach after the latter lost its hold in the Knesset. Despite its failure to achieve this goal, the short-lived movement exposed the structure of the Kahanist movement's violent satellite networks. When joining the State of Judea, members were asked to divulge the details of other organizations to which they belonged. In this manner, it was revealed that the various Kahanist networks numbered a few hundred activists, with much overlap between the various networks. In other words, many activists who declared their membership in the Committee for the Safety of the Roads also reported belonging to other evasive movements, such as Dov (a play on the Hebrew acronym of Dikui Bogdim, "Suppression of Traitors") and the Sicarii (Sikarikin). The former were a group of students formed by Kach activists for the purpose of taking action against left-wing public figures, and the Sicarii were Kach activists who named themselves after the Sicarii rebels during the time of ancient Rome. They protested the disqualification of the Kach list from the Twelfth Knesset elections by setting fire to property and sending threatening letters to media figures, judges, and political leaders from the ultra-Orthodox, moderate right, and left-wing parties.[96]

The establishment of the State of Judea was confirmation of the widespread reports of rising support for Kach among Gush Emunim settlers. Further evidence was provided when a group of students, followers of

Rabbi Zvi Yehuda Kook and members of Gush Emunim, officially joined the State of Judea movement. Two additional indications were the frequent invitation of Michael Ben-Horin to participate in meetings of the Gush Emunim leadership and the publication of articles by Rabbi Scheffler, the designated minister of education for the State of Judea, in *Nekuda*, Gush Emunim's official organ. Even Mercaz Harav Yeshiva, the spiritual bastion of the Gush Emunim movement, supported the idea of the State of Judea after approval from Rabbi Avraham Shapira, who was at the time the Chief Ashkenazi Rabbi of Israel. These were the first signs of the tightening relationship between the various streams of the settlers and their supporters, which found expression, among other things, in several acts of terrorism perpetrated in the 1990s.

THE DISCIPLES

Yoel Lerner was not the only Kahane disciple to mount a terrorist attack without a direct order from the rabbi. In August 1987, stolen weapons, explosives, and ammunition were found in the possession of a soldier serving in the Northern Command of the IDF. He had provided them to Kach activists who came from the Yeshiva of the Jewish Idea, apparently with the intention of harming Arabs.[97] An almost identical incident occurred in 2000, when the GSS learned that IDF-issued weapons and ammunition had been smuggled to students at the Yeshiva of the Jewish Idea, who were forming a group that was to carry out reprisal attacks against Arabs. The group's leader, Yonatan Yosef, persuaded his friends and acquaintances serving in the ultra-Orthodox Nahal unit of the IDF to appropriate munitions for him, but he and his friends did not get the chance to execute their plans.[98] However, the most serious episode of stealing weapons involving a Kach activist was discovered on April 22, 1991. Daniel Pinner, a soldier and Kach activist, smuggled weapons and ammunition to two of his friends in the movement: Kuzriel Meir and Nachshon Walls (Wolf), both residents of Hebron.[99] Wolf, who was twenty-nine at the time of his arrest, used the weapons to commit murder. On August 6, 1990, while traveling in a car near Kiryat Arba, Wolf drew out an M16 rifle and fired at a passing vehicle with Palestinian license plates. Aziza Jaber, a resident of Hebron who had been on her way to the local hospital, was killed.[100] After his capture, Wolf confessed to that act and explained that he had done it to avenge the killings of the two Jewish youths, Lior Tubol and Ronen Karmani, both seventeen, who had been murdered two days before by Palestinian terrorists.[101] It quickly became clear that Wolf had not acted alone. Kuzriel Meir, who had served in the Green Berets in the American army, was suspected of providing logistical assistance for the murder but was ultimately not indicted due to lack of evidence. Nachshon Walls was sentenced to life imprisonment, which was later shortened to fifteen years.[102]

GOD OF VENGEANCE

In November 1990, Kahane was visiting the United States on one of his frequent trips to raise funds and rally support in the Jewish communities. On Monday, November 5, he delivered a lecture at the Marriott Hotel in New York on the obligation of Jews to immigrate to Israel. After Kahane finished speaking, people began to approach him in order to ask questions and speak with him. A young man with a Middle Eastern appearance also moved toward Kahane, and before anyone could notice, he pulled out a gun and shot the rabbi twice at close range. Kahane was hit in the head and the chest and collapsed to the floor. He died a short while later, before reaching the hospital. Kahane's murderer was later identified as an Egyptian named El-Sayid Nosair, a member of Ramzi Yousef's terror network, which was responsible for the first attack against the World Trade Center on February 26, 1993.

A few hours after the murder, a rejoinder came from the other side of the Atlantic Ocean. Ali el Hatib, sixty-five, from the village of Luban e-Sharqiya in the West Bank, was riding his donkey on a dirt road and making his way toward his olive grove. He was shot in the back by people in a yellow Peugeot 404, bearing Israeli license plates, as it drove by at high speed. A few seconds and 500 yards later, gunfire was aimed from the same car at Miriam Salman Rashid, who was standing at the entrance to her home. She was hit in the throat, chest, and abdomen. Both Ali and Miriam died on the spot, and the car quickly disappeared in the direction of the nearby settlement of Eli. Evidence collected by police investigators at the scene of the incident led them to the conclusion that the shootings were perpetrated by Kach activists in retaliation for the assassination of Rabbi Meir Kahane. Police intelligence revealed that immediately after learning of the rabbi's death, Kach members began preparing a list of reprisal targets, which only reinforced the investigators' suspicions that the attack had been carried out by Kahane people. After intensive investigations, the police arrested three Kach activists on suspicion of being involved in the incident: David Ha'ivri, David Cohen, and Ben-Zion Gophstein. However, they were never tried, due to lack of evidence.[103]

The assassination of Kahane marked a significant turning point in the history of the Kach movement. Kahane's closest associates, second-generation members of the party leadership (i.e., Baruch Marzel, Noam Federman, Tiran Pollack, and Michael Ben-Horin), believed that the most effective way to promote the legacy of their assassinated leader was by way of representation in the Knesset, and to this end they were willing to make ideological changes that would preclude the disqualification of their list a second time. Another group, less dominant in its partisan activities, felt that although running in the elections was essential, it was insufficient reason to leave behind their violent operations. Most members of this network were from the Kfar Tapuach settlement, where they had settled as an organized core group after completing their studies at the Yeshiva of the Jewish Idea, founded and headed by Rabbi Kahane. Following differences of opinion, however, three central members of the Kach secretariat—Mike Guzovsky (Yekutiel Ben-Ya'akov), David Ben-Dor, and the Kahane younger son, Binyamin Ze'ev Kahane, announced their departure from the movement. In its place, they established a new faction, Elnakam (God of Vengeance), which later also attempted to run in the Knesset elections under the name Kahane Chai (Kahane Lives).

Despite the many reports in the media about the irreparable rift between the two groups, the fact that many of the members of both groups had studied together in the Yeshiva of the Jewish Idea and had spent their teen years in the Kach movement and Kach summer camps led them to maintain friendly relationships. In the early 1990s, however, members of Kahane Chai displayed a greater commitment in practicing the violent ideology of their rabbi. Exactly two years after the murder of the two elderly Palestinians in Luban e-Sharqiya, they struck again.

Four seventeen-year-olds from Jerusalem—Ze'ev Wolf, Gershon Hershkowitz, Tal Shahar, and Nehemia Meshbaum, all members of the local Kahane Chai network—decided to mark the second anniversary of Rabbi Kahane's death with an act designed to intimidate the Palestinian public.[104] A few weeks earlier they had stolen a fragmentation grenade from a military vehicle in which they had hitched a ride. The four of them plotted the operation in secret and meticulously coordinated their efforts. They decided to lob the grenade at Palestinian passersby in the crowded butchers' street of the Arab market in Jerusalem's Old City. They drew lots to decide who would throw the grenade while the others kept watch at the entrance to the market to make sure no Jews would get hurt. Nehemia Meshbaum was chosen to throw the grenade.[105]

On the day designated for the attack, their plans went awry. The four boys were delayed by the police after participating in a violent demonstration organized by Kahane Chai. However, their detention did not deter them from their plans. They simply decided to postpone the attack by one day. On the early morning of November 16, 1992, they met in order to carry out the attack. Shahar, who had changed his mind, did not join his friends, and they decided to go on without him. Contrary to their original plans, only Hershkowitz remained at the entrance to the market, while Meshbaum and Wolf climbed onto the roof of one of the shops. After ensuring that there were no Jews in the street below, the boys drew out the pin and threw the grenade. Abd al-Razek Adkik, aged sixty-nine, was killed in the explosion. Seven other Palestinians were wounded, and one of them later died of his wounds.[106] Despite their young age and the amateur fashion in which their action was perpetrated, the Jerusalem District police did not manage to track down the boys for eight months. Their evasion of the police was due mainly to the boys' loyalty to one another.

Earlier in this chapter we pointed out the similarity between the Kahanist groups and Salafi jihad groups with respect to the fact that both evolved in the framework of a counterculture of immigrants. The story of this group, whose members dubbed it Sayeret Hanekama (the Vengeance Patrol), draws attention to another similarity to the Salafi jihad networks in Western Europe[107] and even the networks of Palestinian suicide bombers.[108] In most of these cases, there was a spontaneous organizing of youngsters who were already friends and whose social interaction led them to develop similar worldviews. Contrary to the common assumption that terrorism is a strategy carefully chosen by an organization leadership, in these cases there were no such strategic considerations. Such networks were the result of an intensive group dynamic that ultimately found expression in the perpetration of serious violence on a political basis.

■■■■■■■■■■

THE ASSASSINATION OF Prime Minister Yitzhak Rabin on November 4, 1995, an act carried out by a network of young religious Zionist Jews, marked the divorce of Jewish terrorism from both the established Jewish settlement movement and the Kach movement in its many incarnations. The Jewish terrorism accompanying Israel into the twenty-first century was a younger and different version and, in addition to the terrorists' motivations discussed in previous chapters, for the first time was committed blatantly in defiance of the State of Israel itself. The first signs of the transition began to appear immediately after the signing of the Oslo Accords, which were the source of a great crisis for religious Zionists and settlers alike.

THE VENGEANCE UNDERGROUND

The first episode began on the evening of December 10, 1993, when Sa'adi Abdul Mahdi Fatafta, twenty-seven, his brother Mahmoud Abdul Mahdi Fatafta, and their cousin Iskhak Mahmoud Fatafta, both twenty-five, left their workplace in Beit Shemesh, near Jerusalem, and set off for their home in the village of Tarqumiya. They were stopped at an improvised roadblock on a narrow dirt road near the village of Hares. On the side of the road was a vehicle with Israeli license plates. The occupants of the car fired automatic weapons at the men, and all three were killed on the spot.[1] Several hours later, Israel public radio received an anonymous call taking responsibility for the attack. It was described as retaliation for the murder of two settlers a few days earlier by Hamas operatives in Hebron.[2]

Despite a painstaking investigation, more than ten months passed before General Security Service (GSS) agents finally made the breakthrough that pointed them in the direction of several suspects. In early September 1994, an Israel Defense Forces (IDF) officer by the name of Oren Edri was arrested on suspicion of supplying explosives and firearms to a group of settlers from the Hebron area who were involved in terrorist attacks on Palestinians.[3] The GSS investigators concluded that this group, known as the Vengeance Underground, was responsible for the attack against the Fatafta family and that they were also planning a high-profile attack on one of the Arab villages near Hebron. Despite the exhaustive investigation and subsequent arrest of several prominent Kiryat Arba settlers suspected of membership in the group, including Avraham Tibi, Rabbi Ido Elba, and Elyashiv Keller, the only one brought to trial was Edri. He was sentenced to a two-year jail term for stealing IDF explosives.[4] Apparently, the group did not carry out additional operations. Even today, there still seems to be a shroud of secrecy surrounding the way the group was formed, its modus operandi, and its membership. However, it seems that all the elements of our theoretical framework were manifested in the characteristics of the group. It is clear that, similar to earlier terrorist groups, this was a network composed of friends and neighbors from Kiryat Arba.[5] Group members had suffered from Palestinian terrorism and were influenced by the tense and bitter atmosphere prevalent in their community after the Oslo Accords. An additional factor was the internal escalation typical of social networks involving members in distress, a process that apparently led the group to adopt and implement violent tactics.

In the wake of the Vengeance Underground undercover investigation, the GSS found out that two other settlers were planning to assault Arabs. These were the brothers Yehoyada and Eitan Kahalani, both in their twenties and residents of Kiryat Arba. In the summer of 1994, they decided to launch a terrorist campaign against Palestinians in the West Bank. The intention of the Kahalani brothers was to inflame the region and forestall the execution of the terms of the Oslo Accords.[6] On September 2, 1994, their inaugural attempt met with failure when they tried to ambush Palestinians on a dirt road leading from Jerusalem's Malkha Shopping Mall to the nearby village of Batir. The two brothers had stolen M16 rifles from the armory at Kiryat Arba and were waiting for an unsuspecting victim. At approximately 3:00 P.M., they espied Ziad Shami, twenty-two, who was riding to the village on his bicycle. While Yehoyada returned to their car in preparation for a quick getaway, Eitan approached Shami and asked him in Arabic whether he had any money. Before Shami could answer, Eitan raised his rifle and pulled the trigger. But instead of gunfire, there was only a dull click. Stunned, he ran to the car, and the two fled the scene. A few miles later they were stopped by the Border Police and GSS agents. It turned out that the weapons had been made inoperable by GSS agents who had discovered their plans.[7]

In the months that followed, resistance to the Oslo Accords by members of the religious Zionist stream and settler community intensified. They became increasingly radical as the leaders of these countercultures responded severely to the gradual implementations of the accords. For them, the Oslo process was a real threat to the vision of a Greater Land of Israel and ultimately the realization of a Jewish religious state. Thus, a long line of rabbis attacked not only the agreements themselves but also the legitimacy of the Israeli government as a source of authority. They pointed a finger at the heads of the administration, accusing them of being traitors to Zionist ideas and endangering the existence of the Jewish state. Some of them did not even hesitate to spell out the response they felt was necessary. For example, Elyakim Haetzni, one of the prominent leaders of the settler community, compared Rabin's government to the Petain government in France during the Nazi occupation: "A government that is responsible for the death of Jews needs to know that its members may stand trial for treason, the same as in France when Nazi collaborators were sentenced to death."[8] Even Rabbi Yoel Bin-Nun, who is still considered one of the more moderate leaders of the Gush Emunim movement, declared, "There is no more moderate way—just brutal force brought the Palestinian all their achievements. . . . We must clarify to Shimon Peres and his people that we can disrupt the normality of life in this country."[9]

In mid-1995 the rhetoric used among the religious Zionist and settler communities regarding the Oslo agreements was ratcheted up another level. A growing number of pamphlets appeared in synagogues all over the settlements debating whether the Halakhic rules of *din rodef* and *din moser* could be applied to Rabin. The first *din,* or "judgment," refers to a Jew who is willing to endanger the lives of other Jews, and the second refers to a Jew who is willing to hand Jewish property over to gentiles. According to the Halakha, the sentence for both transgressions is death. Moreover, in many of the pamphlets rabbis morally approved revenge attacks on Palestinians, even glorifying acts such as the Goldstein massacre. Finally, in September 1995, shortly before the actual assassination of Rabin, another group of rabbis from various settlements in the West Bank published a Halakhic rule enjoining IDF religious soldiers to disobey any order that dictated the evacuation of settlements and the implementation of the Oslo Accords.

In view of this intense process of catastrophic framing taking place inside the settler and religious Zionist communities, it is hard to be surprised at the emergence of the Yigal Amir group.

THE YIGAL AMIR GROUP

The rally that took place at Kikar Malkhei Yisrael (Kings of Israel Square)[10] on the night of Saturday, November 4, 1995, was regarded as a great success by its organizers. The city of Tel Aviv had not seen such an enormous assembly of supporters for ages. Some claimed it was the largest turnout of Israeli citizens at a political rally since the mass demonstration after the massacre of Palestinians in the Lebanese Sabra and Shatila refugee camps. After two years in which the Israeli right wing had "ruled the town squares" and led a cascade of protests against the Oslo process, the Israeli left had proved that it still had some fight in it. Prime Minister Yitzhak Rabin, who had his doubts before the rally regarding both its necessity and its chances of success, was in buoyant spirits when informed that attendance was estimated at 150,000. This was a number that to a fair extent represented wide sectors of the Israeli public backing the political process he led. "Finally," he said to his associates, "here is the unbeatable answer to all our critics. . . . The people support the peace process."[11]

The atmosphere at the rally was also energized, and the crowd's elation surged still higher when, near the end of the event, Rabin and the leaders of his coalition government appeared on stage to sing the anthem of the peace camp, "Shir Lashalom" ("A Song for Peace").[12] At the close of the rally, the crowd was slow to leave the square, basking in high spirits and heaping praise on the prime minister as he continued to watch his supporters. At that moment, none of the participants could conceive that in just a matter of seconds, a young Jew would aim his Beretta and shoot the prime minister dead with three bullets. Of all the threats made against the Israeli prime minister, also leader and proponent of the Oslo process, the scenario that unfolded was the least probable. Rabin's assassination was the result of a bond formed between young people who were poles apart from the established protest movements. Their motivations were a combination of a desire to retaliate against Palestinians who carried out terrorist attacks, a desperate ambition to halt the transfer of West Bank land to Palestinian sovereignty, and a deep-seated hostility toward the country's institutions and leaders.[13]

Yigal Amir, twenty-five, a law student at Bar-Ilan University, had spent the hours before the assassination at his home in the Neve Amal neighborhood of Herzliya. Friday evening, he worshipped at the Etz Hakhaim (Tree of Life) Synagogue and then joined his family for the traditional Sabbath dinner, where the conversation quickly moved to politics. His parents weren't especially concerned when their son once again repeated the mantra he had been propounding for some time: "Rabin has to be destroyed. . . . He is the one responsible for the disaster that has fallen upon us with this false peace."[14]

On Saturday morning, Amir returned to the synagogue, this time accompanied by his brother Hagai. During the break between prayers, Yigal told his brother of his plans to assassinate Rabin at the rally. Hagai wasn't surprised; he only asked him to use a sniper rifle when carrying out the deed. He was afraid that if his brother shot Rabin at close range, he would be killed by the prime minister's security detail. Despite Hagai's pleas, Amir decided to stick to his original plan: go to the rally, wait for an opportunity, and then get close enough to shoot the prime minister.[15] At 7:45 P.M., Yigal Amir boarded bus number 247 to Tel Aviv carrying a Beretta 9-millimeter short caliber pistol. Before he left his house he took out two types of bullets from his desk drawer: regular and hollow point. His brother had prepared the special hollow point bullets for him.[16] He arranged the bullets in two separate rows and alternately loaded them in the magazine. When he finished, he cocked the weapon and loaded a bullet directly in the barrel so if the gun jammed, he would at least be able to get off one shot. "I was always afraid the gun would jam and nothing would happen. I would get caught and like an idiot, I'd spend the rest of my life in prison."[17] When he arrived at Tel Aviv, he got off the bus at Arlozorov Street and removed the black skullcap he always wore, afraid it would attract the attention of the security forces.[18]

At the square, he stood with the rest of the people in front of the stage where the prime minister would soon appear. He had expected to be able to shoot Rabin from his place in the packed crowd, but realized he was out of range. The fact that the police had formed a barrier between the crowd and the stage gave him further reason to change his plans. He walked over to the Tel Aviv City Hall northern parking lot, next to the square. The stairs descending from the stage ended there, and Amir saw Rabin's and Foreign Minister Shimon Peres's official limousines waiting for them.[19] At first, Amir was afraid the security detail would notice him and ask him to leave the area, but he soon realized that confusion reigned at the scene, and the security forces were not coordinated: "There was bedlam, police, bodyguards. . . . I realized the right hand had no idea what the left hand was doing."[20] To lower the risk of getting caught, Amir tried to draw as little attention as possible and acted as if he were one of the security officers. Some of the police even thought he was one of the drivers and asked him to stand next to his car.[21]

After waiting about forty minutes, Amir saw the minister for foreign affairs, Shimon Peres, descend the stairwell with only one bodyguard accompanying him. Peres approached the bystanders and waved. There were only 10 feet between him and Amir. However, the latter decided to wait for Rabin, his original target. Before entering his car, Peres asked the prime minister's driver where Rabin was; the driver answered that he was on his way. Peres waited a few moments but then thought better of it and instructed his driver to leave. A few minutes later, the prime minister appeared at the top of the stairs with four bodyguards. His wife, Leah, and the head of the GSS personal protection unit were behind him. They saw the prime minister make his way toward the open doors of his car.[22]

At the same moment, Amir got up from the large concrete flowerpot he was sitting on. He saw that one bodyguard was in front of the prime minister, and a second one was moving toward a barrier that kept the crowd away in order to block a gap that had opened there. This left only one agent, who was guarding him from behind. Amir took advantage of the breach; he quickly closed the distance until he was 9 feet from Rabin, raised his arm across the back of the guard, and began to fire. Only 8 inches separated the barrel of the gun from Rabin's back. Two bullets hit Yitzhak Rabin. The head of the security detail, Yoram Rubin, took a bullet in his arm when he tried to cover the prime minister with his own body.[23]

Amir threw the gun away at once to avoid being fired upon. Security personnel and officers pounced on him almost immediately. They dragged him away and held him up against the parking lot wall. But it was too late. Rabin was rushed to the nearby Ichilov Hospital, where he arrived with no pulse or blood pressure, taking his last breaths.[24] The two hollow point bullets had caused extensive damage. The first caused pulmonary embolisms and tore into his right lung; the second ripped through his spleen before hitting the left lung. After more than forty minutes of resuscitation efforts, Prime Minister Yitzhak Rabin was pronounced dead at 10:30 P.M. The director of the Prime Minister Bureau, Eitan Haber, addressed the journalists and citizens crowded around the hospital entrance and made the announcement that became etched into the memories of so many Israelis: "The Government of Israel announces with shock, great sorrow and deep grief, the death of Prime Minister and Minister of Defense Yitzhak Rabin, who was murdered by an assassin tonight in Tel Aviv. May his memory be blessed."[25]

THE PLOT

Yigal Amir hails from an Orthodox Jewish family that emigrated from Yemen. He studied in the state religious school system and then at the Hayishuv Hakhadash Yeshiva, an elite religious high school in Tel Aviv. After graduating, he joined a *hesder* yeshiva at Kerem D'Yavne, where his brother Hagai had studied several years earlier. He served in the Golani Brigade, one of the select infantry units of the Israeli army.[26]

During his military service, Amir began to espouse views that combined religious fanaticism with hatred of Arabs and the Israeli left. During his service, a large part of which he spent in the West Bank, his positions became even more extreme and were manifested in the harsh way he treated the Palestinian population.[27] After his release from the army in the summer of 1992, he was sent to Russia by the Nativ organization, which had been employed by the Israeli government to collect covert intelligence in the Soviet Union. By this time, the organization had turned to the task of trying to persuade young Russian Jews to immigrate to Israel. After about a year, he returned to Israel and began his studies at the prestigious Faculty of Law at the Bar-Ilan University.[28]

As could be expected of one who grew up and was educated in the religious Zionist counterculture, Yigal Amir was highly influenced by the very negative attitudes and teachings of religious Zionist rabbis toward the Oslo Accords. He quickly adopted the stance that the accords were a threat to the continued existence of the Jewish state and that activities for their preclusion should be the highest priority for any Jew. Therefore he rapidly became one of the most prominent political activists to voice his objection to the agreements at Bar-Ilan, the only religious university in Israel.

Amir persistently initiated mass demonstrations of students against the Oslo process and the Rabin government. However, most of his efforts were devoted to a project he had thought up himself, whose goal essentially to get students to visit the settlements. He did this by organizing weekends of worship and lectures for university students in the West Bank and Gaza Strip settlements.[29] Every Friday morning, Amir appeared at a different settlement leading such a group. His charismatic personality already drew dozens of students, but before long the numbers swelled. During the last trip he arranged, the weekend before the assassination, 550 students paid a visit to Netzarim in the Gaza Strip. During these visits, Amir never hesitated in voicing his belief that something must be done about Rabin and that his government must be deposed.[30] Few then had any idea that behind his declarations were concrete intentions.

But Yigal Amir was in fact very serious. By late 1993, he and his older brother Hagai began amassing arms and ammunition. Their goal was to form an underground group that would put a stop to the implementation of the Oslo Accords. They discussed the idea of murdering the prime minister, and assassination quickly became their preferred option.[31] Amir began to collect historical and professional material dealing with the assassinations of political leaders in the past, while his brother dealt with the more practical question of how to get close to the most heavily guarded person in the State of Israel.[32]

FORMATION OF THE NETWORK

Several months after they began plotting, the Amir brothers decided to share their secret with Dror Adani. Yigal Amir and Dror Adani had met when they studied together at the Kerem D'Yavne Yeshiva, and they became close while serving in the IDF. In 1993, Yigal brought Adani home to introduce him to his sister. Although nothing ever developed between the two, Adani and the two brothers continued to see each other. They spent many hours in a small shed behind the nursery school run by the brothers' mother and developed a common philosophy regarding the steps that were necessary to halt the Oslo process.[33] The constant interaction between the three intensified their militancy, and after a short while they decided to act on two separate fronts. On one hand, they would try to kill Prime Minister Rabin, and on the other they would act against Palestinian police officers and civilians. Their objective was to precipitate a crisis between Israel and the Palestinian Authority that was grave enough to stop the peace process.[34]

Adani was very creative in devising ways to carry out the assassination. One of his plans was to booby-trap the prime minister's official car. To evaluate that option, the Amir brothers went to Rabin's neighborhood carrying a package of explosives and explored the possibility of placing it next to the car. To their disappointment, they discovered it was always parked in a secure location. Adani didn't give up. He suggested detonating a car bomb on the route between Rabin's home and the Tel Aviv–Jerusalem highway. The brothers rejected this plan because they were afraid of injuring passersby. Hagai Amir suggested launching an anti-tank missile at Rabin's car, but despite his optimism, they were never able to obtain one.[35]

Probably the most imaginative of their schemes was to insert a chemical substance—nitroglycerine—into the water system of the apartment building where the Rabin family lived in northern Tel Aviv. The three had first thought of introducing poison in this manner, but Adani refused because of the danger to the other residents. He therefore suggested placing explosive nitroglycerine in the pipes. In order to test the feasibility of the plan, the brothers returned to the prime minister's neighborhood. Yigal Amir was able to reach the building's entrance and inspect the water pipe juncture. He even located the pipe leading to the Rabin apartment. However, they realized that they would need a compressor to drill a hole in the pipe. Again, a plan was frustrated because of their inability to get hold of the necessary equipment.[36]

At the same time, Yigal Amir tried to secure the rabbinical authorization for killing the prime minister. How successful was he? The question remains unanswered, although most signs indicate that he received a positive response. Some figures in the religious Zionist camp claim that although the issue was debated, not one rabbi was found who would approve the assassination. Other prominent figures from this camp, such as Rabbi Yoel Ben-Nun, insisted that Amir did receive authorization.[37] Moreover, in his testimony to the police immediately after the assassination, Amir himself declared that he would never have taken on the assassination without rabbinical approval and without being sure that more people were behind him.[38] Whatever the answer is, there is little doubt that the debate in the rabbinical circles of the religious Zionist stream regarding the application of *din rodef* and *din moser* to Rabin, and the fact that at least some rabbis did not reject the use of these terms in describing Rabin's policy, had an important role in persuading Amir that the blood of the prime minister was not only on his own head. As he himself declared during his trial, "I acted according to *din rodef*. . . . It was not a personal act, I just wanted him to be removed from his position. If he would have remained paralyzed, it would have been the same for me."[39]

Although inspired by Adani's bold ideas, the Amir brothers understood that in order to execute them they would need additional operatives. Adani had reservations. He was afraid that by widening the circle, they also would be increasing the danger of infiltration by the GSS. Yigal Amir, the driving force behind the network, ignored his warning and set out to conscript likely candidates from among his fellow demonstrators at Bar-Ilan University (figure 5.1). Most of the recruits were persuaded to participate in antiPalestinian operations; few were involved in the conspiracy to assassinate

FIGURE 5.1 **THE AMIR BROTHERS NETWORK**

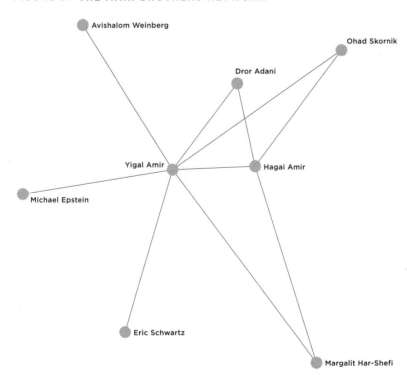

Rabin. Only a fellow law school student, Margalit Har-Shefi—resident of one of the most prestige settlements, Beit El, and daughter of settler nobility—was let in on the finer details of the plan.[40]

Amir first approached Avishalom Weinberg, a friend of his from the *kolel* (yeshiva for men) at the Bar-Ilan University. He suggested they form a cell of ten operatives that would mount violent assaults on Palestinians. Eric Schwartz, another friend of Amir, was appointed the task of procuring arms and explosives. Like Amir, he had served in the Golani Brigade and studied at the Kerem D'Yavne Yeshiva. After the police uncovered his connection to the Amir brothers, they found detonators, grenades, explosives, and more than 2,400 bullets in his possession.[41]

Amir also recruited Ohad Skornik, a law student who had come under Amir's influence, and Margalit Har-Shefi.[42] Amir had met Har-Shefi during their studies in the Faculty of Law, and they had become close friends. This relationship was uncommon in their Orthodox Jewish social circle, which followed strict rules of separation between the genders; Amir apparently hoped the relationship would develop into a romantic one. He trusted her completely and soon told her of their plans to assassinate the prime minister, asking for her help. Among other assignments, she looked into the practicability of breaking into the Beit El settlement armory and also tried to obtain a Halakhic authorization to kill Rabin. Because of their close relationship, Har-Shefi was aware of almost all of Amir's activities that were related to his efforts to assassinate Rabin.[43]

The last one to be recruited by Amir was Michael Epstein, a student in the Department of Computer Science at Bar-Ilan. Epstein, who lived in the Dolev settlement, was taken on apparently for practical reasons. One of Amir's plans was to take out Rabin with sniper fire, which meant he needed a marksman's rifle. Hagai Amir took this task upon himself; he pretended to be a settler and put in a formal request to the IDF for a weapon of self-defense. The IDF refused. As a result, Yigal approached Epstein, who, as a resident of Dolev, had been issued such a rifle by the army.[44] Epstein agreed to lend it to Amir. The next stage in the plan was to scout for a suitable place to stage the firing. At first, Amir hoped to shoot directly from the street into the Rabin family apartment, but he discarded this option when he found out that Rabin lived on the fifth floor.[45] That left him with only one scenario: a close-range hit. However, this idea was rejected by Hagai Amir because he was uncertain his brother would be able to penetrate the security cordon surrounding the prime minister and was also afraid for his brother's life. In the summer of 1995, Hagai's opposition weakened and eventually dissolved. Yigal Amir, for his part, did not bother to hide his intentions. For instance, that summer during a demonstration at Givat Hadagan in Hebron, he proclaimed, "If someone should turn up and kill Rabin, I would salute him and say, 'well done.'"[46] During the same period, he began to bring the subject up during family meals. After the assassination, his father, Shlomo, disclosed the following: "For the past four or five months, my son said that the prime minister should be killed because a *din rodef* was issued against him."[47] Imbued with faith in his mission, Amir attempted to execute the plan. He tried twice to shoot the prime minister but failed both times. He attempted to get close to Rabin on the latter's visit to the Beit Lid Junction after the suicide attack there and then during the dedication ceremony at the Kfar Shmaryahu Interchange. In both instances, he was not successful in penetrating the security shield surrounding Rabin's entourage.[48]

When he heard a peace rally had been set for November 4, he was determined not to miss another opportunity. At first he thought he would be able to mount a sniper attack with Epstein's M16. To this end, he visited Ohad Skornik's student apartment close to the square, hoping for an unobstructed line of fire. When he saw that the angle from the windows and terrace was not suitable, he decided to stage the attack from close range— the consequences be damned.[49]

After Yigal Amir was captured, the activities of the network ceased and all members were arrested. Amir was sentenced to life imprisonment plus sixteen years. His brother Hagai was sentenced to sixteen years, and Dror Adani to seven years. Margalit Har-Shefi was convicted of failing to prevent the murder and sentenced to eighteen months in jail.[50]

Apart from the reverberating shock felt after the Rabin assassination, the act marked a historic watershed for Jewish terrorism in Israel for two reasons. First, the assassination was carried out by a network of anonymous young people who belonged neither to any known terrorist group nor to the two most important ideological and sociopolitical organizational frameworks of the Israeli radical right: the Gush Emunim and Kahanist movements. Second, in contrast to Jewish terrorists who in the past had avoided direct challenges to government institutions and political leadership, Amir's network was completely alienated from Israeli democracy. Its members believed that the government of Israel was acting in diametric opposition to the interests of the people of Israel. A number of years later, this worldview was adopted by the hilltop youth and manifested in the terrorist activities of the Bat Ayin Underground, whose activities are discussed in the next chapter.

Despite these noted differences, however, the radicalization process undergone by Amir's group and its structure resemble those of previous groups and correspond with the premises of the theory we presented. External events that were perceived as catastrophic, communal framing, intragroup socialization, and the individuals' social distance from the majority culture were main factors that led to the emergence of the group and its slide into violence.

Vengeance

█████████████████████

THE AL-AQSA INTIFADA, which broke out in
October 2000, was punctuated by spates of Palestinian violence directed
at Israeli targets all over the country. Consisting mainly of suicide attacks,
this campaign of violence served as a catalyst for the emergence of Jewish
terrorist groups. For students of Jewish terrorism in Israel, this was almost
to be expected. Similar to the reaction that followed past episodes of Palestinian violence, a Jewish response would surely not be long in coming.
However, few expected that a Jewish group would be so brazen as to initiate a terrorist attack as savage as the one that was almost perpetrated on
the night of April 29, 2002, by the group that later came to be known as
the Bat Ayin Underground.

On that night, two Jerusalem police officers, Shimon Cohen and Barak
Segev, were on duty in East Jerusalem. As they patrolled the area around
the Beit Orot Yeshiva near Mount Scopus, they needed a few moments to
digest the incongruous sight of two bearded and skullcap-wearing young
Jews driving a vehicle towing a trailer. Something was wrong with this picture. At the height of the intifada, Jews did not usually wander the streets
of East Jerusalem, populated almost entirely by Palestinians, and there was
certainly no reason for them to be doing so at this time of night. When
questioned, the young men said they were on their way to the yeshiva. Their
suspicions not quieted, the officers nevertheless had no grounds to detain
them and resumed their patrol.[1] They had no idea that the two, Yarden
Morag and Shlomo Dvir-Zeliger, were on their way to carry out a terrorist
attack, and the trailer they were towing contained a powerful explosive
device.[2]

Later, around 3:15 A.M., when the route of their patrol took Cohen and
Segev past the Al-Makassed Hospital and the local girls' school in the Abu
Tor neighborhood, they were surprised to see the car and trailer again. This
time it was clear the two young men were up to something. When the

police got closer, they could see that one of the youths was hunched over the trailer that was now unhitched from the car. The officers decided to surprise the two, turned off the patrol car's blue flashing lights, and parked nearby. They slowly made their way toward the trailer. Yarden Morag, bent over the trailer, was caught unaware when they suddenly asked him what he was doing. He stammered out an unconvincing story about a flat tire. The explanation didn't impress the officers; why would they choose, of all places, one of the least hospitable areas of East Jerusalem to change a tire? Indeed, a quick inspection of the trailer showed that the tires were in satisfactory condition.[3] Their suspicions were further aroused when they asked the two men to open the trailer and produce identification. The suspects maintained they did not have a key, nor did they have identity cards on their person. That, together with a handgun and an Uzi—later found to have been stolen from Israel Defense Forces (IDF) soldiers—discovered during a search of the car made it perfectly clear this was no ordinary occurrence. The police officers called for reinforcements and sappers.[4]

In the meantime, Cohen and Segev isolated the two suspects and informed them that they were being detained. The young men became nervous, realizing their secret was on the verge of being revealed. At this stage, when Yarden Morag understood their plot was going to be exposed, he decided to change his strategy. He approached the officers and informed them that the trailer contained a bomb and explosive bricks. Gil Shabaz, the police sapper who arrived a few minutes later, asked the suspects to help him defuse the bomb.[5] Although Shlomo Dvir-Zeliger refused to cooperate, Morag agreed and sketched the contents of the trailer on paper: two containers of gasoline, a powerful explosive device made of two TNT bricks, and propane gas tanks. The source of electricity was a "virgin," a term denoting a military battery. Using a robot, the sappers immediately began the job of disarming the bombs. They discovered that the entire device was assembled with a detonator timed to go off at 7:35 A.M.[6]

The location where the two were caught with the trailer—directly in front of the entrance to the girls' school—and the time that the bomb was set to go off made it apparent to the police and the General Security Service (GSS), who had also been called to the scene, what the conspirators had intended to do. They had timed the bomb to explode at exactly the time when dozens of girls would have entered the gates of the school, killing many of them. Without a doubt, if the attack had succeeded, it would have been one of the most heinous acts of terrorism ever to take place in the State of Israel and probably would have led to an escalation of the intifada to even greater heights.

The police and GSS quickly found out that, contrary to initial assessments, this was not merely an organized effort designed to carry out a one-off strike in response to Palestinian suicide attacks against Jewish targets during the intifada. It became evident that these two conspirators were part of a social network of activists living in several West Bank settlements and that this specific attack was an additional stage in their campaign of terrorist attacks against Palestinians.

THE HILLTOP YOUTH

The Bat Ayin group was in effect a network of activists composed of various cliques that, for the most part, acted independently and had only limited contact among themselves.[7] The most famous of these cliques, and the one that gave the underground its name, was established by religious young people from the Bat Ayin settlement. Even before their network was exposed, residents of this settlement, which is near the town of Surif in the Hebron area and was established in 1989 by newly observant young people, were considered particularly extremist. They became known for their callous behavior toward Palestinians in neighboring villages. For instance, they aggressively refused to allow any Palestinian to enter or even pass near their settlement.[8]

Although the network structure of the Bat Ayin group was similar to that of earlier Jewish terrorist groups, it was unlike the Jewish Underground or the Kach networks. This conclusion was also reached by the GSS after the discovery of the group's existence:

They are different from members of other Jewish underground groups which came from the mainstream Yesha [Hebrew acronym for "Judea, Samaria and Gaza"] settlement movement, many of whom belonged to the settlement establishment and were associated with the governing elite. The Bat Ayin people, including many of the detainees who have been released in the last few weeks for lack of evidence, were raised on the "hills." Some of them belong to families of newly observant Jews, and none of them are associated with the settler elite.[9]

Although it did not explicitly say so, the GSS meant that the Bat Ayin group was for the most part made up of young people representing a new stream in the settlement enterprise of the new millennium: the hilltop youth. This moniker, fairly common in Israeli discourse in recent years, describes the tendency of third-generation West Bank settlers to establish themselves on desolate hilltops in communal-type farms, working the land to support themselves.

The rationale behind the actions of the hilltop youth reflects not only their desire to reinforce the rule of the Jewish people over all of Eretz Israel by establishing farms on the hills as a means for expanding Jewish-controlled territories in the West Bank but also their longing to promote a lifestyle identical to those of the ancient Hebrews, at least as they perceive it. These activists made a name for themselves among the Israeli public primarily through the violence and militancy they often demonstrate toward their Palestinian neighbors and the antipathy they exhibit toward any sign of sovereign authority of the State of Israel.[10] Many of them have explicitly declared that the State of Israel has come to the end of its days, and a new theocratic state composed of workers of the land should be established and run according to Jewish religious law. Thus, in many respects the principles of the hilltop youth can be regarded as a further radicalization of the Kahanist ideology. Both have aimed at offering a religious, Halakha-based political and cultural alternative to the current Israeli secular regime and its mainstream culture. Yet whereas the Kahanist movement operated from within Israeli society and Israel's political system and by the same token rejected revolutionary sentiments, the hilltop youth are implementing their worldview by creating isolated communities completely detached from the state authorities and mainstream culture. The farms or "outposts" they are building stand in defiance of the state sovereignty and are fostering the delegitimization of the existing sociopolitical order.

It is interesting to note that the most prominent leaders of the hilltop youth and those who developed its underlying ideology are older. Avri Ran and Yehoshafat Tor, for example, were among the first to establish farms on the hills of Samaria in the mid-1990s when they were in their thirties, although they depended on younger people to run the farms.[11] These more experienced members, although lacking all religious authority, rapidly became exemplary figures and a source of moral authority for the younger inhabitants of the small farm communities. They instilled in their young followers the understanding that the current standing of the Zionist project, as manifested both by the secular state and even the mainstream settlement movement, was on the brink of moral and physical collapse, and new alternatives should be developed. Many of these third-generation settlers, looking for alternative ways of self-fulfillment, were subsequently drawn to this new adventure.

In order to get a firsthand look at the hilltop youth, we set out on an early, hot August morning in 2005 and made our way to the Gvaot Olam farm, near the Itamar settlement. The founder of the farm, Avri Ran, is considered the undisputed symbol of the hilltop youth. At the time of our visit, Ran was being hunted by the police for his involvement in a violent attack on Palestinians. However, we thought we might find an opportunity to meet him. As we neared the farm, the road began to twist and turn through hills and boulders. It became increasingly narrow and rough, which only increased our feeling that this was a particularly isolated location.

When we arrived at the outpost, we were welcomed by the young residents who made up the workforce. The commune-like farm consisted of common living quarters, an almost complete absence of personal property, and a communal dining hall serving all the inhabitants. Our tour revealed a settlement with a diverse organic agricultural program that supplied its residents with most of their needs. Most buildings were either picturesque wooden cabins or barns with herds of goats. Its location on the summit of one of the highest hills in the region permitted a strategic view of the whole area and the Arab villages surrounding it. When we asked the young people about relations with their Palestinian neighbors, it became clear that despite the serene and pastoral atmosphere, the hilltop youth were in the midst of a bitter and never-ending conflict with the nearby Palestinian villagers, especially regarding the right to work the agricultural land surrounding the farm. The youths we spoke to harbored no doubts about their own right to the land. As far as they were concerned, in the Bible God bequeathed this land to the people of Israel, and therefore they were the legal heirs. nor did they show any uncertainty about their prerogative to respond with violence when they felt that their Palestinian neighbors were trying to prevent them from realizing this right. In their opinion, the fact that from a modern legal standpoint some of the lands may have belonged to Palestinians had no relevance. Their attitude brought home to us the extreme alienation felt by these people toward the laws of the State of Israel.

Near the end of our visit, we asked about Avri Ran, who had lived here with his family before fleeing from the law. The young settlers, who evidently were still suspicious of us, said that since he had run away they had heard no word of his whereabouts. But, they added, they were absolutely sure he was being persecuted for something he did not do. During our return trip from Gvaot Olam, the thought occurred to us that the outpost, of all places, provided optimal conditions for the radicalization of its residents. The location was remote and isolated from the rest of the world, and there was the ongoing conflict between the residents and their neighbors and their alienation from the Israeli authorities and mainstream culture. Together with the mutual reinforcement of these people's attitudes, here was a situation that cultivated a social dynamic easily leading to an escalation of their extremist beliefs.

THE BAT AYIN GROUP

It is a complex challenge to try to describe how the Bat Ayin group evolved. Even today, only the tip of the iceberg has been exposed. The Israeli security apparatus has even failed to reveal how the group was formed or to obtain convictions against the majority of its members. In fact, except for the two who actually carried out the attack in Abu Tor and several more activists who were charged with abetting them, no other network members have been brought to trial, and it is still not clear how they are connected to the group's activities.

The initial concept of forming an underground group was apparently brought up in the second half of 1998 during a conversation between two eighteen-year-old friends, Shahar Dvir-Zeliger and Sela Tor. The first hilltop youth settlements were established several years earlier, and the two were among the first inhabitants. Dvir-Zeliger lived in the Adei Ad farm, and Tor divided his time between Hebron and the Maon Farm, which his brother Yehoshafat had founded.[12] They both sought to take their militant ideology a step forward by creating a group that would commit acts of violence against the Palestinian population in the West Bank.[13] They especially believed it would be easy to engage in a campaign of drive-by shootings against Palestinian vehicles on West Bank roads. Their plan quickly became concrete as they began collecting weapons and looking for additional collaborators to help take part in organizing the group.[14]

In October of that year, Dvir-Zeliger suggested they recruit Hagai Avikar, whom he had met while studying at the Joseph's Tomb Yeshiva in Nablus from 1993 to 1995. During a meeting that took place at Ein Prat in Wadi Kelt, they offered him the option of joining in the shooting attacks they were planning. Avikar refused, explaining that he didn't share their views. The two didn't give up and suggested he "only" act as a lookout and warn them of the approach of Palestinian vehicles, but Avikar stood his ground.[15]

There is no clear information available about the activities of the two after their failure to recruit Avikar. However, it seems that after the Al-Aqsa Intifada broke out, they were able to lay the foundations for the Bat Ayin network. They particularly focused on enlisting young people from their group of hilltop youth and from the Jewish settlement in Hebron. Their mobilizing efforts in Hebron were not unexpected, taking into account the fact that many hilltop youth originated from the Jewish settlement in this city, which was dominated by the Kahane movement and known for its highly militant educational and religious establishment. At any rate, gradually a number of cliques took shape and began to be active.

The Bat Ayin clique included Shahar's brother, Shlomo Dvir-Zeliger, and Ofer Gamliel, who had served in the IDF Engineering Corps and was therefore of major assistance in preparing the device for the attack on the girls' school in Abu Tor. Yarden Morag, the young man who was caught during the attempt to blow up the school, lived in Bat Ayin and was recruited by Shlomo Dvir-Zeliger. From the Adei Ad farm, Shahar signed on his friend and neighbor Tzuriel Amior, who was then twenty-one years old.[16]

An additional clique included several activists from the Maon Farm, apparently enlisted by Sela Tor.[17] Young Jewish settlers were also recruited from Hebron, some of whom were chosen to help get hold of weapons, whereas others, according to the testimony of Shahar Dvir-Zeliger,[18] were assigned to carry out roadside shootings. Among those who helped obtain weapons were prominent people linked to Gush Emunim and important Kach operatives.[19]

It seems that the most recognizable member of the clique from Hebron was Yitzhak Pass. On March 26, 2001, Yitzhak pushed the stroller of his baby daughter, Shalhevet, down the narrow roads of the Jewish settlement in Hebron. They were on their way to visit her grandparents, who lived in the vicinity. A Palestinian sniper, twenty-six-year-old Mohammad Amro, was observing them from a nearby hill. Seconds later, several shots were fired. The first bullet ended Shalhevet's life, and the following ones wounded her father in both legs. The picture of the tiny body of the ten-month-old baby carried in her father's arms became one of most unforgettable images of the Second Intifada. When the Bat Ayin group was discovered, Pass was convicted for possession of 10 pounds of explosives.

Despite the fact that the idea of forming the group was first introduced in 1998, the members began to put into practice their plans only after the outbreak of the Al-Aqsa Intifada in late 2000. This emphasizes the role of an external event—if perceived by counterculture members as threatening—in the gradual slide to violent activity. At any rate, in early 2001, Bat Ayin members began to carry out two main types of attacks: shooting at passing vehicles and planting explosive devices in public buildings.

Shootings were generally carried out by small cells of two or three members who were careful to choose only secondary roads with little traffic and easy escape routes. The attacks were perpetrated late at night and always followed the same routine.[20] The team members would tailgate the targeted vehicle, make sure the passengers were Palestinian, and then overtake the vehicle and open fire with automatic weapons.[21] Advance planning of escape routes and familiarity with army routine in the area made it possible for them to evade the security forces.

Their most notable shooting attack took place on April 1, 2002, when a cell of three network members fired on a Mercedes truck near Ramallah, north of the Kokhav Hashahar settlement. Immediately after firing, they made a U-turn to return in the direction they had come from, and the perpetrator sitting next to the driver left the vehicle to confirm the killings. The driver of the Mercedes, Allah Abed El Hai, twenty, died on the spot, and the friend sitting next to him, Issa Mahmoud Salim, forty, died later at the Hadassah Ein Kerem Hospital in Jerusalem.[22] Members of the network later claimed responsibility for the attack in the name of a group called Tears of the Widows and the Orphans. The announcement they released to journalists' beepers claimed that the operation was intended to avenge the victims of Palestinian terrorist attacks.[23] After members of the network were arrested, they revealed that they had conducted seven such gunfire operations in which eight Palestinians were killed and sixteen injured.

The network also used the same modus operandi each time it carried out a bomb attack. The chosen targets were public buildings, especially schools. On September 17, 2001, several members of the network planted a powerful explosive device in a schoolyard in Yatta, near Hebron. The operation consisted of two stages. In the first stage, a small 1-pound explosive device was placed next to the water fountain and hidden by rocks and branches. It was set to explode at 10 A.M., during recess. Several minutes later, after teachers and pupils would be drawn to the area, a much larger 22-pound bomb was set to go off in order to cause additional casualties. However, because of a technical malfunction, the first bomb went off at 9:45, fifteen minutes early. The school principal, Yousef Abed-Rabo, described the events at the school: "I was standing at the door of the teachers' room, the pupils were already in the classrooms, when suddenly we heard a strong explosion. . . . I went outside and saw that the water fountain had been destroyed and the tree next to it uprooted; there were several casualties and I immediately phoned the police and the army." Sappers who arrived found and neutralized the second bomb, which had been planted higher in order to hide it more effectively and increase its destructive force. As a result of the single explosion, several pupils were injured.[24]

On March 5, 2002, a Bat Ayin cell executed an almost identical attack, this time in retaliation for a Hamas suicide bombing in the Beit Israel neighborhood of Jerusalem. The target they chose was a boys' school in the Tzur Baher village in East Jerusalem. The cell had gathered intelligence specifying that the gates of the school opened every day at 7:30 A.M. and that the pupils waiting for school would play in the schoolyard until class began. This particular morning, several of the children noticed a pink ice cream carton lying on the ground between two trees. Woolen pillows were on both sides of the carton. The inquisitive children advanced toward the carton but were afraid to open it. In light of previous incidents, they had been warned not to touch suspicious objects in the yard. They called to one of the teachers, Issa Kanter, thirty-one. After examining the carton, he asked the principal, Moussa Pawacha, to phone the police. Unfortunately, at nearly 8 A.M. and just a few minutes before the police arrived, the bomb exploded and ten pupils were slightly injured. Mustafa Ziad Amira, thirteen, was a witness and described what happened: "I was sitting in class next to the window looking at the strange object on the ground, when there was a tremendous boom. The window fell on my foot and I fell to the floor."[25] The subsequent investigation by police sappers determined that the ice cream carton had been rigged with two devices consisting of explosives from an IDF shell and a phosphorus grenade. The bomb also contained pieces of metal, bullets, and bullet casings to make it more lethal. The investigators assumed the attackers had timed the device to explode at 8:00 A.M. because at that moment most of the pupils would have been in the yard for the morning assembly, which included physical exercises.[26] A short while later, an announcement was sent out to the media by a group called Revenge of the Infants, claiming responsibility for the attack. Although in this case the perpetrators were never identified, Yarden Morag testified in court that several weeks after the attack, he had asked Noam Federman why the operation had failed. He claimed that Federman said that the device itself had worked perfectly; it had simply been discovered before it exploded.[27]

Despite the intense activities of the network in 2001 and 2002, Israeli security forces failed to discover who was behind it. The members took extreme precautionary measures. For example, in order to evade GSS surveillance, they refrained from taking part in the activities of the Kach movement. One of the group's leaders explained, "The Kach people do not make up the hard core of the terrorist cells. None of the 'Jewish terrorists' will join in Kach activities, since it is certain they would immediately draw the attention of the Shabak (GSS)."[28]

Another factor that made the security forces' task so difficult was the meticulous compartmentalization of the various cliques, which led the security forces to the incorrect conclusion that several groups were working independently. This incorrect premise was also reinforced by the fact that the network used a variety of names in their press releases (usually when claiming responsibility for a particular attack). Some examples are the "Gilad-Shalhevet Brigades," the "Sword of Gideon," and the "Tears of the Widows and the Orphans."[29]

Despite their previous failures at attacking Arab schools, and in the wake of the escalation of Palestinian terrorism in late 2001 and early 2002, members of the network, especially those from the Bat Ayin clique, concluded the time had come to once more attempt a high-profile act of terrorism. They believed such an event would fulfill the need for Jewish revenge and at the same time deter Palestinians from continuing to attack Jewish targets. It would also prove to the Arabs that there were Jews who were not afraid of practicing an "eye for an eye, a tooth for a tooth."[30] Early in March 2002, Shlomo Dvir-Zeliger and Ofer Gamliel began to discuss various targets for such an attack. In the end, the girls' school in Abu Tor was chosen, as the court verdict stated, "with the intention of causing great suffering by murdering young girls going to learn at school."[31]

After they settled on the target, the conspirators began to search for explosives. Gamliel told Shlomo Dvir-Zeliger that Yarden Morag had possession of explosive bricks and convinced him that Morag should be let in on the plan. When the two approached Morag, Dvir-Zeliger tried to impress him with how determined they were by revealing that they were members of the underground group responsible for drive-by shootings and other operations in which Arabs were harmed. He also told Morag that he had stolen M16 rifles from reserve duty soldiers guarding the settlement. To top it off, he said another group in the underground was intending to carry out a shooting attack the day after the proposed bombing.[32] It seems that despite the self-imposed segregation of the cliques, other members in the network still knew of the upcoming Abu Tor attack.

At this stage, Shlomo Dvir-Zeliger was still not entirely convinced he could count on Gamliel and Morag, who were new to the network. He consulted a third friend, Yosef Ben-Baruch, from the Maon Farm and drew him a general picture of their plans. Ben-Baruch said he could trust the two, but he advised them to pack the explosives in a trailer instead of a car because it had a greater capacity. He even promised to supply the trailer. Ben-Baruch also helped them by getting the money to buy the fuel and propane gas tanks. However, he did ask Dvir-Zeliger to keep his own involvement a secret from the other participants.[33]

After the Passover holiday, and as the day of the attack approached, the three began their preparations in earnest. They invested a great deal of time in putting together the bomb and the other components attached to it. They also conducted preliminary scouting expeditions in Abu Tor to ascertain the optimal location for placing the trailer so the explosion would cause a maximum number of human casualties.[34]

As in their previous attempts, they set the timer so that the booby-trapped trailer would explode during the girls' assembly at 7:30 in the morning. The night of the operation, despite his role in building the bomb due to his experience as an army sapper, Gamliel backed down, explaining that his rabbi had advised him not to participate. However, he did describe to them how to connect the explosives to the trailer.[35] When Morag and Dvir-Zeliger reached Abu Tor in East Jerusalem, it was late at night and the streets were deserted. They parked their vehicle in front of the school on the main artery next to the Al-Makassed Hospital. They got out of the car, unhitched the trailer, and secured it to a pole on the sidewalk with a lock and chain. After leaving the scene, they suddenly remembered that according to plan they should have made a hole in one of the trailer tires. They then returned to the school, but when Morag approached the trailer, the police arrived.

The arrest of Yarden Morag and Shlomo Dvir-Zeliger provided the lead GSS investigators were looking for in order to solve the acts of terrorism committed against Palestinians in the West Bank. Within a week, they had linked Ofer Gamliel and Shahar Dvir-Zeliger to the events at Abu Tor. The detaining order against the four suspects was extended, and the state prosecutors began preparing the case against them.[36]

For the most part, the Israeli security apparatus assumed that the arrest of the four suspects would bring an end to the attacks. However, after several more shooting attacks and another attempt to plant a bomb at a school, it became clear that additional cells were at work in the field.[37] Only with the arrest of nine additional suspects in July 2003, and after an intensive intelligence-gathering effort by the GSS, was the entire network finally unveiled. However, as mentioned earlier, just a small number of network members were convicted. Whereas some blamed the slipshod work of the law enforcement forces, including the state prosecutors, others claimed that the real problem was the stubbornness and willpower of the detainees during interrogations. Members of the group did not cooperate and refused to reveal any information on network activities and operations. In late 2003, Shlomo Dvir-Zeliger and Ofer Gamliel were sentenced to fifteen years in prison, Morag to twelve years, and Shahar Dvir-Zeliger to eight years. Yitzhak Pass and Matityahu Shabo were each sentenced to twenty-four months in prison. The remaining members were sentenced to minor felonies or were not even put on trial.

THE WITHDRAWAL FROM GAZA

Already in late 2003, Israeli Prime Minister Ariel Sharon started to devise a plan for the evacuation of the Jewish settlement and IDF forces from the Gaza Strip. The disengagement plan also included the removal of four small settlements that were located in the northern part of the West Bank (northern Samaria). At this point, Israel was still embroiled in the Second Intifada, and Sharon, similar to many other Israeli policymakers, felt that Israel, along with its military offensive response, should present conciliatory steps in order to break the deadlock between the two sides and also encourage moderate Palestinians to resist prolonging the violence.

In early May 2004, the disengagement plan was approved by the Israeli government, and on October 26, 2004, the Knesset ratified the resolution. As was the case in the early 1980s with the Camp David Accords, as well as a decade later after the signing of the Oslo Accords, the main resistance to the evacuation came from the settler movement and the various religious Zionist streams and groups. They had organized countless rallies, demonstrations, and assemblies against the plan in order to mobilize public support. Rabbis once again insisted that the plan was an intolerable violation of the Jewish heritage and rules of the Halakha and that the evacuation had no moral or other legitimacy. They called on IDF soldiers to disobey the orders of their commanders, and some of them urged even more extreme steps such as illegal resistance. In consequence, the protest increasingly began to involve illegal activities whose intent was to disrupt the public order, such as blocking main highways by crowding them with demonstrators or by putting sharp nails on the road. However, some of the initiatives went one step further and eventually developed into terrorist activities.

The first act of organized terrorism in response to the disengagement from the Gaza Strip and northern Samaria came to light in early May 2005. There were three members in the cell: Rabbi Mordechai (Mordi) Levinstein (Harel), who taught at the Homesh Yeshiva;[38] his brother Elitzur Levinstein; and a yeshiva student, Avraham (Mordechai) Levkowitz. Their plan was not particularly complex, but it was potentially very lethal. The three had intended to douse vehicles with flammable materials and ignite them near the Kibbutz Galuyot Interchange on the Ayalon Highway in Tel Aviv. The operation was planned for the early hours of the morning, when the highway was very congested. The plotters sought to create a tight blockade of the road so that drivers who were behind the burning vehicles would be caught in the firetrap and not be able to escape.[39] When asked by a police investigator what would have happened if the operation had gone as planned, one of the detainees, Avraham Levkowitz, replied that he wouldn't have been particularly sorry if innocent people were harmed "because sometimes in order to obtain a just goal, illegal acts must be carried out during which people might get hurt."[40] These words reveal an important process that was gathering momentum within the religious Zionist stream in the context of the resistance to the disengagement plan. Increasing numbers of religious Zionists, highly disappointed with the persistent inclination of Israeli governments to compromise time and again for almost thirty years and to relinquish parts of the historical Land of Israel, were more likely to adapt elements from the Kahane and hilltop youth ideologies. These elements included mainly alienation from state institutions and symbols and a willingness to accept active and violent resistance.

The most prominent figure in this group was Rabbi Levinstein. The disengagement plan, which included the evacuation of the community of Homesh, greatly agitated him and made him feel that he must do something. In April 2005 he acquired two old, large vehicles that were to be sold to auto parts dealers. Once they were purchased, the terrorist cell that was to carry out the operation began to gain flesh and bones. Levinstein approached his younger brother, Elitzur, who lived in the Yitzhar settlement, one of the most radical in the West Bank,[41] and recruited him for the assignment. Afterwards, he turned to his student, Levkowitz, from the Elon Moreh settlement.[42] Levinstein had made contact with Levkowitz during a rally in the settlement against the disengagement. In his testimony, Levkowitz said, "During the rally, Rabbi Mordi approached me . . . and asked me if I was available late on Monday night. I replied that I was. I already knew that this was about a scouting patrol in order to block a street in the central [Israel] area. I knew it because it was a subject we used to secretly talk about in the yeshiva. . . . In the yeshiva, there are three rabbis. . . . Among these three, Rabbi Mordi was the one who talked about blocking roads. . . . Rabbi Mordi told me he would contact me on Monday."[43]

In the meanwhile, Rabbi Mordi Levinstein continued his preparations for the operation. On May 2, one day before the program was to be executed, he ordered a tow truck and hauled the old vehicles from the Beit El area in the West Bank to De Russi Street near the Kibbutz Galuyot Interchange in Tel Aviv. On the next day, true to his word, Rabbi Mordi called

Levkowitz. In the dead of the night, the three met and set off in the rabbi's car for the interchange. On the way, the rabbi informed his brother and the student of the details of the plan. Elitzur and Levkowitz's role was to drive the old cars on the Ayalon Highway south until they arrived at the designated site of the roadblock. Here, they were to slow down, block the highway with the large vehicles, and set them on fire. After completing their part, they were to leave the area immediately and run to a rendezvous point, where the rabbi would wait for them in his car.[44]

Despite being under significant stress, the three of them withdrew for a short night's sleep. At 6:35 in the morning, they met up and made their way in the rabbi's car to the road where the two old vehicles were parked. Without delay, they began to load up the cars with mattresses soaked in inflammable liquid, paper debris, and other combustible materials. After preparing the vehicles, they went out in the light of day on a round of the area to be blockaded. They were satisfied with what they saw and returned to the starting point, ready for the operation. At 8:15, the rabbi left the two young men and made his way to the getaway point where he was to collect them. The two made last-minute preparations and awaited instructions. When they received word from the rabbi to rev up the automobiles, the plan began to go wrong. Both Levkowitz and Elitzur were unable to start up the engines of the old cars. They informed Rabbi Levinstein of the hitch, and he instructed them to wait there for him. When the rabbi joined the other two conspirators, all three were arrested by a police force that lay in wait for them nearby.[45] It later turned out that a neighbor caught sight of the suspicious vehicles the day before, saw them being loaded with combustible materials, and notified the police. The police first sabotaged the cars and then concealed themselves until the suspects' intentions were clear. After all of them showed up, the police seized them.

In the course of their interrogation, Rabbi Levinstein and his brother Elitzur invoked their right to remain silent. Levkowitz provided police investigators and the GSS with a detailed confession, which he later retracted. An expert who examined the potential danger in igniting the vehicles on the Ayalon Highway wrote in the report requested by the prosecution, "The consequences of such an incident is a rapid release of high energy whose source is in the flammable charge of the pressurized material, the car, the additional containers of petrol, and this may be accompanied by the propulsion of burning objects and may in fact lead to the igniting of nearby vehicles or injury of persons standing outside."[46]

In November 2005, the Tel Aviv District Court sentenced Avraham Levkowitz to twenty-four months in prison. The trial of his two co-conspirators took much longer. Finally, on February 2, 2008, the same court sentenced Rabbi Levinstein to forty months in prison and Elitzur Levinstein to thirty months in prison.

Although some Israelis preferred to regard the actions of Levinstein and his two colleagues as an isolated incident and not a part of a radical-ization trend within the Orthodox Jewish streams, the Israeli security forces found out that the reality was much different. During the same month in which Levinstein's cell was discovered, another daring plot de-vised by Jewish militants to disrupt the disengagement plan was exposed by the GSS. At the core of the initiative were again two brothers and a friend, all Orthodox Jews. Avtalion and Akiva Kadosh's plan was to climb onto the roof of the Returning Sons Yeshiva, which also overlooked the Temple Mount, and from there to shoot an anti-tank missile at the Dome of the Rock Mosque. When police forces arrived at the scene, the two planned to attack them with hand grenades and then commit suicide by means of a pistol shot to the head.[47]

At first Avtalion contacted Eyal Karamani, an acquaintance of his from their visit together at the grave of Rabbi Shimon Hatzadik, and convinced him to help them carry out the operation. Afterwards they approached Rabbi Elior Hen, who headed a Torah study group that the two brothers used to attend, for advice and assistance. Rabbi Hen, who was a religious and moral authority for the brothers, gave his blessing to the planned op-eration and even advised them to take out a bank loan so they would be able to acquire ammunition and weapons from army veterans or criminals.[48] At this stage, Akiva Kadosh decided to withdraw, and Karamani and Avtalion continued on their own. However, they were discovered by the security forces before they were able to secure the necessary arms for the operation. In his interrogation Avtalion claimed that the goals of the group were to prevent the implementation of the disengagement plan, incite violence, and provoke a third intifada—perhaps even a war between Israel and the Arab countries.[49] In any case, the fact that the plan was still far from materializa-tion, and that the GSS was reluctant to reveal its sources during the judicial process, led to a decision not to put all those involved on trial.

GUSH KATIF

The first thing that greeted our eyes when we visited Neve Dkalim about two months before the implementation of the disengagement was a pastoral beach of golden sand and azure waters. However, this peaceful scene was deceptive. Less than 100 yards south, on an old asphalt road, one could make out the Hof Dkalim, or "Palm Beach Hotel." This derelict structure was once designed to be a tourist attraction on the beach of Gaza, but as the date of the disengagement approached, it became the stronghold for dozens of opponents to the plan who flooded the area from all corners of the country and earned it the name Maoz Yam ("Stronghold on the Sea").

In the early morning near the end of June, Maoz Yam appeared almost deserted. Most of its inhabitants, a mixture of youths—some of them almost children—from settlements in Samaria, young men from Chabad yeshivas,[50] long-haired hilltop youth, and even a number of old-timers who stood out in the youthful milieu of the scene, were sound asleep. A group of fifteen youths sluggishly made their way to the dining room, part of which had been converted into a makeshift synagogue. The Shacharit (morning prayer) was led by Michael Ben-Horin, undoubtedly the heart and soul of the place. He was fifty-eight, but the many years he had spent fighting ideological battles did not show on him. He appeared in fine form and full of vitality.

Directly after the prayers were concluded, he informed the youths that he was leaving for a short while. He explained that he was going to bring food to the dozens of young people who occupied an unfinished building owned by Palestinians in the Moasi neighborhood. The takeover of the building was in response to the military authorities' decision to demolish eleven old structures of the Egyptian army that the hilltop youth from the West Bank had intended to occupy in anticipation of evacuation day. Our request to accompany Ben-Horin was first rejected, but he eventually relented.

The trip to the building lasted only several minutes. As we neared the site, we could make out a three-story building that was indeed a peculiar sight. The impression was that a great deal of money had originally been invested in the building, but for one reason or another, construction was never completed. The dissonant appearance of the building couldn't have been more remarkable. Heads of youths covered with large cotton skullcaps suddenly materialized out of ornamented windows built in a distinctive Middle Eastern style. On the northern wall of the building, which faced the neighboring Palestinian house, the words "Mohammed [is a] pig" were sprayed in black. The occupants, who at the sight of Ben-Horin's small, run-down pickup understood that their breakfast had arrived, clustered at the front of the building.

Ben-Horin took advantage of the attention that his arrival had provoked to halfheartedly protest against the graffiti on the wall. He asked them to wipe it off because, in his words, "Our struggle is not against the Arabs but against the government of Israel." When one of the young men asked whether they had to remove the graffiti in support of the Kach movement, which included the inscription "*Koakh*[51]—Gaza to the Jews, a noose for the traitors," Ben-Horin responded in the negative with a smile of satisfaction on his face. Throughout this time, we stole glances at the Palestinian residents, who stood only several meters away from us. They naturally assumed we were Ben-Horin devotees, and the looks we received from them were accordingly spine-chilling. For the first time in our lives, we felt the full impact of the expression "If looks could kill."

About two hours later, while discussing the day's events on our way back north, we concluded that the region could be likened to a powder keg. Indeed, in the afternoon of that same day, the fuse leading to the bomb was lit. The inscription "Mohammed [is a] pig" led dozens of Palestinians who lived nearby to form into groups next to the building. The high levels of tension among the building occupants began to mount, and the presence of Border Police soldiers who were trying to detain several of them for interrogation did not help matters much. Within a short while, the cursing turned into rock throwing on both sides. Ben-Horin's people took advantage of the building's height in order to cast huge rocks onto the Palestinian residents assembled in the street below. Sixteen-year-old Hilal Ziad al-Majaydeh was among the Palestinian demonstrators. After sustaining a blow to his head from a rock, he staggered toward a group of soldiers nearby. One of them took hold of him and led him to shelter behind a concrete wall, but at that very moment several youths from the building attacked them and tried to lynch al-Majaydeh. After several long minutes of struggling, he was rescued and rushed to the hospital in Khan Yunis.[52]

Nearly five hours later, the special counterterrorism team of the Israel Police with a backup of IDF forces stormed the building. At the end of a short struggle during which a burning inner tube was thrown at the police, the occupants were removed.[53] The next day, near noon, Southern Command major general Dan Harel signed a warrant that declared all of Gaza Strip a closed military zone.[54] Near evening, large police and military forces raided the Maoz Yam complex; they evacuated the inhabitants in less than thirty minutes and immediately afterward established an army base on the hotel grounds.

Despite the nearly fatal violence that accompanied the Moasi incident on the same day, this was not a case of genuine terrorism. However, the impression we were left with was that these events were only a sign of things to come. One of the greatest sources of concern had to do with the identity of the rioters. They represented almost every stream of the religious camp in Israel: knitted skullcap–wearing members of the religious Zionism, hilltop youth with their woolen skullcaps and long side locks, yeshiva students from the Chabad movement in their black hats, and Kahane youths in their yellow shirts. On that day we saw how the youths of all streams mixed together and awaited the word from Ben-Horin. In fact, Ben-Horin is one of the most extreme symbols of Kahanist teachings and until only several years ago was pretty much a pariah to the majority of the religious public in Israel. Furthermore, despite the fact that the struggle was territorial, its spirit was entirely religious. Of this we had no doubts. The plan for evacuating the settlements was regarded as a criminal injury to humans during the course of the redemption of the people of Israel.[55]

SA NUR

Three weeks later, on the morning of a particularly scorching summer day, we set our sights on Sa Nur, the most radical settlement in the northern West Bank to be evacuated in the disengagement plan. Whereas the trip to Gush Katif in a private car was fairly trouble-free, the journey to Sa Nur required special preparations. Sa Nur was one of the most isolated Jewish settlements in the heart of a highly populated Palestinian territory. It was erected in the middle of a triangle of large Palestinian cities: in the north, Jenin; in the east, Nablus; and in the west, Tul Karm. The journey to Sa Nur took place on an armor-plated bus that departed from Netanya each morning. Only after two hours of travel, during which the bus collected and dropped off passengers at the biggest settlements, including Avnei Hefetz, Einav, and Shavei Shomron, it finally arrived at its destination.

In July 2005, Sa Nur was at long last "rejuvenated." After twenty years of failed attempts time after time to populate the settlement, ironically, near its evacuation, it seemed as if there was not enough space to contain all the believers trying to prevent the harsh edict. Already from our first glance at the human population of the settlement, we could see that, as in Gush Katif, the battle against the evacuation at Sa Nur crossed movements and varieties of faith. Alongside middle-aged ultra-Orthodox Jews who had recently arrived from the United States and had concentrated their efforts on building a new synagogue in the name of Rafael Eitan,[56] there were also remnants of an artists' group from the former Soviet Union that had tried to establish an artists' village and gallery in this settlement after immigrating in the 1990s. Although the gallery they had built in an old British police building continued to exhibit their works, the majority of the artists had left the settlement several months after their arrival here. The settlement core group that had replaced the Russian artists consisted of Chabad people. Most members of the core group that settled at Sa Nur during the Al-Aqsa Intifada did not stay for long because of severe confrontations with residents of the neighboring Palestinian villages, al-Fandaqumya and Silat e-Dahr. Only isolated survivors remained and welcomed the last wave of settlers who arrived in 2003. Many of the new settlers were former residents of more established settlements who had tired of the comfortable life that the veteran communities provided. They, too, sought to realize the revolutionary ideology of their parents, who had settled the lands of the West Bank in the 1970s. Finally, there were those who joined in 2005, such as the hilltop youth, the followers of Rabbi Kahane, and the rest of the support from the overall settlement project who tried to prevent the evacuation with their own bodies.

When we reached Sa Nur in the early morning, in view of the fact that in four weeks it was to be evacuated we were surprised to find a quiet stillness reigning over the settlement. We found it hard to reconcile the contradiction that lay before our eyes. On one hand, we saw the summer sights of children running along the pathways of the settlement and amusing themselves at the playground; on the other, we recalled the numerous television reports that portrayed Sa Nur as a modern Masada whose inhabitants were hoarding food and bracing themselves for a life-and-death struggle against the soldiers coming to clear them out. About a month before the evacuation of the settlement, the residents of Sa Nur found no contradiction either, as Yaron Adler, a smiling and courteous young man and father of six children who moved here with his family from Kiryat Arba, explained to us. As Adler and his friends perceived the situation, there was no chance that the disengagement plan would be carried out. He believed that the settlers and their children would continue to live there for many more years. We pushed him a little further and asked him what would happen if soldiers nevertheless appeared at the gates to the settlement and asked them to leave. Adler shrugged his shoulders and told us that on the day the order would be carried out, some 15,000 supporters from all over the country were expected to arrive in order to thwart any possibility of evacuation. To our question whether there was a chance that the residents and their supporters might open fire on the soldiers, Adler replied that this scenario did not even come up in the discussions among the residents. However, he admitted that if armed youths came from the outposts on the hills of Samaria or if Rabbi Kahane devotees showed up, it would be very difficult to prevent the slide into violence. About one month later, Adler's forecasts were proved wrong. Sa Nur was evacuated with relative ease. Unfortunately, this was not true for the rest of the withdrawal process.

KFAR TAPUACH

In the early of Thursday, August 4, 2005, less than two weeks before the withdrawal, we set off for Kfar Tapuach, one of the most radical settlements in the West Bank. The purpose of our visit at Tapuach was to meet with David Axlerod (Ha'ivri), follower of Rabbi Meir Kahane and one of the leaders of the Kahane Chai ("Kahane Lives") movement. Trips to the settlements in the West Bank are accompanied by apprehension. In many cases, the roads are in bad repair, and in order to reach the more isolated settlements, the driver has no alternative but to drive straight through the center of Palestinian villages. In the case of Tapuach, however, our fears were unsubstantiated: The trip was comfortable and safe. The settlement is located seven and a half miles east of the city of Ariel, the largest Jewish settlement in the West Bank. In the last few years, the Israeli government has paved a new highway to Ariel, and the casual observer finds it hard to imagine that he or she is right in the middle of an occupied area that has been involved in a bloody forty-year dispute.

The dissonance we felt between the fear of a trip to the out-of-the-way settlement and the tranquil experience of traveling the modern highway only grew as we entered the settlement. The drowsy soldier who opened the gate didn't even bother us with a glance. Several more seconds of driving and we found ourselves in the middle of the settlement, where we were greeted with another surprise. Tapuach was the place that made headlines in January 2004, when its residents engaged in a violent struggle with IDF soldiers after they were dispatched to evacuate an illegal structure where Kahane devotees attempted to put up a synagogue in memory of their rabbi. But now it looked like any other kibbutz or community settlement.

Instead of the anticipated armed youths with large cotton skullcaps, we came upon young mothers pushing baby strollers along the footpaths of the settlement. Even David Ha'ivri did not measure up to our expectations. It wasn't a fierce Kahanist who received us but rather a soft-spoken man in his forties who over the course of nearly two hours lay before us his mollified worldview. In his opinion, he and the other followers of Rabbi Kahane had abandoned the approach of their mentor and rabbi, who throughout his life had not disavowed the use of violence and terrorism in his effort to advance his ideas. After more than thirty years of activities in Israel, they realized that the use of terrorism only did them harm. They had concluded that in order to further their goals they would be better off using extraparliamentary means of protest and not straying from the limits of the law. These were extraordinary words coming from one of the most extreme Jews who had ever been active in the State of Israel and who, according to his own testimony, had taken part in various violent episodes, including a pogrom against the neighboring Palestinian village, Luban e-Sharqiya, some ten years earlier.[57]

In the last few minutes of our meeting, just when we were about to leave, we asked about his feelings in regard to the upcoming disengagement, and then the tone of his speech became harder. As he saw it, the struggle against the prime minister's plan was tantamount to *kiddush Hashem* (literally, "sanctification of the Holy Name," or martyrdom). At the sound of these words, our ears perked up. It was not clear to us how this purportedly reconciled person, who had told us only minutes earlier how he had substituted his violent behavior by founding a legitimate social movement, could so easily start talking with such zeal about *kiddush Hashem*. These two words attested to a person's willingness to sacrifice his or her life for the sake of upholding God's precepts. To make sure we were not misinterpreting him, we asked him exactly what his intention was. This time we were no longer surprised by his reply.

About eleven years ago, Ha'ivri had suffered the loss of one of his colleagues, Dr. Baruch Goldstein, who had perpetrated the massacre at the Cave of the Patriarchs in Hebron. In this fashion, Goldstein became the first Jewish terrorist to sacrifice his life while wreaking his vengeance. Ha'ivri did not try to soften or obscure his interpretation of the term *kiddush Hashem*. His view was that the government-sponsored disengagement was heresy and in denial of God's plan, and therefore it was permitted and in fact worthy that a person who was a believer perform an act similar to that of Goldstein if it was potentially capable of preventing the withdrawal.[58] However, the last part of our conversation probably would have been forgotten if not for the events of that same evening.

At 5:05 P.M., bus number 165 set out from Haifa en route to the Arab city of Shfaram, east of the Haifa suburbs. The bus passengers were Muslim, Druze, and Christian residents of Shfaram commuting home after finishing work or studies in the northern metropolis. Among the passengers was also a young man in an IDF uniform. Nobody on the bus paid him any special attention. This was because many Shfaram (Druze or Bedouin) residents served in the armed forces, and therefore a passenger in uniform carrying a rifle was not an uncommon sight on bus line 165. However, a certain detail was a source of concern for driver Michel Bahus. Unlike the soldiers who were residents of the village, the soldier sitting at the back of the bus wore a skullcap and had a thick beard. Very few Jews used public transportation in order to travel to an Arab city, and therefore Bahus suggested to the Jewish passenger that he get off at Kiryat Ata, the last Jewish town on the bus route before it made its way to Shfaram. However, the young man paid no heed to the driver's suggestion and remained in his seat.[59]

At about 6:00 P.M., as the bus drove down Sheikh Amin Farid Street through the western reaches of the city, also known as the Druze neighborhood, the soldier suddenly got up from his seat. He made his way toward the front of the bus, cocked his M16 assault rifle, and fired upon the driver, who died instantaneously. Then, he turned the rifle toward the rest of the passengers and let off bursts of automatic fire, which ceased only after the magazine of his rifle was completely empty.[60] This break gave the unharmed bus passengers an opportunity to rush the soldier and overcome him. After the bedlam died down, four bodies were strewn in the bus and thirteen wounded awaited the rescue forces. As in the case of Baruch Goldstein, the gunman, Eden Natan-Zada, a nineteen-year-old deserter from the IDF, remained alive at the site of the slaughter and was ultimately killed as the residents of the city lynched him.[61] In this way, he became the second Jewish terrorist to sacrifice his life on the altar of *kiddush Hashem,* even if this wasn't his original intention.

Over the course of the evening, as more details about Zada's past streamed in, David Ha'ivri's words about each Jew's duty to put his or her life on the line in order to prevent the implementation of the disengagement plan resounded in our ears. Zada was among Ha'ivri's followers at Kfar Tapuach and an active member of his movement, Revava. The young Jewish terrorist had been born in the city of Rishon Letzion, which is located south of Tel Aviv, but until the age of eighteen he had showed no interest in politics. In interviews to the press, his classmates described him as a very quiet and introverted person.[62] At the end of his high school studies, Zada began to spend his leisure hours surfing Internet sites of radical religious Jewish movements. Within a short time, his parents began to notice that he was increasingly taking on the signs of a religious Jew. His frequent visits to Kfar Tapuach, where he was received by his peers with open arms and was in fact adopted by a local family, facilitated the process of his becoming a reborn Jew. But then the date of his conscription cut short his journey into the heart of Jewish radicalism. Unwilling to accept this, Zada did everything in his power to be released from the army. His commanders did not accede to his repeated requests, and therefore, two months before his terrorist rampage, he decided to desert his unit. The letter he left behind for his commander opened with the slogan from the campaign against the disengagement plan: "I refuse to obey my orders, *a Jew doesn't expel a Jew.*"[63] Zada never made it back home to his parents in Rishon Letzion. He fled into the hills of the West Bank and took an active part in the struggle against the disengagement. According to the testimonies of his friends, he eventually embarked on his murder spree from the Tapuach settlement almost at precisely the same time we crossed through its gates.

The determination shown by the Israeli government in the evacuation of the Gaza Strip and northern Samaria settlements, and the fact that disengagement opponents were not able to prevent the process but at most confronted soldiers and police several hours before their eviction, sidelined the news of Zada's murder spree. The overall impression was that the evacuation of the settlements was completed in a calm fashion and that Jewish terrorism was not able to rear its head once again.

AMONA

About a half year later, the government of Israel engaged in the removal of settlers who illegally occupied structures in the settlement of Amona. Against all expectations, the confrontations between the settlers and the police during the evacuation efforts of Amona were far more violent than those during the disengagement from Gaza. By the morning of the evacuation, it was clear that the process would encounter difficulties. The security forces learned that during the night, hundreds of youths had made their way to the outpost and occupied the roofs of the buildings earmarked for destruction. In the area of the outpost itself, dozens of youths accompanied by Israeli right-wing members of parliament gathered and also tried to protest the impending evacuation.

At 10:00 A.M., police officers on horseback armed with clubs began to force their way into the outpost. The people on the roof responded with a barrage of rocks, metallic objects, and water mixed with paint. The protesters on the ground tried to prevent the manned horses from advancing toward the structures by blocking them with their own bodies. The police, who were themselves surprised by the intense response, countered with equal force and determination. They began to club the protesters on the ground who tried to prevent them from getting nearer to the buildings. As a result of the fierce violence, more than forty police officers and demonstrators were injured at this stage of the incident. Member of Parliament Effi Eitam was hit in the head by a truncheon, and Member of Parliament Arie Eldad's hand was broken after being struck by one of the horsemen.[64] Although some of the demonstrators tried to lie down in front of the tractor that was about to raze the buildings, by noon the police forces were able to reach the structures. Next, with the use of cranes and ladders, Special Patrol Unit officers climbed onto the roofs and began to forcefully remove the protesters who tried to stop them and threw rocks at them. After four hours, the evacuation of all the buildings was completed; however, the price was high: More than 200 were wounded, and 80 of them were members of the security forces.[65]

The Israeli public was shocked at the violence. A doctor from the emergency room at Hadassah Ein Kerem Hospital, where most of the injured were taken, said, "I have been working for 20 years at the emergency room and I have never seen anything like this before in my life. Terrorists in Nablus are removed with less violence than that which I saw today. I saw 14- and 15-year-old boys beaten hard; it's a miracle that none of the people I treated were injured more severely."[66] The commanders in the field were also taken aback by the violence and the need to deploy thousands of police officers. The chief of the Border Police, whose soldiers were responsible for most of the evacuation work, said that for years he had not seen such ferocity: "The violence they used against the police was unlike anything we had ever seen. . . . The police who climbed the ladders were in genuine risk of their lives. They threw boulders, rocks and pieces of iron at them."[67]

The message that the government of Israel received at Amona was sharp as a razor blade. The helplessness displayed during the Gaza disengagement took the settlers completely by surprise. Up to the very last days of Israeli control at Gaza, many believed that divine intervention would halt the process. Others were afraid to confront soldiers of the army in which they themselves had served or were destined to serve. They also realized that the organization of the resistance left a lot to be desired. They had put their faith in the leaders of the veteran settlers, who had disappointed them. The events at Amona reflected the trauma they had suffered in the summer of 2005 and the degree of hate that burned in their hearts toward the government, which had cleared out the strips of land dearest to them.

The events further confirmed our observation in regard to the struggle against the disengagement plan: that in the last decade a large counterculture collective has taken shape that encompasses formerly different counterculture streams. This new counterculture collective is a combination of hilltop youth, radical Jewish Zionists holding a near-Kahanist ideology, Rabbi Kahane followers themselves, and various ultra-Orthodox groups, primarily from the Chabad movement. This collective is gradually detaching itself from the state, alienating itself from its symbols, heritage, and institutions, and even willing in times of crisis to act against its legitimate proxies. Based on these developments and the scenes and voices broadcast from Amona in the winter of 2006, we estimate that the soldiers and police who will be sent to evacuate settlements in the future will run into a level of violence that the State of Israel has not yet seen.

NO SOCIAL SCIENCE THEORY can encompass all manifestations of the phenomenon it seeks to explain. Our theory is no exception, even if we limit ourselves to the study of Jewish terrorism. The instances of Jewish terrorism that do not fully conform to our theory will be used as control cases, and this chapter will be devoted to analyzing groups and individuals who are responsible for this type of terrorism. We hope it will help us shed light on the causes for terrorism that fall beyond the scope of this book.

UZI MESHULAM CULT

The case that comes closest to fitting the theory we presented is that of the Uzi Meshulam cult in 1994. A group of young settlers, most of them descendants of Yemenite immigrants, gathered under the leadership of the charismatic Rabbi Uzi Meshulam. The group and the rabbi barricaded themselves in his home in the Israeli township of Yehud, not far from Tel Aviv, because of a conflict with Meshulam's neighbors over his intention to expand his property.[1] When the police were summoned, Meshulam's followers responded with violence. In this manner, they took advantage of the wide media coverage to bring to national prominence one of the most perplexing episodes in the history of the State of Israel: the kidnapping of the children of Yemenite immigrants in the early days of the state.[2] Meshulam and his followers announced that they were not willing to surrender until a government commission of inquiry was formed to investigate this painful episode. He also demanded that representatives on his behalf sit on the commission.[3] For forty-five days, the rabbi and his adherents remained barricaded in the house, turning it into a veritable fortress. They used sandbags to fortify positions around the perimeter, posted armed sentries, and stocked up on firearms and explosives. There was no doubt that they were prepared to brazen it out with security forces if they were foolish enough to attempt a raid on the house. Mindful of the presence of women and children in the area, the security forces were willing to try nearly everything to bring about a negotiated end to the siege. However, Meshulam, who was enjoying the media circus immensely, kept making new demands and refused any proposals communicated to him by Knesset members and police negotiators.[4]

After a month and a half of siege, the Israel Police persuaded Meshulam to engage in negotiations at a neighboring hotel. He was arrested when he arrived, but contrary to the expectations of the police, who assumed that the remaining adherents barricaded in the house would surrender, they instead opened fire, even shooting at a police helicopter patrolling above the house and police command post.[5] Only several hours later, after the police turned off the electricity and threatened to demolish the house, Meshulam's wife decided that the siege should end.[6] In large part, her decision was the result of her shock at the death of Shlomo Asulin, one of Meshulam's followers, who was shot by a police sniper during the gunfire exchange.[7]

In the months after Meshulam's arrest, his devotees staged incidents of vandalism and assassination attempts against law enforcement personnel they felt were hostile toward the rabbi. The most noteworthy incident was the attempt to assassinate senior warden Beni Aviram, chief security officer of the Nitzan Prison, where a number of the rabbi's followers were incarcerated. The Meshulam followers had initiated a riot after the performance of a female vocalist at the prison.[8] However, they were particularly surprised when Aviram issued an order to place them in solitary confinement; until this incident, they had been generally indulged and treated with kid gloves.[9] The response of Meshulam's people was not long in coming. On October 30, 1994, at 6:00 A.M., three devotees set out for Aviram's home. Avner Sa'id and Yoav Shabo waited for the warden to leave the house at 6:40. When he did, they got out of the car, aimed their Berettas at Aviram, and fired. Quick to react, Aviram drew his gun, but before he could return fire he was hit in the chest and arm. Though badly wounded, he fired no fewer than thirteen bullets at the two attackers. The driver of their van collected the two injured attackers, dropped them off at the hospital, where they were arrested, and fled the scene.[10]

For months afterward, Meshulam's people continued their violent activities, but because of stepped-up police pressure, the number of aggressions began to decline around mid-1996. By the time Meshulam was released in 1999, his group had ceased to exist.

All the prominent elements of our theory are present in this case. The Meshulam adherents belonged to the fringes of the settler counterculture, and they followed a very charismatic rabbi who succeeded in framing a local dispute as a political issue. Because many of the Meshulam cohorts were of Yemenite origin, they felt that this attack was directed at them. The secluded compound in Yehud where the rabbi's followers barricaded themselves served as a catalyst for the radicalization of the house's occupants. The main aspect in which this case deviates from the groups described in previous chapters is that the violence here was a result of deep feelings of discrimination on the basis of ethnic background, and religious and territorial elements were less pronounced.

The next two groups resemble the Meshulam cult in many senses. Their members were from working-class families and in most cases of Middle Eastern origin. They resented the Israeli elite and hated Arabs. Most prominently, they were committed to defending the Jewish religion and people from threats posed by followers of other religions. They created closed and isolated groups, thus minimizing their ties with people who did not share their worldview. Finally, in each group there was one member who assumed a leadership position and guided the other members along the path to violence.

THE JERUSALEM GROUPS: THE EIN KEREM GROUP AND THE LIFTA GANG

On the night of December 8–9, 1983, grenades were affixed to the doors of three major monasteries in Jerusalem: the Dormition Monastery, Terra Sancta, and the Greek Orthodox Monastery. On that same night, a grenade was also hidden in a mosque in Jerusalem's Arab neighborhood, Beit Safafa. Monks and worshippers discovered all the explosives in time, and these were disarmed before causing any damage.[11] Three days later, on December 12, doors were again booby-trapped in the same fashion. The targets this time were homes in the village of Husan, on the outskirts of Bethlehem. On that morning, the grenades were discovered only after one of them exploded, wounding two Palestinians.[12] The next couple of attacks, two days later, were directed at a mosque and monastery in the Palestinian village of Eizariya, on the Jerusalem–Jericho road.

The mosque's spiritual leader and a nun at the monastery were wounded in the explosions.[13]

On April 9, 1984, the police reported that they had captured the people responsible for all these incidents. The driving force behind the group, which was named the Ein Kerem group after the Jerusalem neighborhood where its members lived,[14] was Amram Deri. He was injured in a traffic accident at age seventeen and was not drafted into the Israel Defense Forces (IDF) because of his disability. While most of his contemporaries were serving in the army, he began to work at an aluminum factory in the settlement of Kiryat Arba, gradually adopting an Orthodox religious lifestyle. After establishing himself financially, he opened a welding shop in Ein Kerem. Upon completing their military service, his brother Abraham and cousin David joined him in the welding shop. They were both deeply influenced by Amram and followed in his footsteps by adopting a religious lifestyle. Uri Benayun, a religious young man from Moshav Ohad in the Negev, joined the Deri family's business soon afterward.[15]

Similar to terrorist networks in other parts of the world, here too the close interaction between the four young men at their workplace contributed to their strong ties. The closer their friendship became, the more it assumed an ideological character. The four listened attentively to political propaganda promoting the need to expel the Arabs from Israel and the obligation to wage a campaign against institutions that were attempting to convert Jews.[16] During a trip to the Jordan Valley, the group found a crate of hand grenades that had been left next to a military bunker. Without hesitation, they grabbed hold of the grenades, and a short time later they began to booby-trap non-Jewish targets in the Jerusalem area, focusing on religious institutions. After their capture, they were sentenced to eight to ten years in prison.[17]

The group, called the Lifta Gang (after the site where they concealed their stockpiles of weapons and explosives), operated during roughly the same period in which the Ein Kerem group was active. Like the Ein Kerem group, they attacked mosques in the Jerusalem area; however, they also sought to blow up the Temple Mount mosques in order to precipitate the redemption of the people of Israel.

On the rain-drenched and stormy night of January 26, 1984, near the abandoned Arab village of Lifta located west of Jerusalem, four young men removed their white robes and dipped into a nearby spring. They were Uzi Mahsaya, Yehuda Limaei, Shimon Barda, and Eliahu Srour. After completing their ritual immersion at approximately 10:00 P.M., they loaded four explosive charges and a number of grenades onto a rented minivan parked at the roadside. They then proceeded through the city and around the Old City walls to the Lion's Gate entrance, on the eastern side of the Temple Mount. Near the gate, with the explosives on their backs, they marched toward the sealed-off Golden Gate. They climbed the adjacent wall using ladders they had left there beforehand and descended down the other side into the Temple Mount compound. They advanced toward the Dome of the Rock Mosque, but after a few dozen meters, as they approached the stairs to the mosque, a Waqf guard noticed them and blew his whistle. The four young men were surprised, but they quickly regained their wits, threw the explosives on the ground, and took flight.[18] When the day dawned, security forces were shocked to discover the large quantity of explosives left behind in the Temple Mount compound: four explosive charges, each composed of twenty-three explosive blocks; TNT; fragmentation grenades; explosive sticks; and an 800-gram charge made of plastic explosives.[19]

Members of the Lifta Gang were the closest any Jewish terrorist group ever came to blowing up the Temple Mount mosques. The leader of the group was Shimon Barda, a native of Tel Aviv who at a young age had become a known criminal. After a traffic accident disqualifying him from military service, he became more involved in crime and emerged as one of the foremost criminals in the Tel Aviv area. In mid-1980, he was arrested and sentenced to eight years in prison for breaking and entering. This event changed his life; he became religious and became obsessed with the idea of building the Third Temple and restoring Jewish sovereignty to the Temple Mount. After his release from prison, he flew to the United States and went to see the Lubavitcher Rebbe (Rabbi Menachem Mendel Schneerson). He was also influenced by the ideas of Christian fundamentalists in regard to the building of the Third Temple as a catalyst for redemption and the Second Coming of Jesus. Upon his return to Israel, Barda joined the Sons of Judah cult. This was a group of eccentrics who lived in deserted caves not far from the abandoned Arab village of Lifta and promoted nebulous mystical ideas involving the people of Israel.[20]

The cult's founders, Yehuda Limaei and Uzi Mahsaya, identified with Barda's ideas, and together with Eliahu Srour, who joined the cult at a later stage, they began perpetrating acts of terrorism against the Arab residents of Jerusalem. Ultimately, the group was caught after police noticed the name "N. Srour" written on one of the knapsacks left behind at the Temple Mount. The police located Nissim Srour, who informed the investigators that he had given his knapsack to his brother Eliahu.[21] In the end, Barda and Srour were charged and sentenced to eight years in prison, and Limaei and Mahsaya were committed to psychiatric institutions after being diagnosed as mentally ill.[22]

Although both the Ein Kerem group and the Lifta Gang acted in the name of ideological principles whose core elements were embedded in wider countercultural norms (i.e., the religious Zionist and ultra-Orthodox streams), it is hard to describe them as a genuine part of these communities. They were too isolated and had no ties with the spiritual leaders of these streams. Members of these two groups were also not part of the settlement movement. Finally, it is hard to pick out the influence of a threatening external event that motivated the group members, and some of them apparently were driven to violent activities by mental illness.

SPONTANEOUS VENGEANCE

The realm of Jewish terrorism also included groups whose actions seemed to be a result of spontaneous vengeance. These groups had no clear ideological framework, and their members were not part of a counterculture community. They acted in response to a specific violent act committed against Jews, with minimal preparation, and in order to unload their anger and frustration. The first example of such circumstances occurred on the night of April 22, 1985. The body of a Palestinian, Hamis Tutanji, thirty-three, was found slumped at the wheel of his taxi, parked on the shoulder of the Jerusalem–Ma'aleh Adumim highway. Tutanji's head was riddled with bullets.[23] Three weeks later, his murderers were found. They were Danny Aizenman, a twenty-seven-year-old police officer; Michal Hillel, twenty-five, a literature and geography student at the Hebrew University; and Gil Foux, twenty, an IDF conscript.[24]

The three met for the first time about two months before the murder at a restaurant at the Jerusalem Central Bus Station. Danny Aizenman was sitting in the restaurant, awaiting the arrival of his soldier friend, Gil Foux, who was serving at an army base in southern Israel. While waiting, he struck up a conversation with Michal and told her that he worked for the General Security Service (GSS) in "eliminating the other side." When Gil Foux arrived, Aizenman introduced him as a senior GSS operative, working undercover as a soldier. The conversation between the three quickly turned to politics, and they discovered that they shared strong anti-Arab sentiments.[25] In the ensuing weeks, the three continued to meet at various Jerusalem bars, reinforcing their friendship bonds.[26] When Jewish taxi driver David Caspi was murdered by a Palestinian, the three decided to respond. A few days after Caspi's murder, Aizenman and Hillel got into Tutanji's taxi and asked him to take them to Ma'aleh Adumim, a satellite suburb east of Jerusalem. Foux drove behind them in Aizenman's police vehicle. On the way, Hillel asked the driver to stop the car because she was not feeling well. Tutanji stopped, and Foux pulled up in the police vehicle near the taxi. He pretended to be a police officer and asked to see Tutanji's identification. While Tutanji was searching for his documents, Aizenman went back to the police car, pulled out Foux's M16 rifle, and shot the taxi driver three times in the head. In March 1986, the three were convicted in the Jerusalem District Court and given life sentences.[27]

Revenge was also the main motive behind the act perpetrated by Danny Tikman and Felix Milner. On the second weekend of October 2000, two weeks after the Second Intifada broke out, the front pages of the afternoon newspapers were covered with gruesome photos of the bodies of lynched Israeli reserve soldiers Vadim Norzich and Yosef Avrahami. On their way to report to their unit near Ramallah, the two got lost and mistakenly entered this Palestinian city, where they were arrested by the Palestinian police and conducted to the local police station. However, the police were not able to provide for their security. Agitated young Palestinian men mobbed the police station and threw out the police officers; they beat the Israeli soldiers to death and mutilated their bodies.[28] Danny Tikman and Felix Milner, two twenty-year-old soldiers from the northern Haifa suburbs, decided it was time to pay the Arabs back in kind.

On the night of Friday, October 12, they drove to the Stella Maris naval base in Haifa, where Tikman was posted. They went to the armory and removed an M16 rifle and a twenty-nine-bullet magazine. Minutes later, they made their way down the slopes of the Carmel Mountain to Yaffo Street, known for its many eateries.[29] According to Aharon Ishah, thirty-two, who was at the scene at one of the food stands, "All of a sudden I heard a burst of gunfire. I saw people hitting the ground and I felt a kind of a slap on my leg, like the snap of a belt. I fell to the floor and my hand was cut by shards of glass."[30] Tikman and Milner drove the length of the road, Tikman holding the rifle and shooting long bursts of gunfire in the direction of the food stands. A worker at one of the restaurants, Fuad Asli, twenty-two, from the Araba village in the Galilee, was very seriously injured. Although their objective was to kill Arabs, some bullets went awry, and three Jewish bystanders were wounded. After the shooting, Tikman returned to his base and turned himself in to the officer on duty.[31] Several hours later, Milner appeared at a police station and also took responsibility for the incident. During his interrogation, Tikman claimed that he had been drunk and had carried out the shooting in retaliation for the lynching in Ramallah.[32] Tikman was sent to prison for fourteen years, and Milner received a ten-year sentence. They both appealed to the Israeli Supreme Court, which left Tickman's sentence in force but gave Milner the benefit of the doubt and acquitted him.

INTERIM SUMMARY: THE EXCEPTIONAL GROUPS

What are the common characteristics of the groups that fall outside our theoretical framework, and what can we learn from them?

To begin with, in all the exceptional cases the association between members of the different groups and the Jewish Orthodox countercultures ranged from weak to nonexistent. In regard to the Meshulam cult, although many members were settlers, they were never considered genuinely representative of the religious Zionist or settler populations. Moreover, spiritual leaders of both countercultures disassociated themselves from the ideology and actions of the Meshulam followers. Thus in the eyes of the Israeli public there was no relationship between the actions of the Meshulam group and the ideological agenda of these two sectors. The members of the two Jerusalem groups essentially operated from within social enclaves with a very limited connection to the religious Zionist mainstream outlook or leaders. Finally, members of the last two groups discussed in this chapter, who acted out of a sheer desire for revenge, were not even Orthodox Jews and had no association with any type of counterculture community. In contrast, the terrorist groups mentioned in former chapters all had deep, intensive relationships with the spiritual leaders of the Jewish Orthodoxy, their members belonged to central communities and organizational frameworks of the different religious counterculture streams, and they were continuously exposed to the socialization mechanisms of these countercultures.

From an ideological–operational perspective, it is hard to find clear, long-term rationalizations and goals behind the actions of these groups. Whereas the vengeance groups and Ein Kerem group had nothing close to a robust ideological vision, the Meshulam group acted in order to advance a specific government resolution (the formation of a state commission of inquiry). Only the Lifta group had a type of mythological vision and some vague, long-term goals; however, it is difficult to consider their activities as part of a long-term plan for promoting their political or religious vision.

It seems that the occurrence of the two aforementioned distinctions in our category of exceptional groups is not just a coincidence. In fact, they can be seen as having a cause-and-effect relationship. In the absence of an ideological framework of a wider counterculture, and of the direction of the counterculture's spiritual leaders, it is difficult to develop a complex ideological rationalization for violence that results in long-term plans and more protracted campaigns of aggression. Therefore it comes as no surprise that the length of the campaigns of these exceptional groups is associated with their proximity to the Orthodox counterculture elements. The vengeance groups whose members were not part of the religious streams were "one-attack wonders," whereas the Meshulam group was able to produce successive attacks over a period of three years.

In addition, the fact that at least three of the five aforementioned groups had cultlike characteristics implies that terrorism that develops outside the scope of our theoretical framework is subject to long-term ingroup socialization and, more than anything, total obligation to the group leader or prominent figure who personally takes part in the perpetration of the violence. In contrast, in our model the spiritual leader is responsible mostly for instilling feelings of threat and fear in members of the counterculture with respect to an external event and for rationalizing the violent response. However, the spiritual leader can be a distant figure for the violent group, and its members won't even need his direct supervision. Indeed, in most of the cases presented in earlier chapters, the spiritual leaders did not take part in the implementation of violence.

We can sum up by indicating a clear similarity between the exceptional groups and the other groups that have been presented throughout the book:

the importance of close social ties and socialization within the group. These in turn reinforce the morality of committing the violent acts, the cohesion and solidarity among group members, and the mindset that enables them to take part in such a demanding activity.

At this stage, we would like to shift our attention to the other variety of Jewish terrorism that is not compatible with our theoretical framework and can generally be called lone wolf terrorism. These perpetrators can be divided into three groups: those who act on the basis of a combination of mental illness and the influence of external events, most often a deteriorating security environment; those who act on the basis of a combination of mental illness and a feeling of vengeance, as well as a commitment to a counterculture; and those who do not have an obvious mental disorder and carry out a spontaneous act of vengeance shortly after people who were meaningful to them were attacked.

MENTAL HEALTH AND EXTERNAL EVENTS

The combination of a mental disturbance and a deteriorating political and security situation has resulted in some of the best-known incidents of Jewish terrorism to be committed by individual perpetrators. The cases of Eliran Golan and Ami Popper are the most notable, mainly because of the targets they chose to attack and the number of people victimized by their violent activities.

The city of Haifa enjoys a long-running reputation for ethnic tolerance because of the undisturbed relations between Arab and Jewish residents of the city. Eliran Golan, twenty-two, broke this quiet by staging a series of terrorist acts against Haifa Arabs in the early 2000s. His declared objective was to strike back at Arabs in reprisal for attacks against Jews in intifada-related incidents. After he was captured, he explained, "I am sorry for what I did. . . . I believed those people threatened the security of the nation. . . . I was afraid, like all Israelis, to die in a terrorist attack. That was my greatest fear. I did not act from anger."[33] Like many of his predecessors, Golan was a peripheral figure from a blue-collar family of Middle Eastern descent. He was educated in the state religious school system and after elementary school was sent by his parents to the Yavneh High School Yeshiva. He studied at this Haifa yeshiva until the ninth grade, when he was expelled. He later tried to enlist in the IDF but was turned down for being unsuitable for army service.[34]

Golan never revealed what caused him to embark on his campaign of terrorism. During his interrogation, he spoke of his deep hatred for Arabs and his frustration at what he defined as the impotence of the state in the face of Palestinian violence during the Second Intifada. Similar to the Meshulam affair, the violence was set off during a conflict between neighbors. Early in July 2001, Eliran's brother was beaten up by a boy named Yousef Mahmid. Eliran suspected that the boy's parents, Iyad Mahmid and Aliza Franco, a Muslim and a Jew, were behind the incident. In fact, he loathed the mixed couple. On July 4, 2001, Iyad Mahmid and Aliza Franco entered their yard to discover a bomb planted under their balcony table. They managed to call the police in time, and the bomb was defused by sappers.[35]

A little more than a month later, a few days after Palestinian suicide bomber Muhammad Nasser blew himself up in the Wall Street Café in Kiryat Motzkin, Golan inexplicably began to suspect that Nasser had been hidden before the attack in the home of an Arab family named Kamir who were living at that time in the Halisa neighborhood of Haifa. Golan decided to retaliate. He put together an improvised bomb and placed it under the family car parked in front of their house. He rigged the bomb to be triggered by the car's ignition, intending to kill its occupants. Once again, his plans met with failure. Two ten-year-old boys playing in the street saw the box with wires sticking out. One of the boys tried to pull it out from under the car, and the bomb exploded, leaving the child with burns on his face and arms.[36]

Ten days later, at noon on Friday, August 28, 2001, Jamila Agbaria went to pray at the El Haj Abdallah Mosque on Isfia Street in lower Haifa, as was her custom every Friday. The area was crowded with people. She went to the entrance of the women's section and tried to open the door. However, it wouldn't budge, so she tugged at it with all her strength. Suddenly, the door flew off its hinges and a huge explosion was heard. Jamila was thrown back, and her hands were burned.[37] Police investigators who arrived at the scene were bewildered. They could not understand the motivation for the attack and failed to tie it to previous incidents. All the same, it was clear to them that the bomb was improvised because the main component was gunpowder, not explosives.

Because of his repeated failures, Golan made up his mind to improve his methods. He thought Alexander Rabinovitch, whom he had met when the two studied together at the Yavne Yeshiva, might help him out.[38] Rabinovitch had emigrated from Ukraine to Israel when he was six years old and, like Golan, was a weak student. Their common academic problems had brought them together, and a friendship developed, but when Golan left school they lost touch. The two renewed their friendship when they met by chance at the Haifa Central Bus Terminal in May 2002, two months after Rabinovitch began his army service.[39] In early 2003, Golan revealed to Rabinovitch that he was responsible for the wave of terrorist acts against the Arab residents of Haifa. Although Rabinovitch's reaction was not clear, he used his post in the Engineering Corps to smuggle regulation explosives out of the camp, and he entrusted them to Golan.[40] Emboldened by the equipment he had amassed, Golan decided to raise the stakes and embarked on an attempt to assassinate Knesset member Issam Makhoul, a resident of Haifa and one of the foremost advocates of Palestinian interests in the Knesset.

This time, Golan planned his steps very carefully. He called Makhoul's home, introduced himself to Makhoul's wife, Suad, while posing as an insurance agent, and persuaded her to give him details of the family car. Early in October 2003, he began surveillance of their house and car. After familiarizing himself with their routine, he felt he was ready to act and started to build an explosive device. On October 24, he attached the bomb underneath the family car, affixing it to the axle so it would go off when the wheels began to turn.[41] On that day, at 12:15 P.M., Makhoul and his wife left the house. Makhoul entered his official government car while his wife, who was on her way to pick up the children from school, got into the booby-trapped car. As she pulled out, the device exploded and the car caught fire. Mrs. Makhoul quickly recovered from the blast and escaped the burning car without injury.[42]

These botched attempts were still not enough to discourage Golan. On January 16, 2004, he planted a bomb under the car of a Haifa Arab resident, Issa Gnaim. Golan suspected Gnaim had abetted the suicide bomber who had blown himself up ten months earlier on the number 37 bus en route to the University of Haifa. Once again, Golan was frustrated: Gnaim discovered the bomb and removed it from the vehicle.[43] Two weeks later, Golan struck for the last time. He placed an explosive device in an apartment building on Pe'er Street, where he knew a woman was having intimate relations with Arabs. The father of the young woman found the bomb in the stairwell and disconnected it before it had a chance to explode.[44]

Eliran Golan was caught on March 4, 2004, after a lengthy investigation. In the wake of the attack at the El Haj Abdallah Mosque, the GSS and the police set up a special team. They soon discovered that almost all the incidents, except for the one against Makhoul, occurred within a small radius between the Jewish neighborhood of Neveh Sha'anan and the Arab neighborhood of Halisa. They began by gathering intelligence about suspicious activities in the area and tried to track down someone with a profile that matched a potential perpetrator. Golan's name soon appeared on their computer screens. Several years before the wave of attacks began, the police had been informed that a neighbor had boasted about how he intended to assault Arabs and had even assembled the explosives to do so. As soon as there was enough evidence against Golan, he was arrested. A search of his basement shelter uncovered two suitcases containing thirty-four bombs ready to be activated.[45]

Golan was unknown even to activists from Haifa's radical right-wing political scene. According to Aviad Visoli, chairman of the Land of Israel organization in Haifa and the north, "At no time did I or any right-wing activists I am acquainted with in the city have contact with or hear of Eliran Golan. I believe he is a disturbed pyromaniac who worked by himself."[46] In the summer of 2005, we were following the case and expected to spend many hours in the Haifa District Court to witness Golan's trial firsthand. But a few days before the opening of deliberations, he hanged himself from the bars of his cell at the Kishon Detention Center on the outskirts of Haifa. On September 7, 2005, after several long days of hovering between life and death, Eliran Golan passed away.[47]

Golan's activities, statements, and eventual suicide led to serious questions about his mental health. In the case of Ami Popper, who was responsible for an act of violence that shocked the Israeli public in May 1990, mental problems were evident a long time before he pursued his deadly operation. On the early morning of May 20, 1990, Popper, a twenty-one-year-old secular Jew from the Tel Aviv suburb of Rishon Letzion, donned his brother's IDF uniform, grabbed his brother's personal Galil rifle, and walked to the Ganei–Vradim Junction, not far from his home. He knew that Palestinian laborers waited every morning at this junction for transportation to their workplace. A few seconds after arriving at the junction, he opened fire, killing seven Palestinians and injuring another twelve. During the police investigation he claimed that his action was in response to the Palestinian violence of the First Intifada, but afterwards claimed he was depressed because his girlfriend left him. In the judicial process later it was revealed that he suffered from a serious mental disorder, which among other factors led him to attempt suicide during his military service. Popper also claimed that when he was thirteen years old he was raped by an Arab and from then on developed profound negative sentiments against Israeli Arabs and Palestinians. In any event, he was condemned to seven life sentences and another twenty years. A few years later, the penalty was commuted to forty years by presidential amnesty.

Ami Popper was a secular Jew, and his radicalization process as well as Golan's did not develop on the fertile ground of a counterculture. However, this was not the case for other mentally disturbed individuals, such as Alan Goodman, Asher Rabo, and Gur Hamel.

VENGEANCE, COUNTERCULTURE, AND MENTAL DISTURBANCES

Alan Goodman was born in Baltimore, Maryland in 1944 to an Orthodox Jewish family. Already as a youth, he was a loner and introvert and had received a diagnosis of paranoid schizophrenia. He arrived in Israel for a short visit after the Six-Day War in 1967 and returned for another visit after the Yom Kippur War in 1973. When he again came in 1978, his plan was to settle down. In Israel, he received his first exposure to Palestinian terrorism. Goodman was particularly shocked by the attack on an Israeli passenger bus on the coastal road in February 1978. The attack, which the Israel public called the "blood (bathed) bus" massacre and ended with the death of thirty-one citizens and the wounding of seventy-one, was the most deadly Palestinian attack in the 1970s. After the attack he "felt a strong need to take revenge on the Arabs."[48] Even though Goodman returned to the United States in the winter of that year, he continued to be obsessed with thoughts of revenge. Upon his return to Israel in the autumn of 1980, he became an Israeli citizen and was drafted into the IDF two years later. However, his thoughts of retaliating against the Arabs never left him, and in early spring of 1982 he took advantage of a furlough during his basic training to act on his desire for revenge.[49]

On April 11, Goodman made his way to the Temple Mount, carrying his army-issued M16 rifle. At the northern entrance to the Temple Mount, he lowered his rifle from his shoulder and fired at the Waqf guard, Riad av-Rumeilah. One bullet caught the guard in the shoulder, and two others hit his waist and leg. Goodman immediately entered the Temple Mount compound and began running toward the Dome of the Rock Mosque. One of the compound guards, Mohammed Hamed, saw him running and took off in pursuit. When Goodman realized he was being chased he halted, turned around, and fired three shots. Hamed was wounded in the chest and right shoulder and collapsed. The crowd of worshippers and tourists who heard the gunshots began to flee while Goodman continued to shoot in all directions. After entering the Dome of the Rock, Goodman turned around and shot a few rounds at the door and windows in order to dissuade security forces from trying to gain access to the building. Only forty-five minutes after the incident began, Yehoshua Caspi, commander of Israel's Southern Police District, along with three police officers and two Border Police, managed to gain entry into the building. Goodman tried to escape, but the officers gave chase and were able to knock him down. At this point he finally raised his hands in surrender.[50] During the incident two men were killed and eleven people were wounded.

Goodman later argued that he had wanted to avenge the murder of dozens of Jews by Arab terrorists in the coastal road incident four years earlier. Goodman's demeanor gave the impression of someone who walked the thin line between sanity and madness. His statement to the police was a concrete illustration of this: "Today I exacted justice on the Temple Mount for all the murdered schoolchildren and Jewish citizens. . . . I liberated the Temple Mount by executing all the Arab occupiers. . . . I did what I did to protest the senseless killing of women and children in the bus on the coastal road, four years ago. . . . I did this for the sake of the liberation of the proud Jewish people. . . . God's orders overcame me. . . . Today I exacted justice on the Temple Mount."[51]

Goodman's trial revolved around the question of his sanity, and psychiatrists who examined him found that he suffered from disorders typical of a borderline personality. The defense claimed he suffered from paranoid schizophrenia. In April 1983, the Jerusalem District Court sentenced Goodman to life plus forty years. President Chaim Herzog later commuted this sentence to twenty-three years, and Goodman was released in 1997, after sitting in jail for 15.5 years.[52]

The cases of Asher Rabo and Gur Hamel are also examples of how a combination of mental disorders and intracommunity socialization could lead some people into violent activities.[53] The first was a newly Orthodox Jew, a resident of Tel Aviv in his early thirties, who waged a campaign of death between 1979 and 1982 against nuns, pilgrims, and doctors who performed abortions. After he was caught in December 1982, it became clear that he had spent a lot of his free time in several radical yeshivas in settlements in the West Bank and that he also suffered from delusions and mental disturbances, which apparently caused him to carry out his religious beliefs in the most cruel ways imaginable. For example, he bludgeoned one of the nuns many times with an ax. In the police interrogations he argued that he was really just God's proxy, and all his acts were actually God's will.[54]

Gur Hamel was a twenty-eight-year-old settler who spent most of his time at the Gvaot Olam farm with his comrades, who all belonged to the hilltop youth. After he was involved in several violent incidents with Palestinians from the neighboring villages, IDF officials issued an administrative expulsion directive against him, preventing him from residing at the farm. As a result, he moved to his sister's home in the settlement of Itamar, a few hundred yards from the farm. On October 26, 1998, he decided to visit his friends at the Gvaot Olam farm, ignoring the expulsion order. On the way he met an elderly Palestinian man who was working in his olive grove, and on an unexplained impulse he decided to kill him. He hit the Palestinian in the arm and then bludgeoned him to death with a 20-pound rock. After he was caught, much evidence was found implying that he had borderline personality disorder; this, combined with the intensive dynamics within the hilltop youth community, brought out his most violent tendencies.[55]

The third type of people drawn to political violence in the realm of Jewish terrorism are those who do not suffer from visible mental problems but who, in a haste and sometimes with a certain degree of planning, decide to avenge Palestinian violence, especially if the aggressive actions were aimed at people dear to them.

THE LONE AVENGERS

The parents of David Ben-Shimol immigrated to Israel from Morocco and settled in the Katamonim neighborhood of Jerusalem, where their ten children were born and raised.[56] Unlike his brothers and sisters, David, who was the second oldest, left school and gave up religious observance at age fourteen, causing his parents heartache. The family relationship deteriorated to the point where he had no alternative but to leave home. Life on the streets exposed him to a strange and alienated world, and he soon found himself involved in criminal activities.[57] At the age of eighteen, Ben-Shimol apparently decided to take responsibility for himself and tried to get back on the right track. He enlisted in the IDF, volunteered for the Golani Infantry Brigade, and became highly esteemed by his commanding officers. Deep beneath the facade of the disciplined soldier, however, Ben-Shimol was undergoing radical changes.

As a soldier, Ben-Shimol enjoyed easy access to munitions. He stole a hand grenade and a shoulder-launched anti-tank rocket from his unit.[58] On September 22, 1984, he threw the grenade into a café on Chain Street in the Muslim Quarter of Jerusalem's Old City. Luckily for the café's patrons, a youth sitting inside noticed the grenade and, before it could explode, picked it up and threw it into a metal garbage can. This quick action saved patrons from death, but eight Palestinians were wounded.[59] On October 28, 1984, Ben-Shimol fired the rocket, and this time the results were more severe. The target Ben-Shimol had chosen was a bus belonging to a Palestinian transportation company. It was carrying about fifty passengers to Hebron and was traveling past the Mishkenot Sha'ananim neighborhood, just south of the Old City. Ben-Shimol's aim was true, and the rocket hit the bus near the back door. One of the passengers described its impact: "I saw something fly toward us and suddenly there was a loud explosion. The whole bus shook. . . . People began screaming hysterically for help."[60] One man, Jamal Ismail al-Matar, a student at the Islamic College of Hebron who worked in Jerusalem, was killed and ten people were wounded.[61] Ben-Shimol, who had been hiding behind some bushes in the garden of Khutzot Hayotzer (Jerusalem's Arts and Crafts Fair), which overlooked the road traveled by the bus, fled the scene. He left behind a note written in red ink stating that his action was in response to the murder of two Israeli students, Revital Seri and Ron Levy, near the Cremisan Monastery, south of Jerusalem. The note also said that such actions would continue until the Israeli government took harsher steps against Arab terrorism.[62]

Whereas Ben-Shimol did not avenge the death or harm of people close to him, most the people in the category of lone wolves did. The following cases of Yisrael Lederman, Yoram Shkolnik, and Irena Starashnatzev illustrate this type of perpetrator.

In early April 1978, Yisrael Lederman was on IDF reserve duty in Jerusalem. On the 4th of the month, Lederman's army buddy, Private Avraham Deutsch, was stabbed to death at a hitchhiking post, and so Lederman decided to avenge Deutsch's death. At 6:00 A.M. the next day, several minutes after completing his guard duty near the Western Wall Plaza, Lederman walked to the nearby Rockefeller Junction, just west of the Old City, and opened fire on a group of Palestinian laborers on their way to work. On this occasion, he wounded twenty-three-year-old Khalil Ben Saud Takhan. Lederman claimed in his interrogation that he had acted in self-defense; he was shaken, confused, and in shock. He was sentenced to twenty years in prison after the court determined that his action had been "a personal act of revenge." Years later, Lederman attained fame as a religious right-wing violent activist after his involvement in a series of provocative acts, such as flinging a cupful of boiling tea that struck the face and chest of Knesset member Yael Dayan in 1996.

Whereas both Lederman and Ben-Shimol acted with some degree of planning, it seems that the attack committed by Yoram Shkolnik was more spontaneous. On the morning of March 24, 1993, Moshe Deutsch, security coordinator for the settlement of Susya, received a message that a young Arab man had been seen observing the settlement from a nearby hilltop, some 200 yards away. Deutsch went with his car to get Yair Essenheim, another resident of Susya, and together they drove to the place where the Arab man had been spotted. After locating the man, they asked his business in the area, and he replied that he was out for a walk. Deutsch and Essenheim decided to put the man in their car anyway, take him back to their settlement, and interrogate him further about his presence there. On the way back to Susya, the man, who was seated in the rear of the vehicle, drew out a knife and stabbed Deutsch in the shoulder. The wound was not deep, and Deutsch managed to stop the car. With Essenheim's assistance he was able to get the knife away from the Arab and restrain him.[63] Deutsch reported the incident immediately, and within a few minutes he was joined by Shlomo Haus, Susya's medic, and Yoram Shkolnik, thirty, a resident of nearby Ma'aleh Hever who drove a children's school bus and had heard the report on the radio in his vehicle.

About fifteen minutes after arriving at the scene, Shkolnik fired his IDF-issued Uzi and killed the man, who was bound hand and foot and lying on the ground beside Deutsch's jeep. When investigated, Shkolnik said he thought the Palestinian was about to activate the grenade that was later found on his body. Later, Shkolnik changed his story and said he acted out of temporary derangement and self-defense. Still, he did not convince the court that his life had been in danger and that he had not acted out of a pure desire for revenge. Shkolnik was sentenced to fifteen years in prison. The Arab shot dead was Musa Abu Sabha, twenty, a resident of the village of Yata, near Hebron.[64]

Of all the cases mentioned so far, it seems that the most straightforward act of vengeance was perpetrated by Irena Starashnatzev. On the morning of the first Saturday in March 2003, Irena Starashnatzev, a divorced mother of twins, drove her blue Peugeot to the Erez Industrial Zone in the Gaza Strip to visit her partner, Alex Gorelik, a Border Police officer.[65] Almost one year earlier, her brother David Smirnov, also in the Border Police, had been shot to death in exactly the same place in a terrorist attack. The visit to the scene of her brother's murder filled her head with painful memories. She noticed a group of Palestinian laborers walking on the shoulder of the road and made a split-second decision to strike them. She swerved her vehicle in their direction and floored the gas pedal. The surprised laborers quickly jumped out of the way and avoided injury.[66]

When she met Alex ten minutes later, Irena told him what she had done but didn't inform him of her decision not to leave before she avenged her brother's murder. Ibrahim Martaga was a random victim. Starashnatzev used all the power of her vehicle to run him down, flinging Martaga so high in the air that he hit the ground with a strong thud. He arrived at the Soroka Medical Center in Be'er Sheva unconscious and was admitted into intensive care, where he has remained ever since, in a coma. After Irena turned herself in and confessed, her parents said she had been traumatized by the death of her brother and claimed her motivation was to avenge his death.[67]

THE MINDSET OF THE LONE WOLVES

The stories of many lone wolves suggest that mental illness is a prominent factor in the slide into terrorist activity. This contention is not new in the field of terrorism studies. Since the late 1970s a large number of scholars have tried to figure out whether terrorists have unique personality traits or suffer from common mental illnesses.[68] They have argued that terrorists are driven to commit acts of violence by psychological forces that are constructed to rationalize acts they are psychologically compelled to commit. Thus people become involved in terrorist activities because they have a mental need to commit violent acts, and ideology and "rational" reasons are negligible. However, the majority of studies have proven that this is not the case. This development led Walter Laqueur and Jonathan White to conclude that although most terrorists are young, their actions and psychological makeup vary according to social and cultural conditions, and it seems impossible to produce a single behavioral profile of a terrorist.[69]

Nevertheless, the cases portrayed in this chapter lead to a possible alternative hypothesis. It is not that all terrorists have similar psychological traits or mental disorders. However, some people who suffer from such mental tribulations find in political or religious violence a path to channel their fury and insanity. More specifically, in other circumstances these disturbed people would express their mental disorders in various ways, sometimes even violent but not necessarily directed against other outgroups. When the polity and the community to which the person belongs face growing security threats, and he or she experiences a decline in personal welfare and safety, this increases the chances that the person's violence will become politicized. It becomes more likely that their violence will be aimed at the "enemies" of the state or the community to which they belong, especially because these are perceived as more legitimate targets. However, it should be noted that mentally unstable people do not always act alone. The case of the Lifta Gang demonstrates that when an individual has a charismatic personality, the possibility that others will follow him or her cannot be ruled out.

Several additional conclusions can be drawn from cases of the lone wolves analyzed in this chapter. First, lone wolves generally are not former members of a group who at a certain time detached from the group and decided to go it alone. Therefore they do not go through the intragroup socialization process, which is a critical stage in the radicalization of groups, as we have shown in previous chapters. Most of them were actually introverted people with limited ties to outside sources of socialization. Similarly, they had no ties to spiritual leaders, did not belong to political or social organizations, and in most cases did not even share their violent intentions with others. This indicates that in order to deepen our understanding of individuals who perpetrate terrorism, we need to look for secondary socialization mechanisms, such as the media and general culture, or we must study the socialization process within the familial framework. Another possible conclusion that should be examined is that the individual's resort to terrorism is more a case of inner personal psychological dynamics, whereas outside influences are negligible.

Second, the individual terrorists described here shared a high level of biographical availability. Although this is a common feature of members of the groups described in previous chapters, it is even more prominent among the lone wolves. Furthermore, in many cases their biographical availability was a result of their inability to become integrated into society. As the cases of David Ben-Shimol, Eliran Golan, Gur Hamel, and Ami Popper illustrate, they were essentially driven to the fringes of society or their communities. Some were unable to enlist in the IDF and carry out their army service (Popper and Golan), an important stage in the lives of every young Israeli, and others were expelled from the educational framework to which they belonged (Golan, Ben-Shimol). Therefore the following question should be examined: Do lone wolves perceive the attacks on their targets as a possible rehabilitation mechanism that will help them recover their status and image in their communities? They might believe that by causing harm to those whom they perceive as enemies of their communities or state, they can earn the appreciation, understanding, and affection of their surroundings and society at large.

Finally, many of the acts were a result of two factors. The first was a personal crisis that had a direct influence on the perpetrator. The second was an opportunity to express the anger, frustration, and desire for vengeance that resulted from the event at the source of the crisis. A personal crisis combined with the opportunity to act and avenge those perceived as responsible for the crisis were evident in the cases of the two soldiers from Haifa (Milner and Tikman) and of both Yisrael Lederman and Irena Starashnatzev. In the case of the first two, the access to munitions and firearms facilitated their revenge attacks, both taking place a short time after the crisis event. In the case of Starashnatzev, her return to the site where her brother was killed, a place crowded with Palestinians, triggered her driving rampage.

AND THE LAND
Reassessment of the Causes of Jewish Terrorism

■■■■■■■■■■■■■■

CRACKING THE BLACK BOX that contains the
various processes that characterize terrorist groups is not a simple matter.
When we initially set out to work on this book, we presumed that a large
part of the potential of its theoretical contribution would reside in com-
prehending the motives for terrorism and, specifically, the question of the
relationship between religion and terrorism. As our research gradually
progressed, however, we realized an interesting fact. Although the underlying reasons for terrorism have gained widespread academic coverage—
which has progressively increased since the events of September 11, 2001—
the structures and processes related to the phenomenon have been thrust
aside to a significant degree. In light of our access to a wide range of resources and the cooperation of the terrorists themselves, most of them already retired, we were granted the opportunity to peer into the depths of
the black box of the terrorist group. On the basis of research conducted on
Jewish terrorist groups in Israel, we found it possible to draw several conclusions that may raise doubts about commonly accepted approaches to the
analysis of the structures and processes in the study of terrorism.

One of the customary assumptions in the field is that terrorism is an
organizational action. Nearly every aggregate of individuals that performs
an act of terrorism is labeled a terrorist organization. But isn't this essentially another analytic failing that can be attributed to us scholars of terrorism? Aren't we attempting, in this case as well, to force the comprising
elements of violent action into a familiar framework that is well embedded
in the academic literature, thus providing us with convenient tools to examine the phenomenon? If we accept the assumption that terrorism is an
action carried out in the context of an organization, we can readily draw on
theories and methods from the field of organization theory in order to clarify
aspects related to this phenomenon. This is no small temptation. Researchers in the field of social and behavioral sciences are often on the watch for

constants that might lead to conclusions and, with the application of generalization, be modeled into a theory. In effect, the notion that terrorist groups operate in much the same manner as political and even business organizations provides the researcher with a degree of consolation. Suddenly, it is possible to find order and logic in actions or events that until recently were viewed as incomprehensible.

However, tracing the development of Jewish terrorist groups has taught us that they lack the certain fundamental qualities of organizations, such as clear-cut structures, a hierarchy, regulated mechanisms that interact with the external environment and, above all, a tendency toward institutionalization. On the other hand, an analysis of these same groups from the more flexible sociological perspective of social networks provided us with a different configuration of structures that, despite lacking the elegance typical of organizations, helped us detect the leadership echelon, subgroups, and division of roles in every group. The social network approach significantly shortened the path for us in understanding the processes that are distinctive of terrorist groups and facilitated the modeling of a theoretical framework for explaining the emergence and formation of religious terrorism, as presented in the Preface.

The case studies investigated in this book illustrate how counterculture communities based on totalistic ideologies are breeding grounds for religious terrorist groups. Most groups discussed in previous chapters emerged from within the framework of the religious Zionist stream, the settler community, and Gush Emunim, and from the Kahanist culture and hilltop youth communities. All these elements advance ideologies, norms, and practices that widely reject the essence of democracy and undermine the state's secular nature. Moreover, all do not accept the liberal assumption that religion is a private matter[1] and that the collective does not have the right to impose religious practices on its members. Accordingly, the groups spawned by these countercultures seek to enforce their values not only on their own community but on all Jews in Israel.

We further found that when these counterculture communities are subject to potentially threatening external events, community leaders play a central role. Presenting and framing the external event as posing a threat to the continued existence of the community and its ability to preserve its values increase the odds that high-density social networks in the community will resort to violent actions. In the cases presented in the book, events such as the two intifadas, the Camp David Accords, and the Oslo process—all of which potentially threatened the realization of the vision of the Greater Land of Israel and the survival of the settlement project—were followed by a catastrophic framing of the events by the communities' spiritual leaders. This in turn aroused intense concern within the counterculture communities.

In most cases, the high-density social networks within the counterculture communities that descended into violence after the community leader's catastrophic framing were primary groups based on family ties or close friendships. In the case of large and intricate networks, the secondary cliques in the network were distinguished by primary relationships. These primary relationships reinforced the process called a circular response in the sociological literature. Individuals in the clique engaged in intensive interaction with each other, and this dynamic led to a situation in which they immediately responded to the behavior of other individuals in the group and reinforced it. Individuals who were not swept along into the circular response did not abandon the network in most cases because they feared the informal social sanctions involved in such a move.

These characteristics are not unique to terrorist networks but also can be observed in other types of social networks, such as urban street gangs[2] and social movements.[3] In all cases, informal ties serve as important recruiting mechanisms, and membership in the network is supported by the community, provides a sense of belonging, and serves as a source of status, identity, cohesion, and self-esteem.[4] Moreover, in both street gangs and social movements,[5] the community's support helps motivate the network to pursue its operations and makes it easier to recruit new members by increasing what Klandermans and Oegema call their mobilization potential.[6] In summary, members who share a common physical space engage in intensive interaction, bolstering their communal commitment and developing a collective mindset that facilitates the slide into extreme activities.

In all the networks we were able to discern central figures who were hubs. Usually there were one or two hubs, and they were the central factor—the motivating and organizing force—behind the network's actions. They were not leaders in the typical sense of the word; they didn't have any privileges or special authority over the rest of the members of the network. However, they were generally perceived as an ideological authority, and they were the ones who tied together all the ends often necessary to carry out the terrorist actions. In addition to the hubs, we discovered that in the majority of the networks, there were groups or cliques of peripheral collaborators who provided environmental support and sometimes logistic aid to the group. The collaborators weren't key activists in the group and, for the most part, were not familiar with all the members of the group, but they had the same ideological outlook and made small contributions to the group without being aware of the larger picture of the group's actions.

At the individual level, the cases examined in the book demonstrated that the perpetrator's descent into violent activity is related both to his or her level of identification with the community's values and alienation toward external elements and to his or her biographical availability. By constructing a biographical dataset of Jewish terrorists, we found that the majority of the terrorists (more than 90 percent) were men, who in traditional societies enjoy more freedom and are less committed to family-related tasks. At least half of them were unemployed (51.3 percent), single (56.9 percent), and under the age of twenty-seven (82 percent). These features are all indicative of the Jewish terrorist's high level of biographical availability.

Another important factor that led the individual to resort to violent activity was a sense of crisis, such as the violent personal loss of loved ones or close peers in the community (as demonstrated in the case of the Jewish Underground), a loss of status in the community or peer group (shown in the cases of Yoel Lerner and some of the hilltop youth), or a crisis stemming from a perceived assault on the person's or community's beliefs and way of life (as effectively shown in the case of the Yigal Amir network). In crises, the commitment of these individuals to the community's values will lead them to adopt a moral imperative in which the community must be protected and defended. Their sense of alienation from the mainstream culture or outgroups that pose a threat to the community will lead them to act on their sense of moral obligation by taking revenge and inflicting harm on those they regard as enemies of the community.

COMPARING JEWISH TERRORISM WITH OTHER MANIFESTATIONS OF RELIGIOUS TERRORISM

Most of the findings on Jewish terrorism networks are pertinent to the study of other contemporary networks of terrorism. This is because of the many similarities between the processes that distinguish Jewish terrorism networks and those of the Salafi jihad networks that have come to light in recent years in Western countries, such as Britain, Holland, Spain, Sweden, and Denmark.[7]

In both cases, terrorists were individuals who belonged to segregated communities and who felt alienated from the values of the majority culture. In both cases, their isolationism was expressed in their consciousness and daily behavior, and in many cases they perceived the culture at large as a threat to the continued existence of the community. Although many members of the networks that operated in Western countries were second-generation immigrants and therefore may have been expected to assimilate in the host Western culture, a more in-depth study found that they reverted to their traditions and, with the encouragement and assistance of local spiritual leaders, tried to take action against elements perceived as threatening to these traditions.[8] In addition, a structural similarity is discernible. Both the Salafi jihad networks and the Jewish networks consisted of nonhierarchical primary social networks that existed well before they became involved in violent activities. The members who were subjected to the extremist teachings of the communities' spiritual leaders underwent radicalization, a process accelerated by means of an intragroup social dynamic (i.e., intensive and frequent interaction between group members).[9]

However, similarities are not limited to elements stressed by the theoretical framework presented in this book. At this stage it therefore seems appropriate to broaden the comparison between Jewish terrorism networks and other types of religious terrorist groups throughout the world. Before embarking on such a comparison, we should emphasize that more than seventy religious groups worldwide are involved in violent struggles, and this limits the quality of an inductive generalization. Therefore, we have decided to focus on several key conflicts that have generated the majority of contemporary religious terrorism (i.e., the Middle East, the Salafi jihad networks, Islamic groups operating in Southeast Asia, and Christian fundamentalist groups in the United States).

The ideological underpinnings of Jewish terrorism seem to resemble many of the ideological principles promoted by religious groups operating in other parts of the world, although several distinctions do exist. As for the similarities, in both cases the religious component of the terrorist ideology is not an exclusive element. As shown in this book, vigilantism and a struggle for political resources were also factors that motivated Jewish terrorists. Similarly, in other fundamentalist groups worldwide, secular elements are involved, mostly territorial and nationalistic. For example, although adhering to a fundamentalist Muslim ideology and supported by the Iranian regime, Hezbollah in Lebanon also incorporates nationalistic ideological elements. These were manifested in Hezbollah's struggle to drive foreign forces out of Lebanon, most notably the Israel Defense Forces but also French and American troops at the beginning of the 1980s. In its struggle against these foreign forces, Hezbollah used a mixed rhetoric of nationalist and religious elements.[10] Another example is the struggle of Muslim religious terrorist groups in Kashmir in the mid-1980s, which was a direct outcome of a territorial conflict and not just religion-based. Then there is the case of the Sikhs in India, whose campaign of violence in the mid-1980s included religious considerations as well political ones, such as the aspiration to an autonomous Sikh state.[11] The Moro Islamic Liberation Front, operating in the southern Philippines, has also assumed such a pattern by combining nationalistic and radical Islamic agendas,[12] and the Hamas and Palestinian Islamic Jihad groups in the West Bank merged the call for jihad with Palestinian nationalism as well. Finally, many scholars argue that the attempt to assert that the exclusive aims of Al-Qaeda and its various derivatives throughout the world are solely religious is somewhat forced, as some of its earlier operations were aimed at driving out the Western presence from the Arabian Peninsula.[13]

On the same note, the impression is that in recent years, and especially with the onset of the new millennium, religious groups are more likely to emphasize their religious motives while minimizing the importance of secular political ones. In the Jewish case, this tendency is apparent in the comparison of the older Jewish Underground and Kahane networks, which did not hesitate to emphasize secular vigilant and political motives along with their religious agenda, with the more recent Bat Ayin group, in which the religious factor was much more prominent. From a more global perspective, it seems that this same process is taking place. This is evident as it becomes increasingly difficult to make out secular–rational motives behind acts such as the March 1995 Aum Shinrikyo nerve gas attack in a Tokyo subway[14] or the attack against the Murrah Federal Building in Oklahoma City a month later, both of which were perpetrated by religious or cultish local networks. The groups that carried out the Tokyo nerve gas attack and the Murrah Building explosion contrast with the more veteran religious groups, such as Hezbollah, the Kashmir terrorist groups, Hamas, and Palestinian Islamic Jihad of the 1980s and early 1990s; the strategy of all the latter was also driven by secular realpolitik considerations.

Another important ideological parallel is that in both Jewish and non-Jewish religious terrorism, many perpetrators are driven by some form of grand vision of a new order, believing that their violent act will be the catalyst for this epic transformation. Juergensmeyer, who studied many manifestations of religious terrorism, calls this a "symbolic" objective.[15] For the Jewish networks, this great change is the redemption of the people of Israel, the construction of the Third Temple, and the establishment of a Halakhic state, whereas for the Salafi jihad groups, it is the creation of a universal Muslim entity. With respect to Aum Shinrikyo, the group's activist goal was to provoke a world-scale apocalypse that would ultimately lead to the creation of a new world order. In all cases, the terrorists see themselves as involved in some type of cosmic war,[16] and the causal links between their violent acts and the long-term goals of the groups are not always clear. Even among fundamentalist Christians, whose struggle is perceived by many as aimed at gaining specific political goals such as the abolishment of abortion, we can detect the existence of a long-term grand vision and orientation toward a supreme cosmic struggle. This is evident, for example, in the ideological manifest of the Aryan Nations, a principal white supremacist group: "We believe there is a battle fought to this day between the Children of Darkness (today known as Jews) and the Children of Light."[17] It is also present among some Christian fundamentalist leaders in the United States who want to engage in a religious revolution that would establish biblical law as the basis for social legislation.[18]

Moreover, both Jewish and non-Jewish religious terrorists see their foremost responsibility in the adherence to God's will, not to secular legal norms and values. They perceive their violent act as a type of divine duty that is executed in response to a theological imperative.[19] In addition, religion-motivated terrorists often are willing to sacrifice their own resources not only to advance their long-term goals (this applies also to secular terrorism) but also because they believe in some sort of reward or compensation in the afterlife.[20] This factor is often an important tool and incentive in the recruitment of individuals to these groups.

In most instances, the justification of violence is based on a radical interpretation of religious and holy writings. In these texts, substantiation is putatively found for the elimination of those who endanger the adherents' way of life and the realization of their religious long-term goals or grand vision. In the case of radical Jews, the obstacle is the Palestinians, whose striving for national liberation jeopardizes the redemption and creation of the Holy Kingdom of Israel. In the case of Hamas and Palestinian Islamic Jihad, Jews living in Palestine are the ones who preclude the creation of an Islamic political entity throughout the Middle East. For the Al-Qaeda networks, the main danger to their grand vision is Western democratic culture, which they argue wants to abolish the worldwide Islamic community.[21] Finally, in the case of Aum Shinrikyo, they claimed that the Japanese government conspired with the United States to destroy religious movements all over the world.[22]

Another important similarity between most religious violent groups all over the world is their common dismissal of any type of reconciliation or process that might lead to a long-term conclusion of the status quo (in contrast to an interim ceasefire, for example).[23] For example, in the last two decades Jewish terrorism has aimed mainly at sabotaging any kind of reconciliation with the Palestinians because it would demand a serious compromise in their theological worldview. On the other side, Palestinian religious groups also intensified their violence after the Oslo Accords were signed between the Palestine Liberation Organization and Israel because they were unwilling to abandon their goals of creating a Muslim Palestinian state as part of the greater Muslim entity in the Middle East. The rejection of conciliation is a dominant feature also in religious terrorism in other parts of the world, as illustrated by a quote from the ideological manifest of the Armed Islamic Group (GIA, an Islamic terrorist group operating in Algeria): "No dialogue, no ceasefire, no reconciliation with the apostate regime."[24] Even in circumstances where groups were willing to negotiate with governments, their ability to abandon their long-term aims is questionable. This is demonstrated in the Philippines, where, even after more than a decade of negotiations (starting in the mid-1990s), a durable peace has yet to be attained between the Moro Islamic Liberation Front and the Philippine government.[25]

Although clear ideological similarities can be found between Jewish terrorist groups and other religious terrorist groups all over the globe, in operational terms there are several notable differences. Many scholars argue that, in comparison to other types of terrorism, religious terrorism tends to be more unrestrained in its methods and shows more inclination to inflict mass casualties.[26] Indeed, it seems that the Muslim type of religious terrorism accords with this contention. Suicide bombings and mass casualty attacks have become the main operational symbol and distinguishing element of religious Islamic terrorism,[27] with a preference for weapons of mass destruction, if available. This was epitomized in the declaration made by Osama bin Laden in 1998: "Acquiring weapons for the defense of Muslims is a religious duty. If I have indeed acquired these weapons [of mass destruction], then I thank God."[28] On the other hand, Jewish terrorism does not conform to this pattern; its objectives are more modest than those of its Muslim counterparts. This is true in regard to its tactics, not only its disinclination to perpetrate mass casualties. The only aggression committed by Jewish terrorists that could fall into the category of a mass casualty attack was the massacre committed by Baruch Goldstein in February 1994, in which twenty-nine people were killed. Moreover, suicide tactics, which have become increasingly popular among religious groups all over the world, are almost entirely absent from the arsenal of Jewish terrorism.

What are the reasons for these differences? Although operational capabilities cannot serve as a compelling enough explanation, a partial account can be found in the fact that Jewish terrorism emerged from an ethnic group that is dominant in the territory where it is operative, and its community did not suffer from prolonged repression, which can often lead to feelings of hopelessness and a collective fear of elimination. This latter predicament is indeed prominent among at least some of the populations that produced fundamentalist groups that initiated suicide bombings and mass casualty attacks. This may also explain why Christian religious terrorists in the United States have never needed to use such radical and drastic tactics as suicide attacks. Another explanation is that whereas most religious terrorists, as noted by Hoffman,[29] do not feel constrained from engaging in any degree of violence because they act mostly in the name of themselves and do not aim to influence their public, Jewish terrorists see themselves as a kind of vanguard group that eventually will be followed by the people of Israel. For fear of alienating themselves from the people of Israel, they cannot allow themselves to perpetrate violent actions that are too radical.

At any rate, in the wake of the attempts of the Bat Ayin group in the early 2000s to execute a mass casualty attack in an Arab schoolyard, we should keep an ear to the ground in order to detect whether some sort of operational radicalization is in progress among Jewish terrorists. In a similar vein, the future will also tell whether the attack on the Murrah Federal Building in Oklahoma City, which killed 168 people and was linked to the Christian Identity movement,[30] indicates a change in the operational features of Christian terrorism or will remain a singular and uncharacteristic attempt by Christian militants to perpetrate a mass casualty attack.

Similarities in the operational features of Jewish terrorism and other types of religious terrorist groups can be found in their methods of recruitment and selection of targets. In regard to the latter, both Jewish and non-Jewish religious terrorists are more likely to attack members of other religions; however, they do not restrict themselves solely to these targets. In some situations, religious terrorists operate against the moderate factions of their own societies. In the case of Jewish terrorism, this was demonstrated by the Yigal Amir network, which assassinated Prime Minister Rabin, and some of the Kahane groups, which preferred to attack figures from the left wing of the Israeli political system. In other types of religious terrorism, one can also observe a tendency to attack the liberal and more secular groups of society. In the United States, violent fundamentalist groups have directed attacks against "liberal" institutions, and in the Arab world many religious terrorist groups, such as the Muslim Brotherhood movement in Egypt and the Groupe Islamique Armé in Algeria, have mounted campaigns of terrorism against their own secular governments.[31] This tendency emphasizes how religious terrorism is not solely the result of a competition between religions and cultures but is also strongly connected to the internal struggle of almost every religion between a moderate, liberal, Western-oriented worldview and that of the more extreme religious factions.

As we have demonstrated throughout this book, recruitment among networks of Jewish terrorists took place within the hubs' closer environment, generally in religious and cultural institutions such as synagogues, yeshivas, and other religious forums. In many cases, recruits were friends and family members. The same pattern can be found in the conscription carried out by many Islamic groups, which adopted a network organizational structure in the last decade. One example is the Hamas and Palestinian Islamic Jihad networks after the Al-Aqsa Intifada; recruiters were based mainly in mosques and welfare institutions.[32] In a similar way, most members of the suicide bomber networks operating in Europe were also recruited in mosques or Islamic learning forums by the friend-brings-a-friend method. However, it should be noted that although this type of recruitment already appeared in Jewish networks in the 1950s, it began to characterize the Palestinian arena and networks of Salafi jihad only after they adopted the network organizational structure in the last decade. We would like to conclude our comparison by noting that religious Muslim and Jewish networks have different operational geographic ranges. Whereas Jewish terrorism networks in Israel generally operate locally, as demonstrated most prominently by the Kahane and Bat Ayin networks, which carried out attacks in neighboring areas, it is hard to detect a consistent pattern among other fundamentalist groups worldwide. Assuredly, some of them are local operators, such as the Hamas networks in the West Bank or some of the Salafi jihad groups, such as the one that carried out the attacks in London in July 2005. However, at the same time, many of the Salafi jihad networks operate internationally and do not confine themselves to one country. The most prominent example is the 9/11 network, which included fanatic Muslim activists from all over Europe. Updated studies on Iraqi insurgents also reveal that Islamic networks in this region consist of volunteers from all over the Muslim world, much like the Taliban in the mid-1980s.

CONCLUDING REMARKS: LOOKING AHEAD

One clear fact uncovered by research on Jewish terrorism in the State of Israel is that the use of terrorism in most cases was not the product of a calculated process involving considerations of cost and benefit. In fact, the opposite was true. Instances of Jewish terrorism were marked by despair, feelings of personal and communal crisis, hatred, a desire to take revenge, and above all a sense of religious vocation. This raises the following question, which at this stage appears altogether hypothetical: If the State of Israel decided to secure itself with defendable borders, and numerous settlements were therefore to be evacuated, would this ultimately bring an end to the era of Jewish terrorism? Our fear is that if the territorial conflict should indeed be resolved, this will herald a new era of terrorism. As mentioned earlier, the second common thread connecting many of the Jewish terrorism groups was the desire to remove the mosques from the Temple Mount. We should not disregard the fact that the last decade has been marked by a rise in interfaith tension.

It is true that radical Islamists to a certain extent justify their terrorism with their aspiration to help the Palestinian nation realize its nationalist goals and by claiming they are responding to the ongoing harm to Palestinians. However, even a movement such as Fatah, all the more so Hamas, Islamic Jihad, Hezbollah, and Al-Qaeda, openly declare that they will not rest until the complete liberation of the Al-Aqsa Mosque is achieved.[33] On the other hand, although in much smaller numbers, there are Jews who regard the very presence of the mosques as an obstacle to the redemption of the people of Israel. A larger number hold a Kahanist worldview, according to which—irrespective of the conflict with the Palestinians—the Jewish state should cast out the Arab minority from within. Some of them are willing to try to implement this goal in a violent way or by means designed to bring about a violent escalation in the relations between Jews and Arabs.[34]

After long years of studying Jewish terrorism in Israel, and in light of our journey to many of its focal points, we must conclude in a pessimistic tone. Despite the fact that in recent decades an almost absolute correspondence is evident between Jewish terrorism and the territorial conflict with the Palestinians, this is not a guarantee that this dependency will go on forever. The potential for Jewish terrorism will remain even if the Israeli–Palestinian conflict finds some sort of resolution. It is possible to assume that, as in the past, Jewish terrorism will continue to be a real thorn in the side for the State of Israel; however, it won't prove to be a strategic challenge. This conclusion should nevertheless be taken with a grain of salt. Harm—and it need not be severe—to the mosques on the Temple Mount by redemption seekers could open the doors to hell.

GLOSSARY

AVRAHAM AVINU NEIGHBORHOOD   A part of the Jewish settlement in the city of Hebron. The neighborhood was established as early as the sixteenth century, and in it the synagogue Avraham Avinu was built, hence the name of the neighborhood. The area was destroyed in 1919, when the Jews left Hebron. It was reestablished in 1979 and consists today of a number of buildings, including the reconstructed synagogue.

CAVE OF THE PATRIARCHS   Jewish tradition claims that the ancient fathers of the Jewish people, Abraham, Isaac, and Jacob, and the matriarchs, Sarah, Rebecca, and Leah, are buried in the cave. The place is holy for the Jews, but also for the Muslims, because Abraham is considered their ancestral father. The building that is built on the cave is situated on the east side of Hebron.

GUSH EMUNIM *(Bloc of Faithful)*   A social–religious–national movement, which stands for the renewal of Jewish settlement in the West Bank. It was established on February 25, 1974, and its aim was to settle all Eretz Israel (Land of Israel). In the early 1980s, it stopped existing as a formal entity. The movement is politically related to the national religious party and consists of people mainly from the religious Zionist population. The movement's spiritual infrastructure comes from the ideas of rabbis Avraham Kook and Zvi Yehuda Kook.

HAGANAH   The Haganah was the largest and central military Jewish organization at the time of the British Mandate. It was established in 1920 by the Achdut Haavoda party as a nationwide organization, which was supposed to provide protection to the Jewish population in the country. Upon the establishment of the State of Israel, the Haganah served as the infrastructure on which the Israel Defense Forces was built.

HALACHA   This encompasses all the judgments in the Jewish tradition that address all aspects of life. It includes laws that refer to a person's life and behavior toward God. The Halacha originated in the commandments and prohibitions that are in the Torah. The Halacha also includes the entire corpus of rules and laws that rabbis have added throughout the years.

ISRAEL-EGYPT PEACE TREATY *(Camp David Accords)*   The peace treaty between Israel and Egypt, which was signed in Washington on March 26, 1979, by Anwar Sadat, Menachem Begin, and Jimmy Carter. The treaty was the last stage in the negotiations for peace between Israel and Egypt that had been initiated at Camp David. Its main points were the mutual recognition of Israel and Egypt and the Israeli withdrawal from the Sinai Peninsula. The treaty was confirmed by the Knesset on March 22, 1979, with vote of 95–18.

KIDUSH HASHEM *(Martyrdom)*   The readiness of every Jew to sacrifice his or her life for the sake of belief. The origin of this principle is found in the book of Daniel (3:16), in which Mishael, Azaria, and Hanania informed King Nebuchadnezzar that they were ready to die rather than ignore the commandments of the Torah.

KOOK, ZVI YEHUDA HACOHEN *(April 23, 1891–March 9, 1982)*   Spiritual leader, rabbi, and head of the Mercaz Harav Yeshiva. He was considered one of the leaders of the religious Zionist stream and the spiritual leader of Gush Emunim. He was the son of Rabbi Avraham Hacohen Kook and edited his father's writings. He regarded the State of Israel as an accomplishment of the vision of the prophets.

MOVEMENT TO HALT THE RETREAT IN SINAI *(Movement for Halting the Withdrawal from Sinai)*   This was an extraparliamentary movement, which was established in order to act against the Israeli withdrawal from the Sinai Peninsula. The head of the movement was Uri Elitzur, and one of its activities was to encourage citizens to sign petitions against the withdrawal. Another activity was transferring families from Israel into Sinai, aiming to prevent the evacuation by physical presence.

OSLO ACCORDS I   The first treaty between Israel and the Palestine Liberation Organization (PLO). The accords stipulated that Israel would recognize the PLO as the representative of the Palestinians, whereas the PLO was committed to recognize Israel's right to exist and to cease its terrorist activity. The accords also stated that Israel would withdraw from the Palestinian territories in the West Bank and Gaza Strip and that a Palestinian state would be established.

OSLO ACCORDS II   A peace treaty between Israel and the Palestinians and a sequel to the Oslo I Accords, also known as the Interim Agreement in the West Bank and the Gaza Strip. The accords were signed in Washington, D.C., on September 28, 1995, and stated that Israel would enable Palestinian self-rule in Palestinian towns in the West Bank and Gaza Strip and rule over about 450 villages. It also agreed on a division of three areas of control and specified who was responsible for each one of them.

PALMACH   The regular military force of the Haganah in Palestine between 1941 and 1948. The Palmach was established on May 15, 1941, in a concentrated decision of the British forces and the leadership of the Jewish population, aiming to establish a military body that would protect the population in case the Germans invaded the country. Although the Palmach was subordinated to the Haganah, politically it was close to the leftist party, Mapam. Upon establishment of the State of Israel, the Palmach bore the main task of fighting until the Israel Defense Forces became organized.

PRIEST *(Cohen)*   According to Judaic history, the Priests are the descendants of Aharon the Priest, Moses's brother, who belonged to the tribe of Levy. The Priests have a special status in Jewish tradition, and their principal mission was to work in the Temple.

REVISIONIST MOVEMENT   One of the most central streams of the Zionist movement. It was established as a reexamination or revision of the modes of operation of the Zionist movement in 1923 by Zeev Jabotinsky, who was its leader and ideologist, after he left the established Zionist movement. Its ideological platform included a twofold struggle, both civil and armed, aimed at bringing about the establishment of the Jewish state in Eretz Israel on both banks of the Jordan River.

SECOND TEMPLE   The most holy site for the Jewish people, which served as the religious–spiritual center of the nation and the place of worship of God. The Temple was headed by the Great Priest. The Second Temple was built by the Jews who returned from the Babylonian Diaspora in 520 B.C.E. It was built on the site of the First Temple, on Moriah Mountain in Jerusalem, where offerings and sacrifices took place through the ages. The Temple existed for about 585 years, until it was destroyed by the Romans in 70 C.E., during the Great Jewish Revolt.

TEMPLE MOUNT Mount Moriah, in Jerusalem. On its summit are the Dome of the Rock and the Al-Aqsa Mosque, which have been there since the seventh century. At one time, the First and Second Temples stood on the mountain, but now only the external wall remains, known as the Wailing Wall or Western Wall. The Temple Mount is considered to be the most holy place in the Jewish religion and the third most holy site in Islam.

YESHIVAT HESDER These are yeshivas that integrate studies of the Torah with an abbreviated military service. Students enter them after graduating from a high school yeshiva, or a religious high school. The hesder yeshivas are a part of religious Zionism and integration into religious ideology. This entails studying the Torah and the will to integrate into Israeli society, including a commitment to serve in the army. The length of the course is five years, out of which the student serves sixteen months in the army and the rest of the time studies at the yeshiva.

YISHUV *(The Pre-State Jewish Community)* The name of Jewish society in Eretz Israel, beginning in the 1880s. At that time, there were about 25,000 inhabitants; when the State was established in 1948, there were about 700,000 Jews living in Israel.

CHRONOLOGY OF ATTACKS AND EVENTS RELATED
TO JEWISH TERRORISM

DATE OF EVENT	DESCRIPTION OF EVENT
9 17 **48**	Count Bernadotte, United Nations mediator between Israel and the Arab states, was murdered as he was riding in a convoy near Armon Hanatziv in Jerusalem. The murder was carried out by the Lehi organization.
12 12 **49**	An attempt was made on the life of Ben Gurion and other members of the government. Avraham Tsfati, a disturbed twenty-three-year-old man, gained entry into the Knesset at a time when its discussions were being conducted at the Kessem movie theater in Tel Aviv. He pulled out his weapon and aimed it at the government table but was stopped at the last minute by Knesset pages.
2 21 **50**	An attempt to place a bomb in the Knesset general assembly chambers.
3 15 **50**	The Kingdom of Israel Underground attempted to hide explosive material in the offices of the Ministry of Education in Jerusalem.
1 18 **51**	In neighborhoods of northern Jerusalem, members of Brith Hakanaim burned private cars whose owners drove on the Sabbath. They also left sacks dipped in gasoline at the Egged Bus Company Garage in Jerusalem.
5 15 **51**	Members of Brith Hakanaim attempted to place a bomb in the Knesset chambers and simultaneously in the Military Induction Center in Jerusalem.
3 28 **52**	Members of the Kingdom of Israel Underground expressing their opposition to the Reparations Agreement sent a booby-trapped parcel to West German Chancellor Adenauer.
4 1 **52**	An attempt to assassinate Prof. Ernest Biham (head of the West German negotiating team to the reparations discussions) by sending a booby-trapped envelope.
6 21 **52**	Secular people tried to assassinate the religious minister of transportation, David Zvi Pinkas, by leaving an explosive near the door of his home in Jerusalem in order to prevent a

coerced halt in public transportation on the Sabbath. There was great property damage, but no one was hurt.

6 24 **52** The Kingdom of Israel attempted to assassinate West German Chancellor Adenauer by sending a booby-trapped parcel, in protest against the Reparations Agreement.

10 5 **52** Dov Shilansky, who belonged to the Herut party, tried to place an explosive device in the offices of the Foreign Ministry in Tel Aviv in protest against the Reparations Agreement.

11 8 **52** Three members of the Kingdom of Israel planted a bomb inside a pail during the evening next to the Czech Embassy in Tal Aviv in protest against Czech government persecution of the Czech Jewish elite.

12 4 **52** Six bombs were discovered near Kfar Shiloakh. Only three exploded. There are no other details about this event. It is thought that the attack was planned by extremist Jews.

12 5 **52** A grenade was tossed at the Czech Consulate in Tel Aviv. Three suspects were arrested in connection with the attack. The Kingdom of Israel claimed responsibility.

2 9 **53** Three people were injured in a blast at the Soviet Legation building in Tel Aviv. The attack was carried out by a small group belonging to the Kingdom of Israel.

4 16 **53** A member of the Kingdom of Israel Underground attacked noted violinist Jascha Heifetz in reaction to his desire to play a work written by German composer Richard Strauss. Heifetz was lightly wounded and left the country.

5 26 **53** Two yeshiva students were arrested under suspicious circumstances. They were found to be carrying explosives. It became clear that they had been planning to do damage to one of the buildings of the Ministry of Education in Jerusalem. Later, the two boys were found to be in the religious wing of the Kingdom of Israel.

6 8 **53** The government announced the existence of the Tzrifin Underground.

7 1 **53** An attempt to set the Czech Consul's car on fire using gasoline took place in Tel Aviv. For some unknown reason the fire was put out with no significant damage to the car. This protest against the treatment of the Jewish elite in the Communist bloc was carried out by Yishayahu Sharabi, a member of the Kingdom of Israel.

9 6 **53** A member of the Kingdom of Israel Underground was caught trying to plant a bomb in the Haifa Port where German boats connected to the Reparations Agreement were going to dock.

3 2 **57**	Members of the former Lehi attacked Israel Kastner, a Mapai sympathizer who was suspected by the Israeli right wing of having aided the Nazis during World War II.
10 29 **57**	Moshe Duek threw a grenade into the Knesset general assembly. Four people were lightly wounded.
8 **72**	It was revealed that Meir Kahane and his colleagues were planning a "bargaining attack" on the Libyan Embassy in Rome.
4 4 **78**	Yisrael Lederman, a reserve soldier, opened fire on Palestinian workers walking near the square of the Western Wall. He was taking revenge for the murder of another reserve soldier, Avraham Deutsch, by Palestinians the day before.
6 2 **80**	An attack on Palestinian mayors on the West Bank by the Jewish Underground. Three people were seriously wounded, two were moderately wounded, and five were lightly wounded.
4 10 **82**	Alan Goodman, a mentally disturbed soldier with a background of extreme right-wing activity, living in Beit Hakerem in Jerusalem, entered the Temple Mount while shooting in every direction with his own weapon. Only after he had entered the Dome of the Rock mosque was he overpowered, and finally the police arrived. In the attack, two people were killed, four were seriously wounded, and seven were lightly wounded.
4 18 **82**	A group of Kach activists were holed up in a bunker in Yamit and threatened to blow themselves up and commit mass suicide if the plan to evacuate the Sinai Peninsula after the Camp David Accords was carried out.
12 1 **82**	Asher Rabo, a resident of Tel Aviv and of the West Bank settlement Elon-Moreh, was arrested while on a shooting spree in Shechem. He was a suspect in four murder cases.
2 11 **83**	Yonah Avrushmi threw a grenade at participants in a demonstration organized by the left-wing Peace Now movement. A peace activist, Emil Greenzweig, was killed and nine others were wounded.
2 22 **83**	Yisrael Fuchs, a twenty-one-year-old Kach activist driving along the Hebron Yatta road with his friends, fired his Kalachnikov rifle and killed a resident of the village of Yatta who was passing his car. He was sentenced to thirty-nine months in prison.
7 8 **83**	As a reaction to the murder of settler Aharon Gross by Palestinians, four shops were set on fire in the Hebron market. The attack was carried out by students at the Shave Zion Yeshiva in Kiryat Arba. The settlers came into the market in a show

of strength and behaved violently toward the local Palestinians, residents of Hebron. No one was wounded, but there was great property damage.

7 26 **83** Three members of the Jewish Underground carried out a shooting attack at the Islamic College in Hebron. Three students were killed and another thirty-three injured.

10 30 **83** Members of the Jewish Underground placed explosive devices in mosques in Hebron.

11 21 **83** Kach activists threw a Molotov cocktail at the building housing the *Al-Fajer* newspaper in East Jerusalem. There were no injuries.

12 9 **83** Members of TNT left an explosive device at the entrance to the Franciscan Monastery on Mount Zion, at the entrance to the Greek Orthodox Seminary on Mount Zion, at the entrance gate to the Church of the Dormition, and at the entrance to the mosque in Beit Safafa.

12 11 **83** A grenade exploded in Jerusalem with no injuries. Members of TNT carried out the attack.

12 11 **83** Members of TNT torched cars belonging to Arabs in Jerusalem.

12 12 **83** Members of TNT left four booby-trapped grenades at the entrances to houses in Kfar Husan, near Bethlehem. Two of the grenades blew up. There were no injuries.

12 20 **83** The Ein Kerem gang left booby-trapped grenades at the entrances to the mosque and Greek Orthodox Church in the village of Azaria. A Muslim sheik and a nun were lightly injured.

1 1 **84** Members of the Jewish Underground left booby-trapped explosives in mosques in Hebron. In the Ali Bekha mosque, the muezzin was lightly injured in the blast.

1 6 **84** An anonymous person set fire to the church on Nevi'im Street in Jerusalem. Two days later, the organization, Yad L'akhim ("A Hand to Brothers") took responsibility for the event. There were no injuries.

1 15 **84** The Ein Kerem group took responsibility for an exploding grenade placed at the door of the apartment of a nun from the monastery at Ein Kerem.

1 26 **84** An attempted mass attack on the Temple Mount by the Lifta Gang was thwarted.

3 5 **84** Members of TNT carried out a shooting attack from an ambush against an Arab bus traveling between the Palestinian town of Mizra'at A-Sharkia to Ramallah. Three people were lightly wounded.

3 5 **84**   A hand grenade exploded near the Hospice Hospital in East Jerusalem. TNT members took responsibility. No one was wounded.

3 27 **84**   Indictments were served for attempts to harm Arabs by throwing a Molotov cocktail in the Shuafat neighborhood of Jerusalem and setting fire to cars in the Alkhatef neighborhood. The prosecution claimed that these acts were to avenge Palestinian attacks on Jews. The suspects were five residents of Beit El. Six people from the Arab village Mizra'at A-Sharkia were lightly wounded in these attacks.

4 29 **84**   Members of the Jewish Underground were caught trying to set explosive devices in five Arab buses from East Jerusalem.

10 22 **84**   A soldier, David Ben Shimol, planted a grenade in a café in the Old City of Jerusalem. A young person sitting in the café hurried to throw the grenade into a trash pail, preventing many deaths. In the explosion, ten people were wounded.

10 29 **84**   David Ben Shimol fired an anti-tank missile at an Arab bus in Jerusalem that was bound for Hebron. In the attack, a Palestinian student, Jamal Ismail Al-Matar, was killed and eight others were seriously wounded. One person was moderately wounded, and one person was lightly wounded.

12 14 **84**   Two Israelis, Eli Vanunu and Nir Efroni, killed an Arab who had stopped at a gas station near Zikhron Yaacov to fill up his car. After they had been caught they claimed that the attack had been in revenge for the murder of Jews in Palestinian terrorist attacks.

5 19 **85**   Near Maaleh Adumim, three suspects—a soldier, an officer, and a student—were arrested for the murder of an Arab taxi driver, Hamis Tutanji, to avenge the murder of a Jewish taxi driver, David Caspi.

7 7 **85**   A spray grenade was found at the entrance to the Center of the Jehovah's Witnesses, at 23 Sheffer Street in Tel Aviv. Before that, a burning tire had been tossed at the building. Yad L'akhim claimed responsibility.

7 17 **85**   An explosive device blew up near the Zim building in Haifa, at a place where Arab workers from the territories gathered. Four suspects were arrested and investigated but were later released.

10 3 **85**   A settler residing in Alon-Moreh was convicted of killing a young girl in Shechem.

1 10 **86**   In revenge for the murder of a Jewish taxi driver, an unknown group planted explosive devices on Jacob Street in Rehovoth,

known as an area where Palestinians lived. Four workers from Khan Younis were moderately wounded.

5 30 **86**   The door of an apartment belonging to an Arab from Jerusalem, on Bar-Kokhba Street in the Givah Hatzorfati (French Hill) neighborhood, was set on fire for nationalist reasons.

7 1 **86**   Four settlers residing in the Jewish sector in Hebron, who were professional guards in the "Association of Guards," were accused of severe attacks and threats. The attacks took place in the center of Hebron, and as a result, one Palestinian was lightly wounded.

10 20 **86**   Khalil Belusha, a cleaning worker from the refugee camp Jabalya in the Gaza Strip, was seriously injured after an anonymous Jewish person stabbed him on the street in Ashdod.

10 21 **86**   Three young residents of Bat-Yam, disguised as police officers, entered a house on Hagiborim Street where Arab cleaning workers were living. They violently attacked the workers. The workers, residents of the Gaza Strip, were temporarily living in Israel. Two were killed as a result of the attack.

11 17 **86**   Four Yeshiva students in Jerusalem were arrested on suspicion of attempting to damage a gas station owned by Arabs. Arabs were beaten, cars were damaged, and Molotov cocktails were thrown. The attack caused property damage, and one Arab was lightly wounded.

11 20 **86**   A fire was set in the apartment of an Arab Israeli living on Maaleh Khaltzia in the Old City of Jerusalem, near the Yeshiva Shuvu Banim. Four yeshiva students, active in Kach, were arrested. Great property damage was caused, and the Arab owner was lightly wounded.

11 24 **86**   During a memorial meeting for yeshiva student Eliyahu Amari, who was murdered by Palestinians, three settlers from an unknown settlement went to Maaleh Khaldia Street in Jerusalem and attacked two Israeli Arabs, who were lightly injured.

12 14 **86**   A suspect, resident of the Sharon, was investigated for shooting at the car of a resident of Kalkilya on the Emanuel–Kalkilya road. The Palestinian was not hurt in the shooting.

12 18 **86**   Two booby-trapped grenades were found near Palestinian homes close to the Dung Gate in Jerusalem.

2 25 **87**   Settler passengers in a bus that had been stoned, together with Kach activists, members of the Committee for Security on the Roads, entered the city of Khalkhul and violently attacked the inhabitants of the city. Great property damage was caused.

6 10 **87**   Four settlers, inhabitants of Kiryat Arba, entered Beit Jalla and tried to stab an Arab resident of Deheishe, a refugee camp near Bethlehem, who was passing by. The Palestinian was lightly wounded.

9 13 **87**   Two young Israelis attacked a Negev Bedouin from the Alaz tribe on nationalist grounds. The Bedouin was moderately injured.

1 11 **88**   Two settlers from the Benjamin area, traveling by car near the village of Beitin, fired on Palestinians who threw stones at them. One of the settlers was Pinchas Wallerstein, the head of the Benjamin Regional Council, and the second was a guard who was traveling with him. As a result, one young Arab was killed, and the second was moderately wounded.

2 7 **88**   An Arab worker, a cousin of Farouk Kaddoumi, spokesman for foreign affairs of the Palestine Liberation Organization, was shot to death by passengers in an Israeli car when they arrived at a roadblock of stones near the Palestinian village of Kaddum. The settlers were arrested, and a police investigation was opened.

2 22 **88**   A resident of the settlement of Hermesh entered the area of the Palestinian village Bik'a Al-Sharkiya and fired at a young Arab girl, a resident of the village, who died of her wounds. The settler was arrested, and a police investigation was opened.

2 26 **88**   Four settlers from Khomesh arrived in the area of the Palestinian village of Burka and attacked residents of the village. The settlers threw a grenade into the village. There was great damage to property, but no one was hurt.

3 16 **88**   About thirty settlers from Mount Grizim arrived in the vicinity of Jenin. The settlers violently attacked local residents and threw stones. As a result of the attack, two local Palestinians were killed.

4 6 **88**   A settler arrived in the vicinity of the Palestinian village of Beita and opened fire. As a result, two Palestinian residents of the village were killed.

5 6 **88**   A settler, a resident of Shiloh, entered the Palestinian village of Turmus and fired at shepherds who were guarding their sheep at the edge of the village. The Palestinians were hit; one died, and the second was moderately wounded.

6 3 **88**   Settlers from an unknown settlement reached the Palestinian village of Shiukh, near Hebron. In a show of strength, they destroyed property. In reaction, the Palestinians protested, and the settlers opened fire. A Palestinian villager was killed.

8 19 **88**   A young Israeli man from the town of Or Yehuda set fire to a shack in which Palestinian workers from Gaza were staying. The Palestinians were killed in the attack.

3 23 **89**   Settlers from Migdalim and Tapuakh shot a young Palestinian boy, a pupil from the town of Itzrin, near his village. The attack was in reaction to a Molotov cocktail attack on an Israeli bus in Samaria. The young Palestinian was killed. The police arrested the settlers and opened an investigation.

4 1 **89**   A settler shot a Palestinian from the village of Al-Azaria to death near his village.

4 11 **89**   An anonymous person wearing an Israeli army uniform opened fire near the Jaffa Gate of the Old City of Jerusalem. He killed an Arab resident and wounded three workers from East Jerusalem. The Sicarii organization claimed responsibility.

4 13 **89**   A settler killed a Palestinian and seriously wounded his friend on the Nahalin–Husan road, while they were on their way to the funeral of those who were killed in an attack during which Border Police killed six Palestinians in the Palestinian town of Nahalin.

5 17 **89**   A settler riding in his car on the outskirts of Jenin shot a Palestinian who was passing through the area. The Palestinian, a teacher from the village of Jilkmus, was killed on the spot.

6 21 **89**   About five settlers from the Yeshivat Kever Yosef ("Joseph's Grave") arrived at the village of Kafel Khars and fired at a young Palestinian girl, a student who lived in the village. The girl was killed.

7 30 **89**   A settler from Rafiah Yam shot and killed an Arab worker from Gaza in the area between the Erez checkpoint and Beit Khanun.

8 21 **89**   A settler from Efrat arrived at the Palestinian village of Tekoah just as a Palestinian was building a barricade at the entrance to his village. The settler shot the Palestinian, a young student from the village. The Palestinian was killed on the spot.

12 11 **89**   Israeli citizens shot two Palestinian boys to death in two separate events. A resident of Gaza was shot not far from the gas station in the city, and in Hebron a young man was shot to death and his friend was seriously wounded.

5 15 **90**   A settler whose car was stoned near Kalkilya shot at a Palestinian student who lived in Kalkilya. The Palestinian was killed.

5 20 **90**   Ami Popper, a young Israeli recently released from the army and living in Rishon L'Zion, arrived at the Vradim Junction

near Rishon L'Zion and opened fire on Palestinians, workers from Gaza who were there at the time. Seven Palestinians were killed, three were seriously injured, and eight were lightly injured.

8 6 **90**   Nakhshon Wolf, a resident of Kiryat Arba, opened fire on a twenty-five-year-old Palestinian woman from Hebron while she was driving her car near Kiryat Arba. The woman was killed.

11 7 **90**   About five settlers from the settlement of Tapuakh entered the fields near the Palestinian village Luban A-Sharkia and fired at two farmers from the village. The two Palestinians were killed.

11 26 **90**   A settler from an unknown settlement reached the vicinity of the Palestinian city of al-Bira and shot a Palestinian taxi driver from the city. The Palestinian was killed.

1 13 **91**   A number of settlers reached the vicinity of the settlement Eilon Moreh and encountered an Arab. They beat him with clubs, and the Palestinian was killed.

6 7 **91**   A settler from Susya shot a Palestinian shepherd to death under unclear circumstances.

6 26 **91**   Three settlers from Bnei Naim shot at a Palestinian taxi on the Hebron–Beersheba road. The Palestinian taxi driver, a resident of Daharia, was seriously wounded. The settlers were arrested, and a police investigation was opened to determine the circumstances of the event.

1 26 **92**   About fifty settlers from the Jewish settlement in Hebron who belonged to the Committee for Safety on the Roads reached the neighborhood of Karat A-Sheikh in the city, and in a show of strength against the local Palestinians, they beat them violently. The settlers fired at the Palestinians, and four Palestinians were wounded; two were moderately wounded, and two were lightly wounded.

11 16 **92**   Members of Elnakam Underground, four young members of Kahana Chai ("Kahane Lives"), tossed a grenade into the butchers' market in Jerusalem. As a result, a Palestinian metalworker was killed and five others were lightly wounded. The victims were residents of the A-Ram neighborhood in northern Jerusalem.

1 19 **93**   A settler from Gush Katif shot a young Palestinian from Sejaya in Gaza to death in response to stone throwing. The event took place on the Gaza bypass road.

3 2 **93**   A Jewish truck driver who was stoned by Palestinians shot to death a Palestinian from Ras-al-Amud in East Jerusalem.

3 9 **93**   After the murder of settler Uri Magidish, another settler from Ganei Tal shot an Arab worker to death and wounded another Palestinian seriously. The attack took place on the Rafiah–Khan Younis road.

3 24 **93**   Yoram Shkolnik, a settler from Susya, shot to death a Palestinian who had been tied up. The Palestinian was tied up because he had previously tried to stab another settler while the two had been traveling in the latter's car.

5 31 **93**   A settler from Ma'akeh Adumim, a professional guard, shot at two Palestinian brothers from A-Ram after they threw stones at settlers. The shooting took place at the A-Ram junction in northern Jerusalem. One of the brothers was killed in the shooting, and the other was lightly wounded.

7 26 **93**   Four settlers ignited a house in the Mesharka Fuka neighborhood in Hebron. One local Palestinian was lightly wounded, and there was great property damage.

10 17 **93**   Dozens of settlers from the Jewish settlement in Hebron, Kach activists belonging to Committee for Security on the Roads, attacked Palestinians and stoned Arabs in the Avraham Avinu neighborhood of Hebron and in the center of the city, Gross Square. As a result, ten local Palestinians were lightly wounded.

11 3 **93**   Four settlers shot at the car of a Palestinian worker from Khalkhul–Hebron who was driving on the Hebron–Jerusalem road. The Palestinian was unhurt.

11 7 **93**   After the murder of settler Efraim Iovi, Rabbi Druckman's driver, a number of disturbances broke out among settlers from the Gush Katif and Hebron areas who were members of Kach. About forty to fifty settlers reached Me'arat Hamachpela ("Cave of the Patriarchs"), near Hebron, and tried to lynch a Palestinian worker, but security forces reached the spot and prevented the lynching. No arrests were made. During the disturbances, six Palestinians were stabbed by settlers with knives. The victims came from the neighborhood of Kharat A-Sheikh in Hebron.

11 9 **93**   Hundreds of setters, both men and women, decided to step up their struggle in reaction to what they called the restraint of the Rabin government in everything connected with the settlement policy. The settlers reached the area of greenhouses near Kfar Darom, where they fired on Palestinian inhabitants. Two Palestinians from Jericho were wounded.

11 16 **93**   Dozens of settlers from the Jewish settlement in Hebron and Kiryat Arba arrived at Me'rat Hamachpela ("Cave of the Patriarchs") and attacked Arabs. The settlers beat the Arabs

violently and stoned them. Eleven Palestinians were wounded, one seriously and the others lightly.

12 5 **93**   Dozens of settlers from Kiryat Arba fired at Palestinians in the center of Hebron and wounded residents of the city, one seriously and three lightly. In addition, the settlers stoned a restaurant near the A-Ram junction in northern Jerusalem. There was property damage, but no one was hurt. The settlers were arrested, and the police opened an investigation into the event. Security forces arrived on the scene to calm things down.

12 5 **93**   About ten settlers from Kiryat Arba who had come to pray near Kharsina Hill noticed a Palestinian who was passing by in his car, and they stopped and confronted him. The Palestinian, from East Jerusalem, was shot by the settlers and was killed. The settlers were not arrested, and the police opened an investigation. Security forces arrived on the scene to calm things down.

12 9 **93**   A sixteen-year-old settler, a student living in Shiloh, went to the fields of the village of Turmus-ai and shot a Palestinian villager to death.

12 11 **93**   A settler went to the center of Hebron and began to shoot in every direction. A Palestinian was killed in the fire. The settler did not stop shooting. Military forces came to calm things down.

12 12 **93**   Two Kach activists from Kiryat Arba killed three Bedouins from the village of Tarkomia in revenge for the deaths of settlers. The murder took place on a dirt road leading to Tarkomia as the Bedouins were on their way home from work.

2 27 **94**   Baruch Goldstein, a Kach activist and a doctor living in Kiryat Arba, opened fire in Me'arat Hamechpela ("Cave of the Patriarchs") while Muslims were praying there. Thirty-nine Palestinians were killed, nine were seriously wounded, ninety-two were moderately wounded, and sixty-eight were lightly wounded.

3 22 **94**   Uzi Meshulam and his colleagues (about 110 people) gathered in his home in Yahud and refused to leave until their demand to set up a government commission to investigate the disappearance of Yemenite children was met. They were armed with submachine guns, clubs, and Molotov cocktails. They threatened to open fire on any person who came near the house. During the siege, which lasted for thirty-one hours, there were exchanges of fire between people in the house and the police. A Molotov cocktail was thrown at Police Major General Gabby List, commander of the Central Sector, whose back was wounded.

3 28 **94**   Daniel Morali, a resident of Kiryat Gat, used his handgun to murder a Palestinian truck driver. The killing was a reaction to the murder of Morali's brother, a settler living at Adorah, by a Palestinian.

3 30 **94**   A settler fired from a passing car in the area of Deir A-Sharaf near Khomesh. He hit a Palestinian boy from the Shechem region, who died of his wounds.

4 14 **94**   Cooling engineer Natan Engelsman, a settler living in Shiloh, was driving through the village of Al-Jib in the district of Ramallah. He shot and killed a pregnant Palestinian woman, a resident of the village.

4 28 **94**   An activist working with Uzi Meshulam threw a gas grenade into a party at the old Tel Aviv port. Two girls were wounded.

5 17 **94**   About thirty settlers, residents of Kiryat Arba and students at the Nir Yeshiva in Hebron, threw stones in Policeman's Square, at the center of Hebron. As a result, four Palestinians were seriously wounded and eleven were lightly wounded.

7 1 **94**   A settler shot a Palestinian to death in the Jerusalem forest. The Palestinian, who transported workers for a living, was a resident of the village of Silwan, East Jerusalem.

9 2 **94**   Two brothers, Yehoyada and Eitan Kahalani, were caught after they tried and failed to murder a Palestinian near the Malha Mall in Jerusalem. Later it became clear that they had been under the surveillance of the General Security Services, who had sabotaged their rifle to prevent the murder.

9 11 **94**   Members of the Revenge Underground were arrested after police found enough evidence to connect them to the murder of three Palestinians. According to the charge, the three drove north of Takumia and shot Palestinian residents of the village to death. When they were arrested, they were on their way to carry out another act of terrorism.

9 18 **94**   Meir Koren, a settler from Kiryat Arba, was arrested after he tried to carry out a shooting attack against Palestinians in Jerusalem.

10 30 **94**   Activists allied with Uzi Meshulam attacked Senior Warden Benny Aviram, the security officer of the Nitzan Prison. As he left his home in the morning, the three activists fired three bullets at him from their car, which was parked nearby. He was wounded in his neck, chest, and face. Despite his wounds he succeeded in firing his handgun, and the attackers fled after two of them had been wounded. The two who were caught were Yoav Shevi and Avner Sa'id.

3 1 **95** A Jewish man from Netanya stabbed an East Jerusalem Arab in the back. The event took place at Gagot Galicia in Jerusalem. The Arab was seriously wounded. The Jewish man maintained that the stabbing had been carried out in revenge for Palestinian terrorist attacks.

8 14 **95** A settler from Beit El, a professional guide, shot and killed a Palestinian resident of the Dura Al-Kera village. The event took place on Artis Hill.

11 5 **95** Yitzhak Rabin, prime minister of Israel, was assassinated in Makhei Israel Square in Tel Aviv. The terrorist was Yigal Amir, a law student at Bat Ilan University.

9 17 **96** A young Jew who belonged to Uzi Meshulam's group stabbed an Arab woman from East Jerusalem. The stabbing took place at the Jaffa Gate in the Old City of Jerusalem. The Palestinian woman was lightly wounded.

1 2 **97** Noam Friedman, a soldier from Maaleh Adumim, opened fire using his personal weapon at Gross Square in the center of Hebron. Seven Palestinian workers from the village of Yatta were wounded; one Palestinian was seriously wounded, two were moderately wounded, and four were lightly wounded.

8 4 **97** A Palestinian from the village of Yatta was shot in southern Hebron, near the settlement of Carmel. The Palestinian died of his wounds.

11 30 **97** A Palestinian was stabbed on Shmuel Hanavi Street, at the corner of Shimon Hatzadik in Jerusalem. The Palestinian was lightly wounded. The police believed that the stabbing was carried out by an ultra-Orthodox man later called "the serial stabber."

12 1 **97** An explosive was set off in the neighborhood of Musrara in Jerusalem near the door of an apartment housing three Arab students. The arsonists left a note saying that the explosive was a message to the Arabs that they were not welcome in the neighborhood.

2 17 **98** A Palestinian youth was stabbed on Batei Warsaw Street in the Mea She'arim neighborhood of Jerusalem. The Palestinian was lightly wounded. The police believed that this was another attack by "the serial stabber."

3 10 **98** A Palestinian youth was stabbed on Reishit Khokhma Street in Jerusalem. The Palestinian was moderately wounded. The police believed that this was another attack by "the serial stabber."

3 12 **98** An Arab was stabbed and moderately wounded in the Mea She'arim neighborhood of Jerusalem. The Palestinian was

lightly wounded. The police believed that this was an attack by "the serial stabber."

4 29 **98** An Arab tourist from Jordan was stabbed in Mea She'arim in Jerusalem. The police believed that this was another attack by "the serial stabber." The Arab was lightly wounded.

5 3 **98** An explosive device was set off on Ido Hanavi Street, near Mea She'arim in Jerusalem, near the door of an apartment rented by three Arab students. The arsonists left a note saying that this was a message to the Arab students that they were not wanted in the neighborhood.

5 7 **98** A Palestinian bakery worker in Jerusalem was stabbed on Beit Yisrael Street. The police believed that this was another attack by "the serial stabber." The Arab died of his wounds.

5 14 **98** A Palestinian Arab worker living in Jerusalem was stabbed. The police believed that this was another attack by "the serial stabber." The Arab died of his wounds.

6 18 **98** Two youths, residents of Beit Haggai near Hebron, admitted to causing the death of a Palestinian. The settlers murdered the Palestinian, from Hebron, by beating him with a stick "just for fun."

7 14 **98** A Palestinian from Shuafat in East Jerusalem was lightly wounded by a bag filled with explosive material near Orient House in Jerusalem.

10 26 **98** Gur Hamal, a youth from the settlement of Itamar, killed an elderly Palestinian whom he met while on his way to one of the hilltop youth settlements.

10 27 **98** A Jewish man from Kibbutz Sa'ad in the Negev, in a reaction to the murder of Jewish guard Danny Vargas, threw stones at a Palestinian worker from Beit Forik in an olive grove near the settlement of Itamar. The Palestinian died of his wounds.

12 2 **98** A Palestinian from Abu-Dis in Jerusalem was stabbed to death on Shmuel Hanavi Street in Jerusalem. The police believed that this was another attack by "the serial stabber."

1 13 **99** A Palestinian living in Ras al-Amudin, East Jerusalem, was stabbed. The police believed that this was another attack by "the serial stabber."

10 7 **00** A settler (along with others) fired at a Palestinian near Kfar Bidiya in Samaria. No other details are known about the terrorists, their number, or where they live. The Palestinian, a village resident, died of his wounds.

10 8 **00** Settlers entered the village of Bidiya and began to throw stones at Palestinians. One of the Palestinians was killed.

10 13 **00** Danny Tickman and Felix Millner, soldiers from Haifa, decided to take revenge for the lynching in Ramallah of two

Israeli reserve soldiers and drove their car to the Arab neighborhoods of the city. There, they opened fire from their automatic weapons at passersby.

10 20 **00** An Arab from Beit Fourik, harvesting olives, was killed by a settler. No further details are known about the event.

10 30 **00** A religious Jewish man from Jerusalem fired at a Palestinian from Jerusalem who was a guard at Augusta Victoria hospital. The Palestinian was lightly wounded.

11 14 **00** Settlers fired at a Palestinian in the area of Kfar Malek in the Ramallah district. The Palestinian, from the refugee camp Askar in the Ramallah district, died as a result of the shooting.

11 14 **00** Thirteen settlers stoned a Palestinian car at the A-Sabkh junction in the region of Kfar Malek. The driver, a vegetable salesman from the refugee camp of Askar, was killed when a stone hit him. It is not known where the settlers came from.

12 7 **00** A settler fired at a Palestinian near the Erez checkpoint. It is not known where the settler was from.

12 9 **00** An unknown number of settlers from the Jewish settlement in Hebron shot a Palestinian in revenge for a terrorist attack in which settlers were shot. The Palestinian was killed.

12 11 **00** A settler from Kiryat Arba, a member of the Regional Council there, was arrested after an attack on a Palestinian child from Hebron. The child was seriously wounded. The attack took place at Kharsina Hill, near Hebron.

12 17 **00** A settler shot a Palestinian from Kfar Aboud near his village. The Palestinian was killed on the spot.

12 22 **00** Settlers shot a Palestinian near the Beit Haggai junction. The Palestinian was killed on the spot.

3 12 **01** Three settlers from Magen David Farm were arrested on suspicion of firing at a Palestinian shepherd but were released due to lack of evidence. The Palestinian was seriously wounded.

4 5 **01** Members of the Bat Ayin group shot and lightly injured two Palestinians from Khalkhul on the Hebron bypass road.

6 20 **01** Bassam Salakh, an Arab worker in the market of Netanya who lived in the village of Akraba, was attacked after the terror attack in Netanya. He was then attacked a second time and moderately wounded by dozens of settlers.

7 4 **01** Eliran Golan, a young resident of Haifa, left an explosive device at the home of a Jewish-Arab couple. The device was discovered and dismantled in time.

7 20 **01** After Palestinians shot two residents of Kiryat Arba to death, five settlers fired on a car with the Rajub family of Kfar Idna

inside. Three were killed, one seriously wounded, and three moderately wounded.

8 18 **01** Eliran Golan, a young resident of Haifa, booby-trapped the car of a family in Haifa whom he suspected of giving help to Arab terrorists. The explosive was blown up when two children found it in time.

8 28 **01** A small explosive device blew up in the Al-Haj Abdallah mosque in Haifa. Jamila Egberia, a city resident, was lightly wounded. The explosive was placed by Eliran Golan, a young Haifa resident.

8 29 **01** Twenty-seven-year-old Gedua Kanaan, from Khizme in the Al-Kuds district, was killed near An'ata, in the district of Al-Kuds, by bullets fired at his car.

9 17 **01** A cell of the Bat Ayin group left explosives in the Palestinian school in Yatta. Seven children were lightly wounded.

9 17 **01** Dozens of settlers attacked Palestinian truck drivers on the Burin–Izhar road after the assassination of Israeli minister Rehavam Zeevi. Although no weapons were used in the attack, one Palestinian was moderately wounded and a second was lightly wounded.

10 11 **01** A cell of the Bat Ayin group fired on a truck on Road 5 near the village of Utzrin in southern Samaria. Two Palestinians riding in the truck were injured.

10 23 **01** Automatic weapon fire was aimed at a moving car in which there were six Palestinians. Five settlers were in the attacking car. The attack took place near the town of Bnei Naim in the Hebron district. Six Palestinians were wounded, one seriously and five moderately. The attack is thought to have been carried out by the Bat Ayin group.

2 15 **02** An explosive device was placed at the entrance to the village of Beit Anun, apparently by the Bat Ayin group.

3 6 **02** A Jewish organization called the "Revenge of the Infants," apparently a cover name for the Bat Ayin group, took responsibility for an explosion at the school at Tzur Bakher.

4 1 **02** A shooting attack at a Palestinian car carried out by a cell of the Bat Ayin group killed two Palestinians.

5 12 **02** Four settlers belonging to the Bat Ayin group left an explosive in the Palestinian school at A-Tur in Jerusalem. The explosive was discovered by security forces.

5 15 **02** Settlers suspected of belonging to the Bat Ayin group, including Noam Friedman, one of the leaders of Kach, and Menachem Levinger, the son of Rabbi Levinger, were questioned for allegedly being involved in planning attacks against Palestinians.

6 14 **02**   Two settlers from Carmei-Tzur arrived at the Palestinian village of Khalkhul after a settler from Carmei-Tzur was killed. They attacked villagers. The settlers prevented farmers from getting to their land to work. As a result, two Palestinians were lightly wounded, one a farmer who had come to work his land and the other an engineer whose family owned the land.

7 28 **02**   More than ten settlers whose residence is not known reached the area of Hebron to avenge the death of settler Eliezer Leibovitch, who was killed by Palestinians. The settlers stabbed a Palestinian boy and beat his brother. The two Palestinians were seriously wounded.

7 28 **02**   More than twenty-five settlers whose places of residence are not known reached the house of the Jimjum family in Hebron to avenge the murder of settler Eliezer Leibovitch and shot the daughter of the family, Nivin, to death. The family was chosen at random, with no connection to those who had killed the settler.

8 15 **02**   An explosive device was discovered and dismantled at the Beit Anun junction with no injuries. It was apparently left by Bat Ayin group.

9 17 **02**   Five students at the Zif School in the village of Yatta, south of Hebron, were wounded by a powerful explosive that was apparently left by the Bat Ayin group.

10 1 **02**   An unknown number of settlers from Tapuach reached the area of the Palestinian village of Yasuf and opened fire to frighten those who were harvesting grapes in the area. One Palestinian was lightly wounded, and Palestinian property was stolen.

10 7 **02**   A settler from Itamar reached the orchards of the Palestinian village of Akraba and opened fire on farmers who were in the orchards. One Palestinian was killed, and two were moderately wounded.

10 7 **02**   Settlers from Itzhar reached the orchards of the village of Burin and attacked a Palestinian farmer who was harvesting olives. The Palestinian was killed in the attack. The weapon used by the settlers is unknown.

10 16 **02**   A number of settlers from Itamar reached the village of Akraba and began a shooting attack at farmers in the village who were in their orchards, harvesting olives. In the attack one Palestinian was killed, and two were moderately wounded.

10 28 **02**   Two unidentified settlers from Pnei Khaver fired at olive harvesters from the village of Bnei Naim. No one was injured.

1 19 **03**   An anonymous group of three settlers attacked a Palestinian tile layer from Hebron with a knife and lightly wounded him.

The attack took place at Me'arat Hamachpela ("Cave of the Patriarchs"), near Hebron.

3 5 **03** David Smirnov, a Border Police officer, was killed a year earlier. In revenge, his sister ran over a Palestinian near the Erez checkpoint and critically wounded him.

10 24 **03** Eliran Golan booby-trapped the car of an Arab member of the Knesset, Issam Makhoul. When the device was activated, Makhoul's wife was in the car, but she succeeded in getting out without being wounded.

1 16 **04** Eliran Golan, a young man from Haifa, tried to booby-trap the car of an Arab Israeli, Issa Ganaim, whom he suspected of trying to help Palestinian terrorists. The explosive was discovered and dismantled in time.

1 30 **04** Eliran Golan, a young man from Haifa, placed an explosive device on the stairs of a building where a young Israeli girl lived who was often seen in the company of Arabs. The device was discovered and dismantled in time.

5 3 **05** Avraham Mordechai Levkowitz, Elitzur Levinstein, and Mordechai Mordi Levinstein were arrested during an attempt to ignite a car on a busy road in Israel, Netivei Ayalon. Their goal was to protest the disengagement from Gaza Plan by causing a number of traffic accidents that would impede the flow of traffic.

5 4 **05** Eden Natan-Zada, an Israeli army deserter, got on an Egged bus traveling from Haifa to the Arab city of Shfaram in northern Israel. When the bus reached Shfaram, he opened fire on the passengers and the driver, killing four and wounding others. Zada was killed as citizens took control of the bus.

8 17 **05** Asher Weissgan shot two Arab workers at the entrance to the settlement of Shiloh in protest against the Disengagement Plan.

5 14 **07** Julian Soufir shot an Arab-Israeli taxi driver. After the taxi had taken him from Jerusalem to Tel Aviv, the murderer invited the driver to his home to drink water and stabbed him with a knife. The murderer was apparently emotionally disturbed.

PREFACE

1. David C. Rapoport, "The Fourth Wave: September 11 in the History of Terrorism," *Current History*, 100 (2001): 419–429; Scott Atran, "The 'Virtual Hand' of Jihad," *Terrorism Monitor*, 3 (May 2005): 8–11; John L. Esposito, *Unholy War* (Oxford: Oxford University Press, 2003); Jonathan Fox, "The Effects of Religion on Domestic Conflicts," *Terrorism and Political Violence*, 11 (1998): 43–63; Jonathan Fox and Josephine Squires, "Threats to Primal Identities: A Comparison of Nationalism and Religion as Impacts on Ethnic Protest and Rebellion," *Terrorism and Political Violence*, 13 (2001), 87–102; Mark Juergensmeyer, *Terror in the Mind of God: The Global Rise of Religious Violence* (Berkeley: University of California Press, 2001); Andreas Hasenclever and Volker Rittberger, "Does Religion Make a Difference; Theoretical Approaches to the Impact of Faith on Political Conflict," *Millennium: Journal of International Studies*, 29 (December 2000): 641–674; Bruce Hoffman, "Holy Terror: The Implications of Terrorism Motivated by Religious Imperative," *Studies in Conflict and Terrorism*, 18, no. 4 (1995): 271; Raphael Israeli, "A Manual of Islamic Fundamentalist Terrorism," *Terrorism and Political Violence*, 14 (2002): 23–40; Walter Laqueur, *The New Terrorism: Fanaticism and the Arms of Mass Destruction* (New York: Oxford University Press, 1999); Bernard Lewis, *The Crisis of Islam: Holy War and Unholy Terror* (New York: Random House, 2004).

2. See Indra De Soysa and Nordas Ragnhild, "Islam's Bloody Innards? Religion and Political Terror, 1980–2000," *International Studies Quarterly*, 51, no. 4 (2007): 927–943.

3. Benjamin R. Barber, *Jihad vs. McWorld: How Globalism and Tribalism Are Reshaping the World* (New York: Ballantine, 1995); Tony Blankley, *The West's Last Chance: Will We Win the Clash of Civilizations?* (Washington, D.C.: Regnery, 2005); Samuel P. Huntington, *The Clash of Civilizations: Remaking of World Order* (New York: Touchstone, 1996); Michael Mousseau, "Market Civilization and Its Clash with Terror," *International Security*, 27, no. 3 (2002): 5–29; Pippa Norris and Ronald Inglehart, "Islamic Culture and Democracy: Testing the 'Clash of Civilizations' Thesis," *Comparative Sociology*, 1, no. 3–4 (2002): 235–263; Reuven Paz, "Is There an 'Islamic Terrorism,'" Institute for Counter Terrorism (1998), see http://www.ict.org.il/home.htm.

4. David C. Cook, *Contemporary Muslim Apocalyptic Literature* (Syracuse: Syracuse University Press, 2002).

5. Paul Berman, *Terror and Liberalism* (New York: W. W. Norton, 2003); John Ikenberry, "Just Like the Rest," *Foreign Affairs*, 76, no. 2 (1997): 162–163; Bruce Russett,

John Oneal, and Michaelene Cox, "Clash of Civilizations, or Realism and Liberalism Déjà Vu? Some Evidence," *Journal of Peace Research,* 37, no. 5 (2000): 583–608; Donald J. Puchala, "International Encounters of Another Kind," *Global Society* (January 1997); Andrej Tusicisny, "Civilizational Conflicts: More Frequent, Longer, and Bloodier?" *Journal of Peace Research,* 41, no. 4 (2004): 485–498; Stephen M. Walt, "Building Up New Bogeymen," *Foreign Policy,* 106 (Spring 1997): 177–189.

6. Scott Atran, "Genesis of Suicide Terrorism," *Science,* 299 (2004): 1534; Mia M. Bloom, "Palestinian Suicide Bombing: Public Support, Market Share and Outbidding," *Political Science Quarterly,* 119, no. 1 (2004): 61–68; Martha Crenshaw, "The Psychology of Terrorism: An Agenda for the 21st Century," *Political Psychology,* 21, no. 2 (2000): 411–415; Walter Enders and Todd Sandler, *The Political Economy of Terrorism* (Cambridge: Cambridge University Press, 2006); Mohammed M. Hafez, "Rationality, Culture and Structure in the Making of Suicide Bombers: A Preliminary Theoretical Synthesis and Illustrative Case Study," *Studies in Conflict and Terrorism,* 29, no. 2 (2006): 165–185; Assaf Moghadam, "Palestinian Suicide Terrorism in the Second Intifada: Motivations and Organizational Aspects," *Studies in Conflict and Terrorism,* 26, no. 2 (2003): 65–92; Robert A. Pape, "The Strategic Logic of Suicide Terrorism," *American Political Science Review,* 97, no. 3 (2003): 344–361; Robert A. Pape, *Dying to Win: The Strategic Logic of Suicide Terrorism* (New York: Random House, 2005).

7. Information based on the National Security Studies Center at the University of Haifa dataset on terrorist groups; see http://nssc.haifa.ac.il/.

8. See Douglas Kellner, "Theorizing September 11: Social Theory, History, and Globalization," *Social Thought & Research,* 25, no. 1–2 (2002): 2–3; Tariq Ali, *The Clash of Fundamentalisms* (London: Verso, 2002).

9. Scot Atran, "The Moral Logic and Growth of Suicide Terrorism," *Washington Quarterly,* 29, no. 2 (2006): 127–147; John Arquilla and David Ronfeldt, *Networks and Netwars: The Future of Terror, Crime, and Militancy* (Santa Monica, Calif.: Rand, 2001); Jonathan D. Farley, "Breaking Al-Qaeda Cells: A Mathematical Analysis of Counterterrorism Operations (A Guide for Risk Assessment and Decision Making)," *Studies in Conflict and Terrorism,* 26, no. 6 (2003): 399–411; David M. Jones, Michael L. Smith, and Mark Weeding, "Looking for the Pattern: Al Qaeda in Southeast Asia—The Genealogy of a Terror Network," *Studies in Conflict and Terrorism,* 26, no. 6 (2003): 443–457; Renate Mayntz, "Hierarchy or Network? On the Organizational Forms of Terrorism," *Berliner Journal Für Soziologie,* 14, no. 2 (2004): 251; Ami Pedahzur and Arie Perliger, "The Changing Nature of Suicide Attacks: A Social Network Perspective," *Social Forces,* 94, no. 4 (2006): 1983–2004; Marc Sageman, *Understanding Terror Networks* (Philadelphia: University of Pennsylvania Press, 2004).

10. Daniel L. Byman, "Al-Qaeda as an Adversary: Do We Understand Our Enemy?" *World Politics,* 56, no. 1 (2003): 145; Assaf Moghadam, "Suicide Terrorism, Occupation, and the Globalization of Martyrdom: A Critique of Dying to Win," *Studies in Conflict and Terrorism,* 29, no. 8 (2006): 707–729; Pedahzur and Perliger, "The Changing Nature of Suicide Attacks," 1983–2004; Yoram Schweitzer and Shaul Shay,

An Expected Surprise: The September 11th Attack and Its Ramifications (Herzliya, Israel: ICT, 2002), 36.

11. Moghadam, "Suicide Terrorism," 707–729; Martha Crenshaw, "Explaining Suicide Terrorism: A Review Essay," *Security Studies*, 16, no. 1 (2007): 133–162; James Hughes, "Chechnya: The Causes of a Protracted Post-Soviet Conflict," *Civil Wars*, 4, no. 4 (2001): 11–48; Alan B. Krueger and Jitka Maleckova, "Education, Poverty, Political Violence, and Terrorism: Is There a Causal Connection?" NBER Working Paper no. 9074, July 2002 (see http://www.nber.org/papers/w9074); Irina Mukhina, "Islamic Terrorism and the Question of National Liberation, or Problems of Contemporary Chechen Terrorism," *Studies in Conflict & Terrorism*, 28, no. 6 (2005): 515–532.

12. Schweitzer and Shay, *An Expected Surprise*, 36; Martin Kremer, "The Moral Logic of Hezbollah," in Walter Reich, ed., *Origins of Terrorism: Psychologies, Ideologies, Theologies, States of Mind* (Baltimore: John Hopkins University Press, 2002), 131–157.

13. Theodore Roszak, *The Making of a Counter Culture* (Garden City, N.Y.: Doubleday, 1969); Dick Anthony, Thomas Robbins, and Steven Barrie-Anthony, "Cult and Anticult Totalism: Reciprocal Escalation and Violence," *Terrorism and Political Violence*, 14, no. 1 (2002): 211–240.

14. See Ken Goffman and Dan Joy, *Counterculture Through the Ages* (New York: Villard Books, 2004); Terry H. Anderson, *The Movement and the Sixties* (Oxford: Oxford University Press, 1995).

15. Roszak, *The Making of a Counter Culture;* Anthony et al., "Cult and Anticult Totalism," 211–240.

16. Alberto Melucci, *Nomads of the Present: Social Movements and Individual Needs in Contemporary Society* (Philadelphia: Temple University Press, 1989); Daniel Pipes, *Militant Islam Reaches America* (New York: W.W. Norton, 2003); Simone Reeve, *The New Jackals* (London: Northeastern University Press, 1998); Sageman, *Understanding Terror Networks;* Verta Taylor and Nancy E. Whittier, "Collective Identity in Social Movement Communities," in A. D. Morris and C. M. Mueller, *Frontiers in Social Movement Theory* (New Haven, Conn.: Yale University Press, 1992), 104–132.

17. Debra Friedman and Doug McAdam, "Collective Action and Activism," in A. D. Morris and C. M. Mueller, *Frontiers in Social Movement Theory* (New Haven, Conn.: Yale University Press, 1992); Doug McAdam and Ronnel Paulsen, "Specifying the Relationship Between Social Ties and Activism," *American Journal of Sociology*, 99 (1993): 640–667; Ami Lacey, "Networked Communities: Social Centers and Activists Spaces in Contemporary Britain," *Space and Culture*, 8, no. 5 (2005): 286–301; Michel Maffesoli, *The Time of the Tribes: The Decline in Individualism in Mass Society* (London: Sage, 1996).

18. See Farhad Khosrokhavar, *Suicide Bombers: Allah's New Martyrs* (London: Pluto Press, 2005), 30–34; Reeve, *The New Jackals*, 130–145.

19. Jeffrey Kaplan, "Something Funny Happened on the Way to the End of the World," *State and Society*, 2, no. 2 (2002): 177–208 (Hebrew); Khosrokhavar, *Suicide Bombers*, 33–34; Terry McDermott, *Perfect Soldiers* (New York: Harper Collins, 2005), 5–20.

20. Juergensmeyer, *Terror in the Mind of God*, 145–150; Khosrokhavar, *Suicide Bombers*, 30–31; McDermott, *Perfect Soldiers*, 5–20.

21. Juergensmeyer, *Terror in the Mind of God*, 145–150; Laqueur, *The New Terrorism*, 81–82. For the cultural and political conditions that can reduce the vulnerability of a society to political violence, see Ehud Sprinzak, *Brother Against Brother* (New York: Free Press, 1999), 317–319.

22. Christopher Browning, Seth L. Feinberg, and Robert Dietz, "The Paradox of Social Organization: Networks, Collective Efficacy, and Violent Crime in Urban Neighborhoods," *Social Forces*, 83, no. 2 (2005): 503–534; John J. Miller, Michael Stone, and Chris Mitchell, *The Cell: Inside the 9/11 Plot, and Why the FBI and CIA Failed to Stop It* (New York: Hyperion, 2002), 250–269; Nikki Ruble and William L. Turner, "A Systematic Analysis of the Dynamics and Organization of Urban Street Gangs," *The American Journal of Family Therapy*, 28, no. 2 (2000): 117–132.

23. Friedman and McAdam, "Collective Action and Activism"; Kaplan, "Something Funny Happened," 177–208; Melucci, *Nomads of the Present*.

24. McAdam and Paulsen, "Specifying the Relationship," 640–667; Bert Klandermans and Dirk Oegema, "Potentials, Networks, Motivations and Barriers: Steps Towards Participation in Social Movements," *American Sociological Review*, 52 (1987).

25. Doug McAdam, "Recruitment to High-Risk Activism: The Case of Freedom Summer," *American Journal of Sociology*, 92 (1986): 64–90; D. B. Tindall, "Social Networks, Identification and Participation in an Environmental Movement: Low Medium Cost Activism Within British Columbia Wilderness Preservation Movement," *Canadian Review of Sociology and Anthropology*, 39, no. 4 (2002): 413–452.

26. Albert Jongman and Alex P. Schmid, *Political Terrorism* (Amsterdam: North Holland, 1983), 5.

27. See The Jerusalem District Court, criminal file 203/84, State of Israel Against the Jewish Underground, or Tel-Aviv Magistrate's Court, criminal file 498/95, the State of Israel Against Yigal Amir.

28. Such as the interview conducted on July 27, 2005 with Yehuda Etzion, the leader of the Jewish Underground, whose story is elaborated on in Chapter 3.

29. The surveys were conducted by the National Security Studies Center at the University of Haifa, Israel in September 2001 and 2003, May 2004 and 2005, and April 2006 and 2007. The surveys were conducted by telephone, and the participation rate was about 50 percent. We do not have any reason to believe that the characteristic of the non-responders differ from those who chose to respond.

30. Our Jewish terrorism dataset consists of a list of terror incidents perpetrated by Jewish terrorists in Israel. It covers a period beginning in 1932 and ending on April 17, 2008. In all, the catalogue includes 309 assaults. The dataset was compiled in several stages and is the property of the National Security Studies Center of the University of Haifa. First, data were collected from various academic sources (articles and books) in order to identify the periods featuring Jewish terrorism. In the second stage, each period was assigned to a researcher who searched for information on the attacks that were relevant to his or her assigned time frame. The sources of information on which

the dataset was established are numerous and diverse: articles and academic texts, databanks found on the Internet, Internet sites dealing with Jewish terrorism, and the broad use of Israeli media sources and interviews. In the final stage, the collected information was encoded in an SPSS file according to the specific variables chosen.

31. The data were gathered mainly from Israeli media publications that tend to elaborate on the life stories of the Jewish terrorists. See Nadav Shragai, "I Wanted the Arabs to Know the Feeling of Collecting Their Children in Bags," *Haaretz,* September 22, 2003, p. B3 (Hebrew); Reuven Shapira, "Yigal Amir and His Friends Considered Blowing Up Rabin's Car with a Powerful Bomb," *Haaretz,* November 14, 1995, p. A4 (Hebrew).

32. See David A. Snow, Louis A. Zurcher, and Sheldon Ekland-Olson, "Social Networks and Social Movements: A Micro-Structural Approach to Differential Recruitments," *American Sociological Review,* 45 (1980): 789.

33. McAdam and Paulsen, "Specifying the Relationship," 640–667; see also review in Klandermans and Oegema, "Potentials," 520.

34. John Scott, *Social Network Analysis* (London: Sage, 2000), 2–5; S. Wasserman and K. Faust, *Social Network Analysis: Methods and Applications* (Cambridge: Cambridge University Press, 1994), 4–10.

CHAPTER ONE **ANCIENT AND MODERN HISTORY: THE FOUNDING MYTHS**

1. Sidney Tedesche, trans., *The First Book of Maccabees* (New York: Harper, 1950), Ch. 2.

2. Sidney Tedesche, trans., *The Second Book of Maccabees* (New York: Harper, 1950), 2–5.

3. One example was the building of a Greek gymnasium in Jerusalem. See Menahem Stern, "The Hasmonean Revolt and Its Place in Jewish History and Religion," in Menahem Stern, ed., *Studies in Jewish History: The Second Temple Period* (Jerusalem: Yad Itzhak Ben-Zvi, 1991), 153 (Hebrew).

4. Ibid., 152.

5. Ibid., 152–153.

6. Jacqueline Schaalje, "Jerusalem: In Search of the Maccabees," *The Jewish Journal,* 27 (1999), http://www.jewishmag.com/27MAG/archi/archi.htm (March 14, 2006).

7. Michael Grant, *The Jews in the Roman World* (London: Weidenfeld and Nicolson, 1973), 28.

8. Stern, *Studies in Jewish History,* 157–159.

9. Uriel Rappaport, *1 Maccabees: Introduction, Translation, and Interpretation* (Jerusalem: Yad Itzhak Ben-Zvi, 2004), 15–28 (Hebrew).

10. For a review of Yehudah's battles, see Menachem Kedem, *Jews in the Second Temple Period* (Tel Aviv: Or Am), 40–44 (Hebrew).

11. Grant, *The Jews in the Roman World,* 1973), 30.

12. Kedem, *Jews in the Second Temple Period,* 49–51.

13. Ian S. Lustick, *For the Land and the Lord* (New York: Council on Foreign Relations), 21.

14. The Sadducees were a Jewish sect active during the Second Temple period. Its followers, most of whom were from the upper classes, centered their beliefs on total adherence to the Torah (the five books of Moses) and partial rejection of the Oral Law.

The Sadducees also rejected the idea of an afterlife and an omnipresent God. The sect disappeared after the fall of the Second Temple because it failed to adjust its religious perceptions to the nonexistence of the Temple in Jewish life. The Pharisees were another Jewish sect active during the Second Temple period, appearing during the Hasmonean kingdom around 150 B.C.E. Its followers, mostly from the lower classes, believed that the Oral Law had been handed down on Mount Sinai, and they accorded it importance equal to that of the written Torah. They also believed in an omnipresent God and the existence of an afterlife. The sect's Torah scholars excelled in adjusting Jewish religious law to suit contemporary needs, so it can be said that the Pharisean approach has been widely adopted by modern Judaism. The two sects were rivals.

15. Aryeh Kasher, "Introduction: The Causal and Circumstantial Background for the Jewish War Against the Romans," in Aryeh Kasher, ed., *The Great Jewish Revolt* (Jerusalem: The Zalman Shazar Center, 1983), 82–83 (Hebrew).

16. Josephus Flavius, *The Jewish War* (Jerusalem: Reuven Mas, 1967), 158 (Hebrew).

17. Menahem Stern, "The Suicide of Elazar Ben Yair and His People on Masada and the 'Fourth Philosophy,'" in Stern, *Studies in Jewish History*, 316.

18. Menahem Stern, "Leadership in Groups of Freedom Fighters at the End of the Second Temple Period," in Kasher, *The Great Jewish Revolt*, 303.

19. Ibid., 305.

20. Martin Hengel, "The Zealots and Sicarians: On the Question of Unity and Division Among Jewish Freedom Movements Between 6–74 AD," in Kasher, *The Great Jewish Revolt*, 345.

21. Ibid., 356.

22. Herod the Great (73–4 B.C.E.) was a pro-Roman Jewish king of Judea. He began his career as a general but later was recognized by Roman statesman Mark Antony as the Jewish national leader. During a war against the Parthians, Herod was deposed, but after fleeing to Rome, he was elected "King of the Jews" by the Roman Senate and provided with soldiers to seize the throne. He was acknowledged as a friend and ally of the Romans and therefore not truly independent, although Rome allowed him to follow his own domestic policy. (http://www.livius.org/he-hg/herodians/herod_the_great1.htm).

23. Stern, "Leadership in Groups of Freedom Fighters," 301.

24. Hengel, "The Zealots and Sicarians," 359; for a review on the Sicarians, see Martin Hengel, *Die Zeloten* (Leiden-Koln: E. J. Bril, 1976).

25. Hengel, "The Zealots and Sicarians," 357.

26. Ibid., 359.

27. Josephus Flavius, *The Jewish Commonwealth: Book 20* (Jerusalem: Bialik Institute, 1953–1955), 369.

28. For a description of Masada, see: Micha Livneh, "And the Name of the Fortress Is Masada," in Irit Zaharoni, *The Road of the Country: Earthenware and Man* (Tel Aviv: Ministry of Defense Publishing House, 1996), 342–359 (Hebrew).

29. Menahem Stern, "Sicarians and Zealots," in Michael Avi-Yona and Zvi Bress, eds., *Society and Religion in the Second Temple Period* (Tel Aviv: Am Oved, 1983), 177–179 (Hebrew).

30. For example, see Flavius, *The Jewish War*, 462.

31. Ibid.

32. Livneh, "And the Name of the Fortress Is Masada," 347.

33. Meir Blumenfeld, "In the Meaning of 'Do Not Rebel' Oath," 1974 (Hebrew), http://www.daat.ac.il/daat/kitveyet/shana/bidvar-4.htm (February 17, 2006).

34. Anna Geifman, *Thou Shalt Kill: Revolutionary Terrorism in Russia, 1894–1917* (Princeton, N.J.: Princeton University Press, 1993), 239.

35. Decter Midge, "Notes from the American Underground," *Commentary*, 73, no. 1 (1982): 27–33.

36. For information on the Bund and its ideology, see Yoav Peled, *Class, Nation and Culture: The Debate over Jewish Nationality in the Russian Revolutionary Movement* (Los Angeles: UCLA, 1983); Geifman, *Thou Shalt Kill*, 101–106.

37. Geifman, *Thou Shalt Kill*, 102.

38. Ibid., 103.

39. Ibid.

CHAPTER TWO EARLY AND MID-TWENTIETH CENTURY: ETHNO-RELIGIOUS TERRORISM

1. Bar-Giora was an underground defense organization in pre-state Palestine, named after Shimon Bar-Giora, one of the commanders of the first Jewish revolt against the Romans. The organization was established in September 1907 in Jaffa by seven recent immigrants to Palestine, including Israel Shohat, Israel Gilady, and Izhak Ben-Zvi, who later served as Israel's second president. The goal of the organization was to replace Arabs and Circassians as guards in Jewish settlements. The group was based in Galilee.

2. Hashomer (the Guard), successor of the Bar-Giora group, was an underground defense organization in pre-state Palestine active between 1909 and 1920. Its purpose was to protect Jewish settlers in Palestine. The heads of the organization were Israel Gilady and Mendel Portugaly. It consisted of a few dozen people and was based mainly in Jewish settlements in the Galilee.

3. Mordechai Naor, "Hashomer: The Myth Was Already Born in the Second Aliya," in Mordechai Naor, ed., *The Second Aliya, 1903–1914* (Jerusalem: Yad Itzhak Ben-Zvi, 1985) (Hebrew), http://lib.cet.ac.il/pages/item.asp?item=12916 (March 12, 2006); Ian S. Lustick, "Terrorism in the Arab–Israeli Conflict: Targets and Audiences," in Martha Crenshaw, ed., *Terrorism in Context* (Pennsylvania State University Press, 1995), 520.

4. For the development of the Haganah doctrine, see Shlomo Lev-Ami, *By Struggle and by Revolt* (Tel Aviv: Ministry of Defense), 88–97 (Hebrew); Ben-Zion Dinor et al., *The Book of the Haganah History: From Defense to Struggle* (Tel Aviv: Maarahot, 1964), 525–528, 614–615 (Hebrew).

5. Pinhas Yurmand and Meir Pail, *The Test of the Zionist Movement 1931–1948* (Tel Aviv: Tcherikover, 2003), 15–17, 64–72 (Hebrew).

6. For the political thought of Ze'ev Jabotinsky, see Raphaela Bilski-Ben-Hur, *Every Individual, a King: The Social and Political Thought of Ze'ev Vladimir Jabotinsky* (Washington, D.C.: B'nai B'rith Books, 1993).

7. Joseph Heller, *Lehi: Ideology and Politics, 1940–1949* (Jerusalem: Keter and Zalman Shazar Center for Jewish History, 1989), 28 (Hebrew).

8. Ibid.

9. Ibid., 33.

10. Ibid., 229.

11. Dinor et al., *The Book of the Haganah History*, 426–432; Aviezer Golan and Shlomo Nakdimon, *Begin* (Jerusalem: Edanim, 1978), 49 (Hebrew).

12. Dinor et al., *The Book of the Haganah History*, 426–427.

13. Yehuda Lapidot, *The Flames of Revolt: The Irgun in Jerusalem* (Ministry of Defense, 1996), 20 (Hebrew).

14. Ibid., 19.

15. Ibid., 21.

16. For a review of the illegal immigration, see Yehuda Lapidot, *The Birth of the Underground: Etzel in the 1930s* (Tel Aviv: Brith Hayalei Etzel, 2001), 124–176 (Hebrew).

17. The Great Arab Revolt took place in Palestine between 1936 and 1939. Among the Jewish settlers, this period was called the Meoraot (events). During the revolt, Arabs carried out hostile acts against Jews, including murder and attacks on fruit orchards and passing cars. During the revolt, a number of attempts were made to bring it to an end, including the Peel Commission (1937) and the Round Table Conference (1939). As a result of the revolt, Britain issued a white paper in 1939 that severely restricted the immigration of Jews into Palestine.

18. Lustick, "Terrorism in the Arab–Israeli Conflict," 524–525.

19. Ibid., 525; Lapidot, *The Birth of the Underground*, 62–63.

20. Sharon is a region along the central coast of Israel and includes such cities as Netanya and Raanana.

21. Yosef Kister, *Hairgun Hazvai Haleumi, 1931–1948* (Tel Aviv: Association of Etzel Museum, 1998), 28 (Hebrew).

22. For a complete list of terror acts committed by Etzel members, see Kister, *Hairgun Hazvai Haleumi*, 26–45.

23. Ibid., 4–5.

24. Dinor et al., *The Book of the Haganah History*, 61–62.

25. The real name of the agent was Meir Zfanya.

26. "Bombs in Jerusalem Radio Station," *Haaretz*, August 3, 1939, p. 1 (Hebrew); Lapidot, *The Birth of the Underground*.

27. Yehuda Lapidot, *At the Height of the Revolt: The Etzel Battles in Jerusalem* (Tel Aviv: Ministry of Defense, 1996), 54 (Hebrew).

28. Lapidot, *The Birth of the Underground*, 53.

29. Lapidot, *At the Height of the Revolt*, 54.

30. Ibid.

31. Kister, *Hairgun Hazvai Haleumi*, 5; Ofer Grosbard, *Menachem Begin: A Portrait of a Leader—A Biography* (Tel Aviv: Resling, 2006), 72 (Hebrew).

32. Dinor et al., *The Book of the Haganah History*, 482; Golan and Nakdimon, *Begin*, 65.

33. Yurmand and Pail, *The Test*, 73.

34. Kister, *Hairgun Hazvai Haleumi*, 15.
35. Lapidot, *The Birth of the Underground.*
36. Yurmand and Pail, *The Test*, 97.
37. "Shocking Crime in Tel Aviv," *Haaretz*, January 21, 1942, p. 1 (Hebrew); "Two More Victims of Tel Aviv Crime," *Haaretz*, January 22, 1942, p. 1 (Hebrew).
38. Golan and Nakdimon, *Begin*, 65.
39. Dinor et al., *The Book of the Haganah History*, 504.
40. Lev-Ami, *By Struggle*, 193.
41. Ibid., 195.
42. Heller, *Lehi*, 160.
43. Lev-Ami, *By Struggle*, 212.
44. Dinor et al., *The Book of the Haganah History*, 511–512.
45. Natan Yellin-Mor, *Lohamey Herut Israel: People, Ideas, Deeds* (Jerusalem: Shikmona, 1974), 136–189 (Hebrew).
46. Ibid., 136–190.
47. Ibid., 136–191.
48. Ibid.
49. Ibid., 136–192.
50. Ibid., 136–194.
51. Ibid., 136–195.
52. "Lord Moyne Killed in Cairo," *Haaretz*, November 7, 1944, p. 1 (Hebrew).
53. Ibid.
54. Joseph Nedava, *Gallows in Cairo* (Jerusalem: Achiasaf, 1963), 13 (Hebrew).
55. "Lord Moyne Killed," 1.
56. Joseph Nedava, "Hakim and Beit-Tsouri Trial in Egypt," *Mahanaim*, 111 (1967): 286–293 (Hebrew).
57. Yellin-Mor, *Lohamey Herut Israel*, 212.
58. Ibid.
59. Ada Ushpiz, "The Endless Morning," *Haaretz*, September 20, 2002 (Hebrew), http://new.haaretz.co.il/hasite/pages/ShArtPE.jhtml?itemNo=210638&contrassID=2&subContrassID=4&sbSubContrassID=0 (March 12, 2006).
60. Yaffa Naker, "60 Years for Avraham Stern Murder," *Knesset*, March 4, 2002 (Hebrew), http://www.miki.org.il/miki/files/shtern.doc (March 12, 2006).
61. Yellin-Mor, *Lohamey Herut Israel*, 212.
62. Ibid., 214.
63. Ibid., 215.
64. Ibid., 216.
65. Ibid., 216–217.
66. Ibid., 218.
67. Ibid.
68. Ibid., 219.
69. Ibid., 220.
70. Heller, *Lehi*, 213.

71. Nedava, "Hakim and Beit-Tsouri Trial," 286–293.

72. Lev-Ami, *By Struggle*, 240, 242; Grosbard, *Menachem Begin*, 83.

73. For a review of the Season, see Yehuda Lapidot, *"Season": Hunting Brothers* (Jerusalem: Jabotinsky Institute, 1994) (Hebrew).

74. Lev-Ami, *By Struggle*, 250–253.

75. Heller, *Lehi*, 211.

76. Grosbard, *Menachem Begin*, 84.

77. Dinor et al., *The Book of the Haganah History*, 540–541.

78. For additional information on the United Resistance Movement, see Yurmand and Pail, *The Test*, 153–208.

79. Golan and Nakdimon, *Begin*, 111.

80. "British Army Engages in Large Campaign Against Yishuv," *Haaretz*, June 30, 1946, p. 1 (Hebrew).

81. Dinor et al., *The Book of the Haganah History*, 810–812.

82. "Massive Casualties in Attack on Government and Army Offices in Jerusalem," *Haaretz*, July 23, 1946, p. 1 (Hebrew).

83. Yellin-Mor, *Lohamey Herut Israel*, 306.

84. Dinor et al., *The Book of the Haganah History*, 879.

85. Yellin-Mor, *Lohamey Herut Israel*, 306.

86. Dinor et al., *The Book of the Haganah History*, 899–901.

87. Grosbard, *Menachem Begin*, 92.

88. "Comprehensive Search to Find Two Sergeants," *Haaretz*, July 13, 1947, p. 1 (Hebrew); "Military Supervision in Netanya Postponed for 24 Hours," *Haaretz*, July 14, 1947, p. 1 (Hebrew).

89. Golan and Nakdimon, *Begin*, 172–173.

90. Eitan Livni, *Etzel: Operations and Undergrounds* (Jerusalem: Edanim, 1987), 238–240 (Hebrew); "Akko Prison: Fourteen Jews and Arabs Killed in Terrorist Attack on Akko Prison," *Haaretz*, May 5, 1947, p. 1 (Hebrew).

91. "Akko Prison," p. 1 (Hebrew); "183 Arabs and 33 Jews Escaped from Akko Prison," *Haaretz*, May 6, 1947, p. 1 (Hebrew).

92. Yellin-Mor, *Lohamey Herut Israel*, 424.

93. Ibid., 428.

94. Dinor et al., *The Book of the Haganah History*, 1599.

95. Shlomo Nakdimon, *Altalena* (Jerusalem: Edanim, 1978), 311 (Hebrew).

96. For a complete review of the *Altalena* affair, see Nakdimon, *Altalena;* Uri Brenner, *Altalena: A Political and Military Study* (Tel Aviv: Hakibbutz Hameuchad, 1978) (Hebrew).

97. Brenner, *Altalena*, 180–189 (Hebrew).

98. Nakdimon, *Altalena*, 175–324.

99. "Additional Arrests of Lehi People," *Haaretz*, September 21, 1948, p. 1 (Hebrew).

100. Heller, *Lehi*, 446–447.

101. Ehud Sprinzak, *Brother Against Brother: Violence and Extremism in Israeli Politics from Altalena to the Rabin Assassination* (New York: Free Press, 1999), 446–447.

102. Asher Lazar, "Folke Bernadotte Murder Shocked the World," *Haaretz*, September 19, 1948, p. 1 (Hebrew).

103. Sprinzak, *Brother Against Brother*, 446–447.

104. Isser Harel, *Security and Democracy* (Tel Aviv: Edanim, 1989), 109 (Hebrew).

105. "Orders for Wiping Out Terrorism Published," *Haaretz*, September 21, 1948, p. 1 (Hebrew).

106. "246 Lehi Members Arrested," *Haaretz*, September 22, 1948, p. X (Hebrew); "Arrests and Searches in the Country," *Haaretz*, September 20, 1948, p. 1 (Hebrew); "Etzel Brigade Ceased to Exist," *Haaretz*, September 22, 1948, pp. 1, 2 (Hebrew); Yehuda Litani, "Black Notepad," *Ofakim*, 23 (August 2005) (Hebrew), http://ofakim.org.il/zope/home/he/1121712720/1122454467 (March 17, 2006).

107. Harel, *Security and Democracy*, 112.

108. Litani, "Black Notepad," 23.

109. Nachman Ben-Yehuda, *Political Assassinations by Jews* (New York: SUNY, 1993), 278–284.

110. Harel, *Security and Democracy*, 106.

111. Isser Harel, *The Truth About the Kastner Murder: Jewish Terror in the State of Israel* (Jerusalem: Edanim, 1985), 105–120 (Hebrew).

112. Sprinzak, *Brother Against Brother*, 71; Harel, *The Truth About the Kastner Murder*, 105–107.

113. Sprinzak, *Brother Against Brother*, 74.

114. Harel, *The Truth About the Kastner Murder*, 105.

115. For a review of the Kastner trial, see Shalom Rosenfeld, *Criminal Case 124: Greenwald–Kastner Trial* (Tel Aviv: Karni, 1956) (Hebrew); Harel, *The Truth About the Kastner Murder*, 326–333.

116. Yoel Brand and Hansi Brand, *The Devil and the Soul* (Tel Aviv: Ledori, 1960), 209–210 (Hebrew).

117. Harel, *Security and Democracy*, 197.

118. "Explosion in Soviet Embassy Building," *Haaretz*, February 10, 1953, p. 1 (Hebrew).

119. Harel, *Security and Democracy*, 194.

120. "Attempt to Blow Up One of the Foreign Ministry Buildings Thwarted—One Man Arrested," *Haaretz*, October 6, 1952, p. 1 (Hebrew).

121. "Two Youngsters Caught with Explosives, Suspected of Trying to Blow Up Ministry of Education," *Haaretz*, May 27, 1953, p. 4 (Hebrew).

122. "Advancing in the Investigation of the Attempt to Plant Bomb in the Ministry of Education," *Haaretz*, May 28, 1953, p. 4 (Hebrew).

123. This name came from the Zrifin Camp, which was the military camp where the trial of the network members was conducted.

124. Interview with Ya'akov Heruti, March 22, 2006.

125. Yaacov Roey, *USSR–Israel Relations, 1945–1947* (Jerusalem: Hebrew University, 1972), 353 (Hebrew).

126. The "Doctors' Plot" was an alleged conspiracy by a group of Jewish physicians to poison top Soviet leaders in the early 1950s. At the beginning of 1952, Soviet security

services began investigating these doctors, suspected of attempting to murder Stalin, Zhdanov, and other Communist Party officials and military commanders. The investigation had a significant anti-Semitic nature and was part of the "war against cosmopolitanism" that was prevalent in the Soviet Union between 1947 and 1953.

127. The Prague trials: were showcase trials against the general secretary of the Czech Communist Party, Rudolf Slansky. He was accused of conspiracy for changing the leadership of the country and removing its current leaders. See Sprinzak, *Brother Against Brother*, 67.

128. For a detailed review of the Tzrifin Underground, see Avraham Daskal, *Oppositional Ex-Parliamentary Behavior in the Beginning of the State, the Brit Hakanaim and the Malhut Israel* (Ramat Gan, Israel: Bar-Ilan University, 1990) (Hebrew).

129. Ibid., 33.

130. "42 Suspects Arrested on Suspicion to Blow Up Knesset," *Haaretz*, May 16, 1951, p. 1 (Hebrew).

131. Ibid.

132. Sprinzak, *Brother Against Brother*, 64.

133. Amos Nevo, "Wise Person Mordechai and His Way," *Yedioth Ahronoth*, April 11, 1985, p. 6 (Hebrew).

134. Tom Segev, *Days of the Anemones: Palestine Under British Mandate* (Jerusalem: Keter, 1999), 219–222, 223–225 (Hebrew).

135. Nevo, "Wise Person Mordechai," 6.

136. Ibid.

137. "Brit Hakanaim Investigation Near Its End: More Than 1000 Documents in Court," *Hazofe,* June 19, 1951, p. 2 (Hebrew).

138. Ibid.

139. "Four Leaders of Brit Hakanaim Underground Sentenced to 6, 10, and 12 Months," *Haaretz*, March 26, 1952, p. 4 (Hebrew).

140. "Vague Details on the Plan to Bomb Knesset," *Hazofe*, May 16, 1951, p. 1 (Hebrew).

141. "Police Officers Give Testimony on How They Collected Confessions from Brit Hakanaim Suspects," *Hazofe*, June 2, 1951, p. 4 (Hebrew).

142. Harel, *Security and Democracy*, 184.

143. Sprinzak, *Brother Against Brother*, 65.

144. Nakdimon, *Altalena*, 254–255.

145. Michael Bar-Zohar, *The Supervisor: Isser Harel and the Israeli Secret Service* (Jerusalem: Widenfeld and Nicholson, 1971), 96 (Hebrew); Ehud Sprinzak, *Political Violence in Israel* (Jerusalem: The Jerusalem Institute for Israeli Studies, 1995), 34 (Hebrew).

146. Harel, *Security and Democracy*, 186.

CHAPTER THREE **THE CAMP DAVID ACCORDS: THE STRUGGLE OVER THE PROMISED LAND**

1. Shabtai Ben-Dov (1924–1979) was a Jewish revolutionist who was active in the Lehi organization. In his writings, he presented a new vision for a future Kingdom of Israel after the Third Temple was to be built. In 1960 his main book was published: *The Salvation of Israel in the Crisis of the State* (Zfat, Israel: Hamatmid).

2. With the liberation of the Old City of Jerusalem during the Six-Day War, the Eshkol government, with the backing of the Knesset, extended Israeli law, jurisdiction, and administration to the eastern part of Jerusalem on June 27, 1967. Although Israeli sovereignty applied to the Temple Mount, Israel agreed that administration of the compound would continue to be maintained by the Jordanian Waqf, under the Jordanian Ministry of Religious Endowments.

3. The process of redemption includes the gathering of all Jews in the Land of Israel, the construction of the Third Temple, and the coming of the Jewish Messiah. During this process there will be a Gog and Magog war (mythical victorious war of Israel over its enemies before the coming of the Messiah), after which an eternal Jewish kingdom will be established. There is disagreement between various factions of Judaism as to whether this process will be speedy or prolonged.

4. Tofiq Khuri, "Both Cars Were Booby-Trapped in an Identical Method—And Within 45 Minutes Two of the Leaders of the West Bank Were Wounded," *Yedioth Ahronoth* Saturday Supplement, June 3, 1980, pp. 9, 33 (Hebrew).

5. Ibid.

6. Eitan Haber, "The Escalation in the Occupied Territories Brought About the Attacks on the Mayors; Within Minutes Two of the Leaders of the West Bank Were Wounded," *Yedioth Ahronoth*, June 3, 1980, p. 2 (Hebrew); Khuri, "Both Cars Were Booby-Trapped," 9, 33; Yehuda Litani, "Mayors Assassinated in West Bank," *Haaretz*, June 3, 1980, p. 3 (Hebrew).

7. Carmi Gillon, *Shabak Among the Shreds* (Tel Aviv: Yedioth Ahronoth, 2000), 101–102 (Hebrew); Hagai Segal, *Dear Brothers: The Story of the Jewish Underground* (Jerusalem: Keter, 1987), 96–100 (Hebrew); Khuri, "Both Cars Were Booby-Trapped," 9, 33; "Investigation Hypothesis: Three–Four Small Groups of Excellent 'Professionals' from an Unknown Group Committed Assassinations," *Maariv*, June 3, 1980, pp. 1, 15 (Hebrew).

8. The National Steering Committee operated in the West Bank and Gaza Strip between 1978 and 1982. It was composed of twenty-one members representing the elite of Palestinian society: physicians, lawyers, newspaper editors, and mayors. Among its members were mayors Fahed Kawasma, Bassam Shaka, and Karim Halaf. The objective of this body was to represent the Arab population in the occupied territories and act against the Camp David Accords, signed between Israel and Egypt, which were supported by both Egypt and Jordan. The committee organized protest strikes and the collective resignation of the municipal civil Palestinian leadership. Israel objected to the nationalist character of the organization, and Jordan and the Palestine Liberation Organization followed suit, although for different reasons: They regarded it as a rival to their leadership over the Palestinian population in the West Bank and Gaza Strip.

9. Jerusalem Regional Court, Criminal File 203/84, 431–433.

10. Yosef Vaksman, "The Assassins Did Not Intend to Kill, But to Hurt," *Maariv*, June 5, 1980, p. 3 (Hebrew).

11. Ian S. Lustick, *For the Land and the Lord* (New York: Council on Foreign Relations), 40. In addition, before his election to prime minister in 1977, Menachem Begin stated,

"There will be a lot of Elon Moreh [settlements]." Also, during his term in office, his government transferred more then $1 billion to settlements in the occupied territories.

12. The Ein Vered Circle was formed after the Six-Day War to support the ideology of the Greater Land of Israel (i.e., annexation of the occupied territories). Its members believed that only a large and strong Israel would be able to absorb the Jewish people, which was of the utmost importance for the future growth of the nation. The group consisted of second-generation Labor Party members, settlers from new Golan Heights settlements, and members of Kibbutz Ein Harod. The group closely identified with the settlement enterprise in Hebron and other places but did not participate in founding illegal settlements because its members believed it was the role of the State of Israel to decide when and whether these settlements should be founded.

13. Hatkhalata De'Geula is part of the process of the coming of the Messiah. There is conjecture in religious Zionism that Jewish settlement of the country is supposed to eventually bring about the establishment of the Kingdom of Israel, whose ruler will be a descendant of King David; Ian S. Lustick, "Israel's Dangerous Fundamentalists," *Foreign Policy*, 68 (Fall 1987): 119.

14. Ibid.

15. Ehud Sprinzak, *Fundamentalism, Terrorism, and Democracy: The Case of the Gush Emunim Underground* (Washington, D.C.: Smithsonian Institution, 1987), 198–199.

16. On the notion of the frontier culture, see Naomi Gal-Or, *The Jewish Underground: Our Terrorism* (Tel Aviv: Hakibbutz Hameuchad, 1990), 58 (Hebrew).

17. Oren Yiftachel, "Ethnocracy: The Politics of Judaizing Israel/Palestine," *Constellations*, 6 (1999): 364–391.

18. Gal-Or, *The Jewish Underground*, 58.

19. Danny Rubinstein, *Gush Emunim* (Tel Aviv: Hakibbutz Hameuchad, 1982), 55 (Hebrew).

20. Ibid., 56.

21. Ehud Sprinzak, "Gush Emunim: The Tip of the Iceberg," *Jerusalem Quarterly*, 21 (1981); Lustick, *For the Land and the Lord*, 134.

22. Lustick, "Israel's Dangerous Fundamentalists," 126–127; Lustick, *For the Land and the Lord*, 48.

23. For the struggle between the settlers and the army in Yamit, see Hagai Segal, *Yamit, the End. The Struggle for Stopping the Withdrawal from Sinai* (Israel: Beit El Library, 1999), 147–300 (Hebrew); Lustick, *For the Land and the Lord*, 59–61.

24. Idith Zertal and Akiva Eldar, *Lords of the Land* (Tel Aviv: Kinneret Zmora-Bitan Dvir, 2004), 101 (Hebrew).

25. Aryeh Naor, *Begin in Power: Personal Testimony* (Tel Aviv: Yedioth Ahronoth, 1993), 183 (Hebrew).

26. "A Prayer in Order to Prevent the Evacuation," *Hazofe Daily News*, April 22, 1982, A1 (Hebrew).

27. Zertal and Eldar, *Lords of the Land*, 93.

28. Segal, *Dear Brothers*, 39–40.

29. For example, Rabbi Zvi Yehuda Kook stated in 1983 that a peace agreement between Israel and Egypt would not be legitimate and called it "governmental betrayal." From Naor, *Begin in Power,* 183.

30. "It's Not Over Yet," *Hazofe Daily News,* April 28, 1982, A1 (Hebrew).

31. The hub is the actor at the center of the network where most connections either lead to or derive from. In contrast to the concept of organizational leadership, which is identifiable and established and includes a hierarchical structure, the hub is invariably a local operative who is not particularly well known, may be replaced frequently, and occasionally shares his or her influence over the network with other operatives or hubs.

32. Aviva Shabi, "A Limited Regret," *Yedioth Ahronoth* Saturday Supplement, June 16, 1989, p. 11 (Hebrew).

33. Judge Dr. Zvi Cohen headed the panel of judges, which included Justices Finkleman and Bazak, who presided over Criminal File 203/84, which included the indictments that were submitted against members of the Jewish Underground.

34. Jerusalem Regional Court, Criminal File 203/84, 447.

35. Sprinzak, *Fundamentalism,* 198.

36. Ibid.

37. Gillon, *Shabak Among the Shreds,* 127.

38. Jerusalem Regional Court, Criminal File (203/84), 361.

39. "After Lifting the Publication Ban, for the First Time a Full List Is Published of Members Accused of Participation in West Bank Jewish Terrorist Underground, Its Organization and Modus Operandi in Each Attack, and the Terrorist Plans They're Suspected Of," *Haaretz,* June 19, 1984, p. 13 (Hebrew).

40. Lustick, *For the Land and the Lord,* 70.

41. The ancient Jewish court system was called the Sanhedrin. The Great Sanhedrin was the supreme religious body in Palestine during the time of the Holy Temple (First Temple). There were also smaller religious Sanhedrins in every town in Palestine and a civil–political democratic Sanhedrin. These Sanhedrins existed until the abolition of the rabbinic patriarchate in about 425 C.E.

42. Jerusalem Regional Court, Criminal File 203/84, 331.

43. Ibid., 348.

44. In an interview we conducted with him, he indicated that in his estimation the underground had to recruit at least forty activists for this purpose.

45. Jerusalem Regional Court, Criminal File 203/84, 405.

46. Ibid., 361.

47. Nadav Shragai, "First Publication of Second Defendant's Statement: 'If We Do Not Take Revenge Now, They [Will] Keep Raising Their Head,'" *Haaretz,* June 4, 1984, p. 1 (Hebrew).

48. Jerusalem Regional Court, Criminal File 203/84, 361.

49. Shragai, "First Publication," 1.

50. Jerusalem Regional Court, Criminal File 203/84, 361–362.

51. Gillon, *Shabak Among the Shreds,* 100.

52. Ibid.

53. Ibid., 101.

54. Jerusalem Regional Court, Criminal File 203/84, 356.

55. Khuri, "Both Cars Were Booby-Trapped," 9, 33.

56. "Egyptian People's Assembly Condemns Israeli Attacks on Palestinian Mayors," *Xinhua*, June 4, 1980.

57. Nadav Shragai, "Menachem Livni and Pragmatic Terrorism," *Haaretz*, May 8, 1985, p. 7 (Hebrew); Jerusalem Regional Court, Criminal File 203/84.

58. Gillon, *Shabak Among the Shreds*, 122–123; Ehud Sprinzak, *Political Violence in Israel* (Jerusalem: The Jerusalem Institute for Israeli Studies, 1995), 79 (Hebrew).

59. Jerusalem Regional Court, Criminal File 203/84, 433.

60. Segal, *Dear Brothers*.

61. Gillon, *Shabak Among the Shreds*, 104.

62. Jerusalem Regional Court, Criminal File 203/84, 433.

63. Ibid., 409.

64. Interview with Yehuda Etzion, July 27, 2005.

65. Jerusalem Regional Court, Criminal File 203/84, 393.

66. Zertal and Eldar, *Lords of the Land*, 116.

67. Ibid., 116–117 (Hebrew).

68. Jerusalem Regional Court, Criminal File 203/84, 392.

69. Interview with Yehuda Etzion, July 27, 2005.

70. Jerusalem Regional Court, Criminal File 203/84, 393.

71. Ibid., 416.

72. Gillon, *Shabak Among the Shreds*, 129.

73. Jerusalem Regional Court, Criminal File 203/84, 392.

74. A small town near Jerusalem.

75. Shragai, "First Publication," 1.

76. Jerusalem Regional Court, Criminal File 203/84, 352.

77. Gillon, *Shabak Among the Shreds*, 130.

78. Ibid., 131.

79. The youth movement of the religious Zionism stream.

80. Gillon, *Shabak Among the Shreds*, 131.

81. "After Lifting the Publication Ban," 13; "Another Accused Member of [Jewish] Underground Confessed in Plea Bargain," *Haaretz*, August 27, 1984, p. 1 (Hebrew).

82. "After Lifting the Publication Ban," 13; "Another Accused Member," 1.

83. Jerusalem Regional Court, Criminal File 203/84, 354.

84. Ibid., 380.

85. Sprinzak, *Political Violence in Israel*, 79.

86. Babylonian Talmud, Tractate Ketubot.

87. Jerusalem Regional Court, Criminal File 203/84, 393.

88. Ibid., 419.

89. Segal, *Dear Brothers*, 102.

90. Ibid., 115 (Hebrew).

91. Ibid., 116 (Hebrew).

92. Jerusalem Regional Court, Criminal File 203/84, 393.

93. Ibid., 349.

94. Segal, *Dear Brothers*, 115.

95. Ibid., 52.

96. Ibid., 137.

97. Ibid., 207.

98. Ibid., 278–279.

99. Interview with Yehuda Etzion, July 27, 2005.

100. Paley continued to teach at the Keshet Field School in the Golan Heights, and Neuberger returned to his work as a gardener. Some of the others eventually took up senior positions in the settlement movement. Uri Meir became the managing director of the Economic Company of the Golan Heights, and Natan Natanzon was appointed secretary general of Gush Emunim. Bohaz and Ya'akov Henman focused their energies on Gush Emunim's political campaign to halt the disengagement from Sinai.

101. Jerusalem Regional Court, Criminal File 203/84, 395.

102. Ibid., 422.

103. Roni Shaked and Gabi Baron, "Three Men in Kaffiyehs Shot in All Directions—And the Students Bled," *Yedioth Ahronoth*, July 27, 1983, pp. 1, 3 (Hebrew).

104. Zvi Barel, "Fear of Unruliness and Murders Followed Terror Attack in Hebron," *Haaretz*, July 27, 1983, p. 1 (Hebrew).

105. Shaked and Baron, "Three Men in Kaffiyehs," 1, 3.

106. Ibid.

107. Shaked and Baron, "Three Men in Kaffiyehs," 1, 3; Barel, "Fear of Unruliness," 1; Gillon, *Shabak Among the Shreds*, 108; Jerusalem Regional Court, Criminal File 203/84, 365.

108. Gillon, *Shabak Among the Shreds*, 108.

109. Ibid., 105; Barel, "Fear of Unruliness," 1.

110. Jerusalem Regional Court, Criminal File 203/84, 367.

111. Ibid., 396.

112. Ibid., 369.

113. Ibid.

114. Ibid.

115. Ibid., 401.

116. Segal, *Dear Brothers*, 159.

117. Zvi Barel, "Those Suspected in Attempt to Bomb Arab Buses—From the West Bank and Golan Heights," *Haaretz*, April 29, 1984, p. 1 (Hebrew); the company was owned by an Arab called Muhammad Juliani from East Jerusalem.

118. Menachem Livni said at the trial, "The goal was to prevent, as much as possible, the spread of the wave of explosions external to the bus itself. In addition, the detonators and the primers were put at the bottom in order to create a wave of explosion upwards, again, in order to prevent, as much as possible, the spread of the shock wave" (Jerusalem District Court, Criminal File 203/84, 371).

119. Barel, "Those Suspected in Attempt to Bomb Arab Buses," 1; Roni Shaked, "Shortly Before Sunrise, Bombs Were Dismantled in Six Buses; The Seventh Was on Its Way," *Yedioth Ahronoth,* April 29, 1984, p. 3 (Hebrew).

120. According to Carmi Gilon, Shaul Nir was the one who offered to help in dismantling the explosives (Gillon, *Shabak Among the Shreds,* 114). According to the written press, the Shabak agent helped in dismantling the explosives (Barel, "Those Suspected in an Attempt to Bomb Arab Buses," 1; Zvi Barel, "This Is How the Jewish Underground Operated," *Haaretz,* May 11, 1984, pp. 1, 2 (Hebrew)). Therefore, it seems that the agent was Shaul Nir.

121. Segal, *Dear Brothers,* 157.

122. Zvi Barel, "Indictments Against the Detainees of the Bus Affair Are Soon to Be Submitted," *Haaretz,* April 30, 1984, p. 1 (Hebrew); Gabi Baron, Gad Lior, and Roni Shaked, "Head of GSS Reported to Shamir: We Prevented a Grave National Disaster," *Yedioth Ahronoth* Saturday Supplement, May 4, 1984, p. 1 (Hebrew).

123. Gad Lior, "A Lead: The Security Authorities' Surveillance Found That Stolen Weapons from IDF Were Directed to a Number of Settlers," *Yedioth Ahronoth,* April 30, 1984, p. 4 (Hebrew).

124. For a description of the discovery of the underground, see Gillon, *Shabak Among the Shreds,* 102–115.

125. Zvi Barel, "GSS Followed Underground Members for Three Years," *Haaretz,* May 8, 1984, p. 1 (Hebrew).

126. Menachem Horowitz, "Shock in Golan Heights," *Haaretz,* April 29, 1984, p. 2 (Hebrew).

127. Baron et al., "Head of GSS Reported to Shamir," 1.

CHAPTER FOUR **MEIR KAHANE AND THE KACH MOVEMENT: JEWS AGAINST ISRAELIS**

1. Investigation Commission for the Matter of the Massacre at the Cave of Patriarchs in Hebron, *Commission Report* (Jerusalem: The Commission, 1994), 28 (Hebrew).

2. Bill Hutman, Alon Pinkas, and Judy Siegal, "Wave of Riots After Hebron Massacre. Kiryat Arba Doctor Slays 39; Over 20 Palestinians Die in Aftermath," *The Jerusalem Post,* February 27, 1994, p. 1.

3. Hutman et al., "Wave of Riots," p. 1; Ehud Sprinzak, *Political Violence in Israel* (Jerusalem: The Jerusalem Institute for Israeli Studies, 1995), 101 (Hebrew).

4. Investigation Commission, *Commission Report* (Jerusalem, 1994), 78–80 (Hebrew).

5. Ibid.

6. Ibid., 76; Allan C. Brownfeld, *Facing the Future: The Need to Promote Free Speech and Confront Extremism in the Jewish Community* (Ponte Vedra Beach, Fla.: The American Council for Judaism, 2005), http://www.acjna.org/acjna/articles_detail.aspx?id=358 (March 24, 2006).

7. Investigation Commission, *Committee Report,* 76.

8. Ibid.

9. Zvi Zinger and Yael Gvirz, "Doctor and Murderer," *Yedioth Ahronoth* 24 Hours Supplement, February 27, 1994, pp. 2–3 (Hebrew).

10. Prevention of Terror Ordinance (Command No. 33, 1948). The ordinance deals with the definition of a terrorist organization and the ways in which the state copes with it. Among other things, it establishes, in paragraph 8, that the decision of declaring a political organization to be a terrorist organization is in the hands of the government.

10. Gideon Alon, "Rabin: Even in My Worst Nightmares I Had Not Thought About a Massacre," *Haaretz*, March 1, 1994, p. 1 (Hebrew).

11. The exact name of the hotel is Nahar el Haled.

12. David Wilder, "Forty Years in the Desert," the Jewish Settlement in Hebron Web site, http://www.hebron.org.il/hebrew/article.php?id=486 (Hebrew).

13. Kiryat Arba is a local council that is located near the city of Hebron, and its area of jurisdiction is 3,500 square miles. It was declared as a Local Council in 1979. According to the Central Bureau of Statistics, as of September 2003, there were 6,500 inhabitants in Kiryat Arba.

14. In September 1988, Levinger's car was attacked by stones. He got out of his car and killed a young Palestinian who was probably not connected to the stone throwers.

15. B'tselem, *Area H-2 in Hebron, Abandonment of Palestinians as a Result of the Presence of Settlers in Town* (B'tselem series of reports, August 2003) (Hebrew).

16. Ibid.

17. Ibid.

18. Ehud Sprinzak, *The Ascendance of Israel's Radical Right* (New York: Oxford University Press, 1991); Ehud Sprinzak, *Brother Against Brother: Violence and Extremism in Israeli Politics from Altalena to the Rabin Assassination* (New York: Free Press, 1999); Judith Tydor Baumel, "Kahane in America: An Exercise in Right-Wing Urban Terror," *Studies in Conflict and Terrorism*, 22 (October 1999): 311–329; Anti-Defamation League, "The Violent Record of the Kahane Movement and Its Offshoots, 1995," http://www.adl.org/extremism/kahane1.pdf (March 26, 2006).

19. Robert I. Friedman, *The False Prophet: Rabbi Meir Kahane: From FBI Informant to Knesset Member* (London: Faber and Faber, 1990); Raphael Cohen-Almagor, *The Boundaries of Liberty and Tolerance: The Struggle Against Kahanism in Israel* (Gainesville: University Press of Florida, 1994); Raphael Mergui and Philippe Simonnot, *Israel's Ayatollahs: Meir Kahane and the Far Right in Israel* (London: Saqi, 1990); S. Daniel Breslauer, *Meir Kahane, Ideologue, Hero, Thinker* (Lewiston, N.Y.: E. Mellen, 1990); Yair Kotler, *Heil Kahane* (New York: Adama, 1986); Ruth Gavison, *The Ideology of Meir Kahane and His Supporters* (Jerusalem: Van Leer Institute, 1986) (Hebrew).

20. Reb Yudel Web page, March 23, 2006, http://www.shmoozenet.com/yudel/mtarchives/001610.html (April 17, 2006).

21. The all-channel form is illustrated by the current network of the global jihad, in which there are no hubs and all nodes are connected to all others.

22. For a review of the global Salafi jihad, see Marc Sageman, *Understanding Terror Networks* (Philadelphia: University of Pennsylvania Press, 2004).

23. Ibid.

24. Ehud Sprinzak, "Kach and Meir Kahane: The Emergence of Jewish Quasi-Fascism," *Patterns of Prejudice*, 19, no. 3–4 (1985), http://www.geocities.com/alabasters_archive/kach_and_kahane.html#bottom#bottom (April 15, 2006).

25. The JDL slogan "Never Again" was once the slogan of Jewish resistance fighters in the Warsaw ghetto. It was interpreted as a cry never to allow the Holocaust to happen again, or never to allow the destruction of Israel, or never to allow genocide to be perpetrated against any other people.

26. Meir Kahane, *The Story of the Jewish Defense League* (Jerusalem: The Institute for the Publication of the Writings of Meir Kahane, 2002), 21.

27. Ibid.

28. Ibid.

29. "New York Jewish Youth in Anti-Soviet Move," *The Jerusalem Post*, December 31, 1969, p. 2.

30. For instance, in 1961 Kahane founded together with Joseph Churba an investigation institute by the name of "Consultant Research," and in 1963 he was asked by the Federal Bureau of Investigation to penetrate the John Birch Society, an extremist right-wing association, with the aim of exposing its financial resources (Kotler, *Heil Kahane*, 36–37). Kahane was also associated with Joseph Colombo, the head of an Italian crime family. The connection between them started in 1971, when Kahane needed money to bail himself out of prison. Over time a relationship developed between them, and it was expressed in the connections the JDL had with the Italian-American Civil Rights League, which was headed by Colombo. The connection between the two started to weaken after Colombo's injury in 1971 (Kotler, *Heil Kahane*, 79–86).

31. Ibid., 79–86.

32. "From Throwing Tomatoes to Weapon Smuggling," *Haaretz*, April 23, 1980 (Hebrew).

33. Kotler, *Heil Kahane*, 94–95.

34. Ibid., 100.

35. Sprinzak, "Kach and Meir Kahane."

36. The African Hebrew Israelite Nation of Jerusalem is a small religious group whose members believe that they are descendants of one of the Ten Lost Jewish Tribes. Most group members live in their community in the city of Dimona, which is located in the south of Israel, about 22 miles south of Be'er Sheba. The community in Dimona is the largest and has approximately 2,000 members, but there are other communities in Arad and Tiberias also.

37. Ehud Sprinzak, *The Origins of the Politics of Delegitimation in Israel, 1967–73* (Jerusalem: Hebrew University of Jerusalem, 1975), 26 (Hebrew).

38. Kotler, *Heil Kahane*, 125.

39. Ibid., 133.

40. Ibid.

41. Friedman, *The False Prophet*, 149–153.

42. Kotler, *Heil Kahane*, 133.

43. Ibid.

44. The split between Yossi Dayan and Kahane took place in 1981 after Dayan published a leaflet of questions and answers in which he wrote that Kach was not a one-man movement. A few months later, Dayan had to leave Kach. From Sprinzak, "Kach and Meir Kahane."

45. Interview with Yoel Lerner, December 25, 2005.

46. Nadav Shragai, *The Temple Mount Conflict* (Jerusalem: Keter, 1995), 85–86 (Hebrew).

47. Yaron Avituv, "The Predictor of the State," *Kol Ha'ir*, August 4, 1989 (Hebrew).

48. Interview with Yoel Lerner, December 25, 2005.

49. Ibid.

50. Ibid.

51. Religious Zionist youth movement.

52. Interview with Yoel Lerner, December 25, 2005.

53. Jerusalem Regional Court, Criminal File 255/78.

54. Interview with Yoel Lerner, December 25, 2005.

55. Ibid.

56. Avituv, "The Predictor of the State."

57. Interview with Yoel Lerner, December 25, 2005.

58. Rabbi Moshe Zvi Segal was an important figure in religious Zionist and right-wing circles. Born in Poltava in the Ukraine, Rabbi Segal was first a member of the Haganah and later of the Etzel and Lehi pre-state Jewish militias. In 1937 he was arrested by the British for blowing a shofar at the Western Wall to mark the close of Yom Kippur. He led the right-wing Brit Hashmonaim youth movement before the establishment of the State of Israel and renewed its activities in the early 1980s. He was a member of the Towards the Mountain of God movement, which led campaigns to allow Jewish prayer on the Temple Mount, although he never tried to enter the Temple Mount himself and concentrated instead on raising awareness of this issue. He was the first Jew to settle in the Old City of Jerusalem in 1967 after the war.

59. Interview with Yoel Lerner, December 25, 2005.

60. "Israeli Convicted of Plotting to Destroy Mosque," UPI, October 26, 1982; Interview with Yoel Lerner, December 25, 2005.

61. Shragai, *The Temple Mount Conflict*, 93.

62. Interview with Yoel Lerner, December 25, 2005.

63. Ibid.

64. A building constructed on the Temple Mount, close to the Dome of the Rock mosque, on its eastern side.

65. Interview with Yoel Lerner, December 25, 2005.

66. Jerusalem Regional Court, Criminal File 420/82.

67. Interview with Yoel Lerner, December 25, 2005.

68. Shragai, *The Temple Mount Conflict*, 92.

69. Sprinzak, *Political Violence*, 82.

70. Carmi Gillon, *Shabak Amongst the Shreds* (Tel Aviv: Yedioth Ahronoth, 2000), 89 (Hebrew).

71. Nadav Shragai, "In the Evacuation of Yamit, Yehuda Richter Hid in the 'Suicide Bunker'; Now He Is Preparing for a Rerun in Tens of Settlements," *Haaretz*, June 10, 2005 (Hebrew), http://www.haaretz.co.il/hasite/pages/ShArtSR.jhtml?itemNo= 597365 (April 15, 2006).

72. Ibid.

73. Gillon, *Shabak Amongst the Shreds*, 89.

74. Ibid.

75. In Israel there are two chief rabbis, Ashkenazi and Sephardic, corresponding with the division into Jews of European origin and Jews from Asia and Africa. Chief rabbis are elected for a ten-year term, and they stand at the head of the Chief Rabbinate, which governs religious matters in Israel.

76. Angus Deming, Milan J. Kubic, Ray Wilkinson, and Julian Nundy, "Bombs and Bulldozers," *Newsweek*, May 3, 1982.

77. William Claiborne, "Israel's Cabinet Votes to Complete Sinai Withdrawal; Most Holdouts Forced from Seaside Town," *The Washington Post*, April 21, 1982.

78. William Claiborne, "Last Nationalist Holdouts Evicted from Sinai Town," *The Washington Post*, April 24, 1982.

79. "Four Very Good Boys," *Yedioth Ahronoth* Saturday Supplement, March 9, 1984, p. 8 (Hebrew).

80. Robert I. Friedman, "Kahane's Commandos," *APF*, 10 (1987), http://www.aliciapat terson.org/APF1005/Friedman/Friedman.html (March 11, 2006).

81. "American Charged with Attacking Arabs in Israel," UPI, January 16, 1986.

82. Ibid.

83. There is no clear-cut knowledge about who notified the press. For another opinion on this, see Friedman, "Kahane's Commandos."

84. Sprinzak, *The Ascendance of Israel's Radical Right*, 236.

85. Kotler, *Heil Kahane*, 316.

86. Sprinzak, *The Ascendance of Israel's Radical Right*, 236.

87. Jesus Rangel, "Man Sought in Israel for Attacks on Arabs Is Seized," *The New York Times*, January 16, 1986.

88. Friedman, "Kahane's Commandos."

89. "Israeli Legislator Compares Jewish Settlers' Trial to Goetz Case," AP, June 17, 1987.

90. Masha Hamilton, "Jewish Settlers Form New Committee to Patrol West Bank Roads," AP, July 24, 1987.

91. "Jewish Settlers Storm West Bank Palestinian Refugee Camp," UPI, June 7, 1987.

92. Nadav Shragai, "We Broke, Set Fire, Poisoned, Uprooted," *Haaretz*, November 23, 1993, p. B2 (Hebrew).

93. In 1986 the Basic Law: The Knesset was amended and paragraph 7a was added. This paragraph states that a list of candidates will not participate in the elections to the Knesset if the goals or actions of the list or of a person (whichever is relevant) negates, explicitly or implicitly, the existence of the State of Israel as a Jewish and a democratic

state, incites to racism, or supports the armed struggle of an enemy state or terrorist organization against the State of Israel. Disqualification of the list according to the amendment had to receive the approval of the Supreme Court.

94. Interview with Yoel Lerner, December 25, 2005.

95. The group was probably also involved in a shooting incident in which Palestinians were targeted at the Jaffa Gate in Jerusalem on April 10, 1988. The group took responsibility for this shooting, but the fact that eyewitnesses testified that the shooting was executed by a man in a uniform and the fact that most of its activities were aimed at Jews rather than directly at Palestinians raise doubts about its involvement in this incident.

96. Arie Kisel, Zvi Zinger, and Izhak Rabbi-Yhiye, "Soldier Who Smuggled Weapon to Kach Sentenced to Two Years in Jail," *Yedioth Aharonoth,* August 5, 1987, p. 1 (Hebrew).

97. Heidi J. Gleit, "Yosef Released to House Arrest. Police Arrest Another Suspect," *The Jerusalem Post,* February 11, 2000.

98. Uri Sharon and Onn Levy, "I Wanted Them to Stop Laughing at Me, Said an Immigrant Soldier, Who Stole a Weapon for Kach," *Davar,* April 23, 1991, p. 3 (Hebrew).

99. Karin Laub, "Palestinian Woman Killed in Apparent Revenge for Slayings of Jews," AP, August 7, 1990.

100. Tel Aviv Regional Court, Criminal File 135/91, 79.

101. Michael Rotem, "Two Kiryat Arba Men Remanded in Slaying of Arab Woman," *The Jerusalem Post,* March 10, 1991.

102. Eileen Powell, "Slayings of Palestinians Linked to Kahane Assassination," AP, November 6, 1990; Sergei Sharghorodsky, "Kahane Follower Suspected of Revenge Killing of Elderly Arabs," AP, November 9, 1990; Ron Kampeas and Michael Rotem, "Kach Man Held in Arab Deaths," *The Jerusalem Post,* November 11, 1990; Evelyn Gordon, "Court Upholds Detention of Two Kach Activists," *The Jerusalem Post,* July 13, 1994.

103. "Four Boys Who Threw Grenade in Butcher's Market Convicted of Murder," *Haaretz,* December 21, 1994, p. A7 (Hebrew).

104. Yossi Torpstein, Eitan Rabin, and Nadav Shragai, "Arab Killed and Twelve Injured from Grenade Thrown in Central Jerusalem; Suspicion: Jews Committed Crime," *Haaretz,* November 17, 1992, p. 1 (Hebrew); "Four Boys Who Threw Grenade," A7.

105. Torpstein et al., "Arab Killed," 1.

106. Sageman, *Understanding Terror Networks.*

107. Ami Pedahzur and Arie Perliger, "The Changing Nature of Suicide Attacks: A Social Network Perspective," *Social Forces,* 84 (2006): 1987–2008.

CHAPTER FIVE **THE ASSASSINATION OF YITZHAK RABIN**

1. Bill Hutman and Jon Immanuel, "Police Have Lead on Killers of Three Palestinians, Says Shahal. Car Involved in Attack Found Near Beit Shemesh," *The Jerusalem Post,* December 12, 1993.

2. "Jewish Settlers Gun Down Three Palestinians in Revenge Attack," *Mideast Mirror*, December 10, 1993.

3. "Accused Member of Jewish Underground Acquitted of Most Charges," AP, January 31, 1995.

4. Bill Hutman and David Rudge, "Edri Hospitalized, Complains of Weariness," *The Jerusalem Post*, September 11, 1994.

5. Ibid.

6. Israel High Court, Criminal Objection 1368/96, 2–3.

7. Ibid., 1–2.

8. Michael Karpin and Ina Friedman, *Murder in the Name of God* (Tel Aviv: Zmora-Bitan, 1999), 100 (Hebrew).

9. Idith Zertal and Akiva Eldar, *Lords of the Land* (Or Yehuda, Israel: Kinneret, Zmora-Bitan, Dvir, 2004), 187 (Hebrew).

10. After the assassination, the name was changed to Rabin Square.

11. Amnon Kapeliouk, *Rabin: Political Murder* (Tel Aviv: Sifriat Poalim, 1996), 9 (Hebrew).

12. Over time the song has become an informal hymn of the peace movement, and it is commonly sung at assemblies and demonstrations.

13. *Report: State Commission of Inquiry into the Matter of the Murder of the Late Prime Minister Yitzhak Rabin* (Jerusalem: Stata, 1996), 88–89 (Hebrew).

14. Kapeliouk, *Rabin*, 11.

15. Karpin and Friedman, *Murder in the Name of God*, 213–214.

16. Yossi Hatoni and Reuven Shapira, "Murder Investigation Concentrates on Connections Between Amir Brothers and Far Right Members," *Haaretz*, November 8, 1995, p. A2 (Hebrew).

17. Kapeliouk, *Rabin*, 12.

18. *Report: State Commission of Inquiry*, 26.

19. Ibid., 28 (Hebrew).

20. Kapeliouk, *Rabin*, 13.

21. Karin Laub, "International News," AP, November 5, 1995.

22. Tel Aviv Regional Court, Criminal File 498/95, 8.

23. Ibid., 12.

24. Dianna Cahn, "Rabin Killed by Assassin's Bullets," AP, November 4, 1995.

25. "Government of Israel Announces with Shock," *Haaretz*, November 4, 1995, p. 1.

26. *Report: State Commission of Inquiry*, 88.

27. Kapeliouk, *Rabin*, 21.

28. Ehud Sprinzak, "Israel's Radical Right and the Countdown to Rabin's Assassination," in Yoram Peri, ed., *The Assassination of Yitzhak Rabin* (Stanford, Calif.: Stanford University Press, 2000), 122.

29. Yaron Kaner, "Eyal Seminar in Hebron, The Organizer: Yigal Amir," *Yedioth Ahronoth* Seven Days Supplement, November 10, 1995, p. 12 (Hebrew).

30. Ibid.

31. Kapeliouk, *Rabin*, 38.

32. Ibid.

33. Linda Gradstein, "Court Rules Rabin Assassination Part of Conspiracy," NPR, September 11, 1996.

34. Ibid.

35. Reuven Shapira, "Yigal Amir and His Friends Considered Blowing Up Rabin's Car with Powerful Bomb," *Haaretz,* November 14, 1995, p. A4 (Hebrew); Zvi Barel, "Prosecutor: Amir Considered Shooting Lau Missile at Rabin's Car," *Haaretz,* December 6, 1995, p. A4 (Hebrew).

36. Eitan Rabin, "Yigal Amir Planned to Blow Up Rabin's House by Injecting Nitroglycerine into Water Pipe," *Haaretz,* November 19, 1995, pp. A1, A2 (Hebrew).

37. Tel Aviv Regional Court, Criminal File 498/95, 28.

38. Eitan Rabin and Shragai Nadav, "The GSS Investigate if Rabbis Gave Religious Authorization to Rabin's Assassin," *Haaretz,* November 9, 1995, pp. A1, A2 (Hebrew).

39. Tel Aviv Regional Court, Criminal Objection 4253/98.

40. Ibid., 1.

41. Alon Pinkas, "Soldier Indicted for Supplying Arms, Ammunition to Amir. First Indictment in Connection with Rabin Assassination," *The Jerusalem Post,* December 5, 1995.

42. Kapeliouk, *Rabin,* 40; Margalit Har-Shefi is the only member of the network who was convicted for not having prevented the murder of Rabin.

43. Pinkas, "Soldier Indicted"; Reuven Shapira, Yossi Hatoni, and Or Keshet, "Settler from Beit El, Student in Bar-Ilan, Arrested Under Suspicion of Involvement in Rabin Murder," *Haaretz,* November 16, 1995, p. 1 (Hebrew); Reuven Shapira and Yossi Hatoni, "Investigator: Involvement of Settler from Beit El in Rabin Murder—Dominant," *Haaretz,* November 16, 1995, p. A3 (Hebrew); Yossi Hatoni, Reuven Shapira, and Eitan Rabin, "Police Will Soon Investigate Four Additional Rabbis on Suspicion of Incitement to Rabin Murder," *Haaretz,* November 27, 1995, p.A1 (Hebrew).

44. Settlers who live in settlements in the occupied territories behind the Green Line are entitled to receive permission to carry a weapon in self-defense from the Ministry of Interior. After they receive the permit, they may approach the military authorities and obtain the weapon from them.

45. Karpin and Friedman, *Murder in the Name of God,* 226.

46. Kapeliouk, *Rabin,* 25.

47. Ibid., 29.

48. Tel Aviv Regional Court, Criminal File 498/95, 8; Reuven Shapira, Yossi Hatoni, Aluf Benn, Eitan Rabin, Orna Eridor, and Akiva Eldar, "Prime Minister Yitzhak Rabin Killed by Assassin," *Haaretz,* p. 1 (Hebrew).

49. Karpin and Friedman, *Murder in the Name of God,* 224.

50. Tel Aviv Regional Court, Criminal File 498/95, 56; Tel Aviv Regional Court, Criminal Objection 4253/98, 1–2, 39; Dan Izenberg, "Amir Brothers' Sentences Increased," *The Jerusalem Post,* August 30, 1999; Danny Ben-Tal, "Rabin's Assassin: I Should Have Done It Sooner," AP, October 3, 1996.

CHAPTER SIX **THE SECOND INTIFADA: VENGEANCE**

1. Yonatan Liss, "Four Settlers Suspected in Attempt to Blow Up Arab School in East Jerusalem," *Haaretz*, May 12, 2002, p. A6 (Hebrew).

2. Jerusalem Regional Court, Criminal File 5034/02, 2.

3. Liss, "Four Settlers Suspected," A6.

4. Ibid.

5. Daniel Ben Simon, "In the Name of Jewish Pride," *Haaretz*, April 25, 2003, p. B2 (Hebrew); Jerusalem Regional Court, Criminal File 5034/02, 2.

6. Ben Simon, "In the Name of Jewish Pride," B2.

7. For a review of the connections between members of the network, see Jerusalem Regional Court, Criminal Files 5034/02, 5035/03, 216/03, 619/03, 3075/02, and 198/03.

8. Ben Simon, "In the Name of Jewish Pride," B2.

9. Nadav Shragai, "The Judges Raised the Punishment Bar, Their Objective: Deterrence," *Haaretz*, October 1, 2003, p. A4 (Hebrew).

10. Baruch Shay, "The Difficult Grain," NRG, June 12, 2003 (Hebrew), http://www.nrg .co.il/online/archive/ART/493/494.html (April 12, 2006).

11. Nava Tzuriel, "GSS and Its War on Hilltop Youth," NRG, October 11, 2002 (Hebrew), http://www.nrg.co.il/online/archive/ART/361/556.html (April 12, 2006); Michal Kafra, "Nati Would Have Wanted It This Way," *Maariv*, January 24, 2003 (Hebrew), http://www.nrg.co.il/online/archive/ART/424/133.html (April 12, 2006).

12. Yossi Levi, "School for Investigators," NRG, January 4, 2003 (Hebrew), http://www .nrg.co.il/online/archive/ART/600/081.html (April 12, 2006).

13. Jerusalem Regional Court, Criminal File 216/03, http://www.takdinet.co.il (May 9, 2006).

14. Ibid.

15. Ibid.

16. Jerusalem Regional Court, Criminal File 619/03, http://www.takdinet.co.il (May 9, 2006).

17. Nadav Shragai and Yair Ettinger, "Network Members Hid Tremendous Quantities of Weapons in Caves Near Adei Ad," *Haaretz*, September 21, 2003, p. A4 (Hebrew).

18. Because of contradictions, the testimony was disqualified in court.

19. Yonatan Liss and Nadav Shragai, "Suspicion: Federman and Menashe Levinger Members of Terror Group," *Haaretz*, May 15, 2002, p. 1 (Hebrew).

20. Yonatan Liss, "Investigation into Murder of Two Palestinians Near Ramallah at Dead End," *Haaretz*, April 4, 2002, p. A8 (Hebrew).

21. Yonatan Liss, "Attacks Against Palestinians: Most Perpetrators Evade Capture," *Haaretz*, June 23, 2002, p. A5 (Hebrew).

22. Liss, "Investigation into Murder," A8.

23. Amos Harel and Yonatan Liss, "Palestinian Killed and One Injured Near Ramallah; The Suspicion: Shot by Jews," *Haaretz*, April 2, 2002, p. A10 (Hebrew).

24. Roni Shaked, "Suspicion: Jews Detonated Explosive in Arab School," *Yedioth Ahronoth*, September 18, 2002, p. 2 (Hebrew).

25. Yonatan Liss and Amos Harel, "Security Authorities: Jewish Group Put Two Explosive Charges in Beita School," *Haaretz*, September 18, 2002, p. 1 (Hebrew).

26. Ibid.

27. Moshe Rainfeld, "Attorney's Office: Accused in Jewish Terrorism Also Committed Zur Baher Bombing," *Haaretz*, June 3, 2002, p. A5 (Hebrew).

28. Yonatan Liss, "Shabak Failed to Expose Jewish Terror Groups; Suspects: Looking Under Flashlight," *Haaretz*, April 11, 2003, p. A12 (Hebrew).

29. Shragai and Ettinger, "Network Members," A4.

30. Nadav Shragai, "I Wanted the Arabs to Know the Feeling of Collecting Their Children in Bags," *Haaretz*, September 22, 2003, p. B3 (Hebrew).

31. Ibid.

32. Yonatan Liss, "Gamliel and Dvir Decided on the Method and Destination of Attack," *Haaretz*, October 1, 2003, p. A4 (Hebrew).

33. Jerusalem Regional Court, Criminal File 216/03, http://www.takdinet.co.il (May 9, 2006).

34. Shragai, "I Wanted the Arabs to Know," B3.

35. Ibid.

36. Yonatan Liss, "Detention of Another Suspect of Attacking Arabs Extended," *Haaretz*, May 9, 2002, p. A6 (Hebrew).

37. Liss, "Shabak Failed," A12.

38. Homesh is a settlement in northern Samaria. The settlement was set up by a Nahal core group (*gar'in*) in 1978 and became a civilian settlement two years later.

39. Chen Kotz-Bar, "The Spark," *Maariv* Weekend Supplement, July 1, 2005, p. 1 (Hebrew).

40. Ibid.

41. Yitzhar is a settlement in Samaria on the Jerusalem–Nablus road. It was founded by an IDF Nahal core group and transformed into a civilian settlement in 1983 by a number of families that established a community on the site. The majority of the inhabitants are nationalist Haredim. The settlement gained publicity in the wake of their violent aggressions against Palestinians who lived in the area and the IDF when it attempted to evacuate illegal outposts erected around the settlement.

42. This was the first settlement to be constructed in Samaria and also the biggest. Elon Moreh gained publicity after the ongoing (seven years) and intensive struggle of the Gush Emunim people to build it. The original core group that constructed the settlement in 1977 consisted of a number of families and bachelors, most of them leaders of Gush Emunim.

43. Kotz-Bar, "The Spark," 1.

44. Ibid.

45. Ibid.

46. Ibid.

47. Amos Harel and Yonatan Liss, "The GSS Exposed a Jewish Organization Which Intended to Attack the Temple Mount," *Haaretz*, May 17, 2005, p. 1 (Hebrew).

48. Ibid.

49. Ibid.
50. Chabad is one the largest branches of Hasidic Judaism in Israel and around the world. Its name is an acronym based on three Hebrew words, *chokhma* ("wisdom"), *bina* ("understanding"), and *da'at* ("knowledge"), which refer to the higher numerations of the Kabbalah. The name was chosen by the founder of Chabad, Rabbi Schneur Zalman of Liadi, who was called the Old Admor and Baal Hatanya by his followers. Rabbi Menachem Mendel Schneerson (April 18, 1902–June 12, 1994), the seventh Chabad Admor, was the spiritual leader of the Chabad movement from 1951 until his death in 1994. The adoration of his adherents only increased during his reign, and in his later years he was addressed as the Messiah King.
51. Meaning "power" and also an acronym of "Kahane Lives."
52. Ronny Sofer and Efrat Weiss, "Palestinian Critically Wounded at Tal Yam: 'It Was a Lynch,'" *Ynet,* June 29, 2005 (Hebrew), http://www.ynet.co.il/articles/0,7340, L-3105629,00.html (April 15, 2006).
53. Ronny Sofer and Efrat Weiss, "Extremist Stronghold in Moasi Evacuated by Army and Police," *Ynet,* June 29, 2005 (Hebrew), http://www.ynet.co.il/articles/0,7340, L-3105843,00.html (April 15, 2006).
54. Ronny Sofer and Hanan Greenberg, "Gaza Strip Closed by Army Order: The Hotel Is in Our Sights," *Ynet,* June 30, 2005 (Hebrew), http://www.ynet.co.il/articles/0,7340, L-3106099,00.html (April 15, 2006).
55. For example, Michael Ben-Horin is quoted as saying, "The Jewish People and their connection to the Land of Israel came before the Israeli governments." From Efrat Weiss, "Extreme Right: We Will Disengage from Israel and Establish the 'State of Judea,'" *Ynet,* June 7, 2004 (Hebrew), http://www.ynet.co.il/articles/0,7340,L-2928254, 00.html (April 17, 2006).
56. Eitan was one of the more prominent leaders of the Israeli right wing toward the end of the 1980s and the beginning of the 1990s. He was the IDF chief of staff between 1978 and 1983. After completing his duty, he founded Tzomet, a political party with an extreme right-wing agenda. He spearheaded the party between 1984 and 1989, until he retired from political life.
57. Interview with David Ha'ivri, August 4, 2005.
58. Ibid.
59. Scott Wilson, "Jewish Settler Kills Four Israeli Arabs in Attack on Bus," *Washington Post,* August 5, 2005, p. A01.
60. Yaakov Katz et al., "Far-Right Soldier Slays 4 Arabs in Shfaram. Mob Lynches Gunman Who Had Gone to Protest Pullout," *The Jerusalem Post,* August 5, 2005, p. 1.
61. Ibid.
62. "The Terrorist Left a Letter: I Will Not Expel Jews," *Ynet,* August 4, 2005 (Hebrew), http://www.ynet.co.il/articles/0,7340,L-3122803,00.html (April 10, 2006).
63. Ibid.
64. Mital Yashur Beit-Or, "Eitam: Olmert Ordered a Pogrom," *Ynet,* February 1, 2006 (Hebrew), http://www.ynet.co.il/articles/0,7340,L-3209443,00.html (April 10, 2006).
65. Ibid.

66. Hanan Greenberg and Meital Yas'ur-Beit Or, "Commander of the Border Police: 'Five Years We Haven't Seen Such Violence Against the Police,'" *Ynet*, February 1, 2006 (Hebrew), http://www.ynet.co.il/articles/0,7340,L-3209427,00.html (April 17, 2006).

67. Ibid.

CHAPTER SEVEN ECCENTRIC CULTS, VENGEANCES, AND LONE WOLVES

1. Israel High Court, Criminal Objection 1294/96, 1; Reuven Shapira and Moshe Tovel, "'If the Police Will Enter, a Lot of Blood Will Be Spilled,'" *Haaretz*, March 25, 1994, p. A2 (Hebrew); Moshe Tovel and Reuven Shapira, "Shots Fired Between Police and Dozens of People Barricaded in the House in Yehud; One Man Wounded," *Haaretz*, March 25, 1994, pp. A1, A10 (Hebrew).

2. Yoav Appel, "Third Judicial Inquiry on Missing Children Places No Blame," AP, November 5, 2001.

3. Raine Marcus, "Meshulam Signs Pact, Surrenders," *The Jerusalem Post*, March 28, 1994.

4. For further details on the Meshulam affair, see Israel High Court, Criminal Objection 1632/95.

5. Reuven Shapira and Moshe Tovel, "Meshulam Supporters Shot at Helicopter and Police That Surrounded the House," *Haaretz*, May 11, 1994, p. A9 (Hebrew).

6. Moshe Tovel, "Thirty-Six Meshulam Supporters Surrendered to Police," *Haaretz*, May 12, 1994, p. A9 (Hebrew).

7. Raine Marcus, "Meshulam, 20 of His Followers, Remanded for 12 More Days," *The Jerusalem Post*, May 25, 1994; Shapira and Tovel, "Meshulam Supporters Shot at Helicopter," A9.

8. Among Meshulam's followers, as among sectors of the religious Zionist camp, it is forbidden for a man to listen to a woman singing because it is considered immodest.

9. For example, Uzi Meshulam gave an interview to the newspapers when he was jailed.

10. Reuven Shapira, "Ramle Prison Security Officer Shot and Wounded; Attackers Probably Uzi Meshulam People," *Haaretz*, October 31, 1994, p. 1 (Hebrew).

11. "Grenades Found in Three Christian Centers in Jerusalem," AP, December 9, 1983.

12. "Hand Grenade Explodes in Arab Village, Linked to Jewish Movement," AP, December 12, 1983.

13. Mel Laytner, "Grenades Explode in Jerusalem Mosque and Monastery," UPI, December 20, 1983.

14. "Foreign News Briefs," UPI, April 9, 1984.

15. Izhar Be'er, "Gang of Bombers," *Kol Hair*, April 19, 1995, pp. 21–25 (Hebrew).

16. "Six Years Imprisonment for Ein Kerem Gang," *Haaretz*, November 21, 1984, p. 3 (Hebrew).

17. Ibid.

18. Jerusalem District Court, Criminal File 262/84.

19. Nadav Shragai, *The Temple Mount Conflict* (Jerusalem: Keter, 1995), 172 (Hebrew).

20. Jerusalem District Court, Criminal File 262/84.

21. Ibid., 10.

22. "Israel: In Brief; Trial of Suspected Temple Mount Terrorists," *BBC Summary of World Broadcasts,* June 16, 1984.

23. "Jerusalem Taxi Driver Killed, Second in Four Days," AP, April 23, 1985.

24. "Policeman, Soldier and Student Arrested in Suspicion of Murder of Taxi Driver," *Haaretz,* May 19, 1985, p. 1 (Hebrew).

25. "Three Jewish Killers of Arab Taxi Driver Given Life Imprisonment," *Haaretz,* December 4, 1986, p. 6 (Hebrew).

26. Ibid.

27. Ibid.

28. Louis Meixler, "Palestinian Photo Angers Israelis," AP, October 13, 2000.

29. "Fourteen Years in Prison for Soldiers Who Tried to Avenge the Death of Soldiers," *Ynet,* June 6, 2002 (Hebrew), http://www.ynet.co.il/articles/0,7340,L-1626888,00.html (April 21, 2006).

30. Ibid.

31. Tal Eyal, "I Wanted to Take Revenge—So I Shot Them," NRG, October 15, 2001 (Hebrew), http://www.nrg.co.il/online/archive/ART74/648.html (April 18, 2006).

32. Yonatan Hilleli, "'I Was Drunk and Unconscious' Said Soldier Who Shot Bystanders in Haifa," NRG, July 5, 2001 (Hebrew), http://www.nrg.co.il/online/archive/ART/161/867.html (April 18, 2006).

33. "'I Don't Hate Arabs, I Believed They Harm Israeli Security,'" *Ynet,* March 30, 2004 (Hebrew), http://www.ynet.co.il/articles/0,7340,L-2896343,00.html (April 17, 2006).

34. David Rudge, "Haifa Jews Held for Attacks on Arabs," *The Jerusalem Post,* March 5, 2004.

35. Haifa Regional Court, Criminal File 1035/04, 2.

36. Ibid.; "'I Don't Hate Arabs.'"

37. Haifa Regional Court, Criminal File 1035/04, 2; "'I Don't Hate Arabs.'"

38. Haifa Regional Court, Criminal File 1034/04, 4.

39. Ibid.

40. Ibid., 2.

41. Ibid.

42. Rudge, "Haifa Jews Held."

43. Ibid.

44. Haifa Regional Court, Criminal File 1035/04, 3.

45. Rudge, "Haifa Jews Held."

46. David Ratner, "Suspicion: Rabbis Knew About Bombs in Haifa," *Haaretz,* March 19, 2004, p. 1 (Hebrew).

47. Ahiya Rabad, "After a Week Unconscious, Eliran Golan Died," *Ynet,* September 8, 2005 (Hebrew), http://www.ynet.co.il/articles/0,7340,L-3139523,00.html (April 18, 2006).

48. Shragai, *The Temple Mount Conflict,* 166–167.

49. Ibid., 167.

50. Ibid., 163.

51. Ibid.

52. Rona S. Hirsch, "Temple Mount Shooter's Release Rekindles Memories," *Baltimore Jewish Times*, November 7, 1997, p. 2.

53. Tel Aviv Regional Court, Criminal File 4144/98, 2.

54. Ibid.

55. Ibid.

56. Gad Lior, "Is Joy at the Revenge on Arabs a Sin? Kahane Asked His Investigators," *Yedioth Ahronoth* Saturday Supplement, November 22, 1984, p. 8 (Hebrew).

57. Nadav Shragai, "Family of Rocket Shooter on Arab Bus Shocked: He Was Never Involved in Politics," *Haaretz,* November 5, 1984, p. 2 (Hebrew).

58. Ibid.

59. Ariel Ben-Ami, "The War Against Palestinians Has Begun," *Davar,* September 23, 1984, p. 1 (Hebrew).

60. Gad Lior and Roni Shaked, "'Passengers Started Jumping from the Windows' Said Driver of Arab Bus, 'Everything Was Soaked in Blood,'" *Yedioth Ahronoth,* October 29, 1984, p. 3 (Hebrew); Nadav Shragai, "Shooters on Arab Bus in Jerusalem Are Professionals," *Haaretz,* October 29, 1984, pp. 1, 2 (Hebrew).

61. Lior and Shaked, "'Passengers Started Jumping,'" 3; Shragai, "Shooters on Arab Bus," 1, 2.

62. Lior and Shaked, "'Passengers Started Jumping,'" 3; Shragai, "Shooters on Arab Bus,'" 1, 2.

63. Jon Immanuel, "Settler Held in Killing of Captured Terrorist; Shooting Took Place After Man Was Bound Hand and Foot," *The Jerusalem Post,* March 24, 1993; Joel Greenberg, "An Arab, Tied Up, Is Shot to Death," *The New York Times,* March 24, 1993; "Settler Arrested, Palestinian Killed as Violence Continues," UPI, March 24, 1993.

64. Immanuel, "Settler Held in Killing"; Greenberg, "An Arab, Tied Up"; "Settler Arrested."

65. Be'er Sheva Regional Court, Criminal File 20430/03, 1.

66. Reuven Kaplan and Eli Bohadana, "Charge Sheet: Tried to Avenge the Killing of Brother," NRG, March 5, 2003 (Hebrew), http://www.nrg.co.il/online/archive/ART/443/981.html (April 14, 2006).

67. Reuven Kaplan, "Tattooed the Same Tattoo as Her Late Brother," NRG, March 5, 2003 (Hebrew), http://www.nrg.co.il/online/archive/ART/443/913.html (April 14, 2006).

68. M. Jerrold Post, "Terrorist Psycho-logic: Terrorist Behavior as a Product of Psychological Forces," in Walter Reich, ed., *The Origins of Terrorism* (Washington, D.C.: Woodrow Wilson Center Press, 1990), 25–40.

69. Walter Laqueur, *The New Terrorism: Fanaticism and the Arms of Mass Destruction* (New York: Oxford University Press, 1999), 38–40; Jonathan R. White, *Terrorism: An Introduction* (Belmont, Calif.: Wadsworth, 2002), 26.

CHAPTER EIGHT **IN THE NAME OF GOD, THE PEOPLE, AND THE LAND:**
REASSESSMENT OF THE CAUSES OF JEWISH TERRORISM

1. Rikki Tessler, "Religious Radicalism Between/in the Defensive Democracy, Defensive Politics and Defensive Citizenship," *State and Society,* 1, no. 3 (2003): 585–619 (Hebrew).

2. Bert Klandermans and Dirk Oegema, "Potentials, Networks, Motivations and Barriers: Steps Towards Participation in Social Movements," *American Sociological Review,* 52 (1987): 519–532.

3. A. D. Morris and C. M. Mueller, *Frontiers in Social Movement Theory* (New Haven, Conn.: Yale University Press, 1992), 104–132.

4. Christopher R. Browning, Seth L. Feinberg, and Robert D. Dietz, "The Paradox of Social Organization: Networks, Collective Efficacy, and Violent Crime in Urban Neighborhoods," *Social Forces,* 83, no. 2 (2005): 503–534; Nikki M. Ruble and William L. Turner, "A Systematic Analysis of the Dynamics and Organization of Urban Street Gangs," *The American Journal of Family Therapy,* 28, no. 2 (2000): 117–132.

5. Ruble and L. Turner "A Systematic Analysis," 117–132; A. Venkatesh Sudhir, "The Gang in the Community," in Ronald C. Huff, ed., *Gangs in America* (Newbury Park, Calif.: Sage, 1996), 241–255.

6. Klandermans and Oegema, "Potentials," 52.

7. Marc Sageman, *Understanding Terror Networks* (Philadelphia: University of Pennsylvania Press, 2004); Ami Pedahzur and Arie Perliger, "The Changing Nature of Suicide Attacks: A Social Network Perspective," *Social Forces,* 84, no. 4 (2006): 1983–2004.

8. Marc Sageman, *Leaderless Giahd* (Philadelphia: University of Pennsylvania Press, 2007); Ami Pedahzur and Arie Perliger, "Understanding Contemporary Islamic Terrorist Networks," paper presented at the American Political Science Association Meeting, Chicago, September 2007.

9. Sageman, *Leaderless Giahd;* Sageman, *Understanding Terror Networks;* Pedahzur and Perliger, "Understanding Contemporary Islamic Terrorist Networks."

10. Nizar Hamzeh, "Lebanon's Hezbollah: From Islamic Revolution to Parliamentary Accommodation," *Third World Quarterly,* 14, no. 2 (1993): 321–337.

11. Mark Burges, "Explaining Religious Terrorism Part I: The Axis of Good and Evil," CDI.org, 6.

12. Zachary Abuza, "The Moro Islamic Liberation Front," *Studies in Conflict and Terrorism,* 28 (2005): 453–479.

13. John L. Esposito, *Unholy War* (Oxford: Oxford University Press, 2002), 22; Daniel L. Byman, "Al-Qaeda as an Adversary: Do We Understand Our Enemy?" *World Politics,* 56, no. 1 (2003): 145; Yoram Schweitzer and Shaul Shay, *An Expected Surprise: The September 11th Attack and Its Ramifications* (Herzliya, Israel: ICT, 2002), 36.

14. Mark Juergensmeyer, *Terror in the Mind of God: The Global Rise of Religious Violence* (Berkeley: University of California Press, 2000), 123.

15. Ibid.

16. Ibid., 148–153.

17. Bruce Hoffman, "Holy Terror: The Implications of Terrorism Motivated by a Religious Imperative," *Studies in Conflict and Terrorism*, 18 (1995): 273.

18. Juergensmeyer, *Terror in the Mind of God*, 29.

19. Hoffman, "Holy Terror," 272.

20. Juergensmeyer, *Terror in the Mind of God*, 70–71.

21. Esposito, *Unholy War*, 21.

22. Ian Reader, "Specters and Shadows: Aum Shinrikyo and the Road to Megiddo," *Terrorism and Political Violence*, 14, no. 1 (2002): 147–186.

23. It should be noted that short-term ceasefires were adopted by several religious violent groups, especially for tactical reasons, such as regrouping and rehabilitation.

24. Mohammed Hafez, "Armed Islamic Movements and Political Violence in Algeria," *The Middle East Journal*, 54, no. 4 (2000): 577.

25. Abuza, "The Moro Islamic Liberation Front," 453–479.

26. Burges, "Explaining Religious Terrorism Part I," 6, note 1; Juergensmeyer, *Terror in the Mind of God*, 29.

27. Bruce Hoffman, "Rethinking Terrorism and Counterterrorism Since 9/11," *Studies in Conflict and Terrorism*, 25, no. 5 (2002): 303–316.

28. Burges, "Explaining Religious Terrorism Part I," 6.

29. Hoffman, "Holy Terror," 273.

30. Burges, "Explaining Religious Terrorism Part I," 5.

31. Ibid.

32. Pedahzur and Perliger, "The Changing Nature of Suicide Attacks," 1983–2004.

33. For example, refer to the Covenant of the Islamic Resistance Movement (Hamas), http://www.yale.edu/lawweb/avalon/mideast/hamas.htm (April 18, 2006).

34. Anat Shihor-Aharonson, "Charge: Desecration of the Holy Place," NRG, September 4, 2005 (Hebrew), http://www.nrg.co.il/online/1/ART/979/446.html (April 18, 2006).

Abed-Rabo, Yousef, 119
Abu Tor school attack (2002), 111–13, 117, 121–22, 169
Adani, Dror, 105–9
Adei Ad farm, 116, 117
Adkik, Abd al-Razek, 97
Adler, Yaron, 131
African Hebrew Israelite Nation of Jerusalem, 212n36
Agbaria, Jamila, 148
Aizenman, Danny, 143–44
Akko (Acre) prison raid (1947), 25
Alexander the Great, 1
Algeria, 166, 168
Ali Baka mosque attack (1983), 65, 178
all-channel networks, 76, 211n21
Altalena (ship), 26–27
Amari, Eliyahu, 180
Amior, Tzuriel, 117
Amir, Yigal and Hagai, 101–10, 168; alienation from Israeli democracy, 109–10; assassination of Yitzhak Rabin, 101–6, 187; background, 104–5; contrast between Amir group and Gush Emunim and Kahane movement, 109–10; formation of terrorist network, 105–10; ideology, 104–5; rabbinical endorsement sought for killing Rabin, 106–7; radicalization of group, 105, 110; social networks, 107–8
Amira, Mustafa Ziad, 119
Amona settlement, 135–37
Amro, Mohammad, 118

El Anti, Zohair, 64
Antiochus III, 2–3
Antiochus IV, 1
Apelles, 1
Apphus, Yonatan (Jonathan), 3–4
Al-Aqsa Intifada. See Intifada, Second
Al-Aqsa Mosque, 38, 170, 173
Ariel, Israel, 77, 81, 87
Armed Islamic Group (GIA), 166
Aryan Nations, 165
Asli, Fuad, 145
assassinations: in ancient Israel, 1, 6–7; British Mandate era, 14–15, 17–22, 27–28; early statehood era, 28–31; modern era (see targets of Jewish terrorism); and Russian Revolution, 8–9
Asulin, Shlomo, 139
Atiah, Mordechai, 48
Aum Shinrikyo, 164, 165, 166
Avikar, Hagai, 117
Avinar, Shlomo, 59–60
Aviram, Beni, 139, 186
Avraham Avinu neighborhood (Hebron), 89, 171, 184
Avrahami, Yosef, 144
Axlerod, David (Ha'ivri), 131–34
Ayalon Highway plot (2005), 123–25, 192
Azran, Edmund, 77, 84

Bachar, Shimon, 32
Bahus, Michel, 133
Barda, Shimon, 142–43

Bar Giora, Shimon, 5, 199n1

Bar-Giora organization, 10, 199n1

Barker, Ronald, 15

Basic Law, 91, 214n93

Bat Ayin group, 164; Abu Tor school attack (2002), 111–13, 117, 121–22, 169; arrests and convictions of members, 122; contrast to Jewish Underground and Kach networks, 113–14; formation and evolution, 116–22; ideology, 113–14, 116; leadership clique, 117; radicalization, 118; recruitment of members, 117; social networks, 113; terrorist attacks, 111–13, 117–22, 169, 189–90. *See also* hilltop youth

Bat Ayin settlement, 113

Bedouins, 181, 185

Be'eri, Dan: and attack on West Bank mayors, 54; and Kahane movement, 77; and modern Hasmonean Revolt, 85; and social network structure of Jewish Underground, 47–49; and Temple Mount operation, 55, 57, 61

Begin, Menachem: and *Altalena* incident, 26–27; and Camp David Accords, 42, 44; and Etzel organization, 23, 26–27; and Herut Movement, 44, 75; and Kahane movement, 74–75; and Yamit suicide pact, 88

Beit Hadassah attack (1980), 50–55

Beit Safafa mosque attack (1983), 178

Beit-Tsouri, Eliahu, 19, 21–22

Ben Avkulos, Zechariah, 5

Benayun, Uri, 141

Ben-Baruch, Yosef, 121

Ben-David, Haim, 47, 49, 59, 60, 66

Ben-Dor, David, 96

Ben-Dov, Shabtai, 49, 61, 85, 204n1

Ben-Dov, Yael, 85

Ben-Eliezer, Binyamin, 40

Ben-Gurion, David, 26–29, 35, 175

Ben Hanan, Hanan and Hezekiah, 7

Ben-Hananiah, Elazar, 4, 7

Ben-Horin, Michael, 220n55; and Gush Emunim movement, 93, 94; and Gush Katif settlement, 127–29; and Kach movement, 93, 96; and State of Judea movement, 77

Ben-Nun, Yoel, 60, 100, 106

Ben-Shimol, David, 153–55, 158, 179

Ben Shimon, Elazar, 5

Ben-Shushan, Yeshua, 47–49, 54, 55

Ben-Ya'akov, Yekutiel, 77

Ben Yair, Elazar, 7

Ben-Yishai, Samuel, 77, 90, 92

Ben-Yosef, Baruch, 77

Ben-Zvi, Izhak, 199n1

Bernadotte, Count Folke, 27–28

Betar Movement, 12

Biham, Ernest, 175

bin Laden, Osama, 167

biographical availability of terrorists, xii, 158, 162

Black Sabbath (June 29, 1946), 23

Blumenthal, Ya'akov, 33

Bnei Akiva youth movement, 83

Bogrov, Dmitri, 8

Brit Hakanaim (Covenant of the Zealots), 33–37, 175

Brit Hashmonaim movement, 84–85, 213n58

British Mandate, 11–28, 84, 200n17; Black Sabbath (June 29, 1946), 23; Etzel's objections to immigration policies of, 13; Etzel terrorist acts, 13–14, 24–25; the Hunting Season, 23; Lehi terrorist acts, 17–22, 26; United Resistance Movement, 23; UN Partition Plan, 25–28; and WWII, 15–16. *See also* Etzel organization (Irgun); Haganah organization; Lehi organization (Stern Gang); Palmach

Bund movement, 9

Camp David Accords, 171, 205n8; and Brit Hashmonaim movement, 85; and emergence of Jewish Underground,

41–45; and Kahane movement, 74–75, 86–88
Carnes, Ralph, 14–15
Casey, Richard, 19
Caspi, David, 144, 179
Caspi, Yehoshua, 152
catastrophic/precipitating events, xi, 34, 144, 162; Beit Dagan Junction bus incident (1987), 90; Beit Hadassah attack (1980), 50–55; "blood bus" attack (1978), 151–52; Camp David Accords, 41–45, 74–75, 86–88; establishment of the modern state of Israel and objections to its policies, 25–29, 34–36; examples, xii; First Intifada (1987), 92; framing by community leaders, xi, 44, 51, 100–101, 138, 140, 146, 160–61; Gaza disengagement plan, 122–37; Greenwald slander trial, 30; Kahane assassination, 95; kidnapping of Yemeni immigrant children, 138, 140; and lone avengers, 155, 156, 158; Munich Olympics massacre, 80; No. 18 bus attack (1984), 89; Oslo Accords, 70, 98–101, 105–6; personal losses (see vengeance); Second Intifada (2000), 111, 117–18, 147–48; and sense of threat, xi–xii, 34, 44, 67, 100, 160–61. See also motives for terrorist acts; vengeance
Catrieli, Avinoam, 47, 58
Cave of the Patriarchs (Hebron): and Six Day War, 42; terrorist attacks, 69–70, 171, 184–85, 192
Chabad movement, 127, 129, 130; defined, 220n50; and recent counterculture collective, 136–37
Christian fundamentalism, 165, 167, 168
Christian institutions as targets of Jewish terrorism, 82, 140–41, 178
chronology of events, 175–92
Churba, Joseph, 212n30
Churchill, Winston, 22

circular response process, 161
Coen, Yehuda, 47
Cohen, David, 96
Cohen, Shimon, 111
Cohen, Yehoshua, 18, 58
Cohen, Zvi, 207n33
Colombo, Joseph, 212n30
Committee for the Safety of the Roads, 90–94, 183–84
communities. See countercultures; hilltop youth; settler community; social networks; ultra-Orthodox community; Zionists, religious
community/religious leaders, 163; framing of precipitating events, xi, 44, 51, 100–101, 138, 140, 146, 160–61; rabbinical endorsement for attack on West Bank mayors, 51; rabbinical endorsement for Temple Mount operation sought but not given, 59–61, 68; rabbinical endorsement not given for Abu Tor girls' school attack, 121; rabbinical endorsement sought for killing Rabin, 106–7; and resistance to Gaza disengagement plan, 123, 124; and resistance to Oslo Accords, 100–101, 104. See also leadership in terrorist groups; specific groups
Corfu, Haim, 15
countercultures: defined/described, x–xi; and mental illness, 151–53; and radicalization, xi–xii (see also radicalization); recent developments, 136–37; social distance from majority culture, xii, 76, 113–14, 116, 162, 163. See also hilltop youth; ideology; immigrant countercultures; Jewish Underground; Kahane movement; leadership in terrorist groups; social networks; terrorist groups, exceptional cases
counterterrorism: Ayalon Highway plot foiled (2005), 125; and Bat Ayin group,

counterterrorism (*continued*)
111–14, 120, 122; British Mandate era, 20, 23; bus attacks foiled, 66–67, 90; and Camp David Accords, 40; early statehood era, 27–28, 30–31, 36; and Haifa attacks in the early 2000s, 150; and Jewish Defense League, 78; Prevention of Terrorism Ordinance, 28, 71, 211n10. *See also specific plots under* Temple Mount
Covenant of the Zealots (Brit Hakanaim), 33–37
crises leading to terrorist acts. *See* catastrophic/precipitating events
cults. *See* terrorist groups, exceptional cases
cultural (primordial) approach to the study of terrorism, ix
Czech Embassy bombing, 176

Dakkak, Ibrahim, 41
Dayan, Yael, 155
Dayan, Yosef, 77, 81, 213n44
Deheishe refugee camp, 91
demographics, 75–76, 82, 162. *See also* social networks; *specific groups*
Deri, Abraham, 141
Deri, Amram, 141
Deri, David, 141
Deutsch, Avraham, 155, 177
Dimona, 80, 212n36
din rodef, din moser, 100, 106–7, 109
Disciples, the, 94–95
Dkalim, Neve, 127
Dome of the Rock. *See* Temple Mount
Dormition Monastery (Jerusalem), 140
Dov movement, 93
Druckman, Haim, 45
Dueik, Moshe, 28, 177
Dvir-Zeliger, Shahar, 116–17
Dvir-Zeliger, Shlomo, 111–13, 117, 121–22

Eckstein, Ze'ev, 31
Edri, Oren, 98–99

Edri, Yosef, 47
Efroni, Nir, 179
Egypt, 18–22, 41–45, 168
Eichmann, Adolf, 30
Ein Kerem group, 140–41, 146, 178
Ein Vered Circle, 42, 206n12
Eitam, Effi, 135
Eitan, Rafael, 130, 220n56
Eizariya, 140
Elba, Ido, 99
Eldad, Arie, 135
Eldad, Yisrael, 16–17
Eliyahu, Mordechai, 33–36
Elnakam (God of Vengeance) Underground, 96, 183
Elon Moreh settlement, 124, 219n42
Engelsman, Natan, 186
Epstein, Michael, 107–8
Erez, Haim, 88
Essenheim, Yair, 155
Etzel organization (Irgun), 11–15, 213n58; and *Altalena* incident, 26–27; early activities, 12–13; and the Hunting Season, 23; ideology, 11; origins and objectives, 11–12; social dynamics contributing to radicalization, 12; social networks, 12; split with Lehi, 15–18; terrorist acts, 13–15, 24–25; units dismantled, 27; warfare doctrine, 16; and WWII, 15–16
Etzion, Yehuda, 38, 48–50; and attack on West Bank mayors, 51, 53–54; on Beit Hadassah attack, 50; and Islamic College massacre, 63–64; perspective on past events, 62; recruitment of Jewish Underground members, 52; and social network structure of Jewish Underground, 47–50; and Temple Mount operation, 55–56, 59, 61–62
Europe, 163, 169

Faglin, Amichai, 80
Fatafta, Iskhak Mahmoud, 98

Fatafta, Mahmoud Abdul Mahdi, 98
Fatafta, Sa'adi Abdul Mahdi, 98
Fatah, 50–55, 170
Federman, Noam, 77, 92, 96, 120
First Intifada (1987), 92
Florus, Gessius, 4
Foux, Gil, 143–44
Franco, Aliza, 148
Fridman, Ze'ev, 47, 53
Friedman, Noam, 187, 190
Fuchs, Yisrael, 177

Gafner, Benjamin, 20–21
Galili, Menachem and Yehudah, 6
Gal underground, 83–84
Gamliel, Ofer, 117, 121–22
Ganiram, Yitzhak: and Islamic College
    massacre, 64, 65; recruitment of Jewish
    Underground members, 51, 53; and
    social network structure, 47; and
    Temple Mount operation, 49–50, 59
Gaza Strip: Amir's student trips to, 105;
    Gush Katif settlement, 127–29; Maoz
    Yam complex, 127–29; National
    Steering Committee, 41, 205n8;
    resistance to disengagement plan,
    122–37; terrorist attacks, 156, 180,
    182–83. See also Oslo Accords
General Security Service (GSS): and Bat
    Ayin/hilltop youth, 113–14, 120, 122; bus
    attacks foiled, 66–67, 90; Dome of the
    Rock plot foiled, 126; and Haifa attacks
    in the early 2000s, 150; and Lerner's Gal
    underground, 84; Vengeance
    Underground investigation, 98–99
GIA. See Armed Islamic Group
Giladi, Eliyahu, 16
Gilad-Shalhevet Brigades, 120
Gilady, Israel, 199nn 1,2
Gillon, Carmi, 210n120
Gilo, Aaron, 47, 52, 53
Gnaim, Issa, 149
God of Vengeance movement, 95–97

Golan, Eliran, 147–50, 158, 189–90, 192
Golan Heights: and Gush Emunim
    movement, 43–44. See also Jewish
    Underground
Golani Brigade, 104, 108
Goldberg, Leonard, 77
Goldstein, Baruch, 81, 133, 167; background,
    70–71; Cave of the Patriarchs massacre,
    69–70; ideology, 70; motives for
    massacre, 70; and social network, 77
Goldstein, Bat-Sheva, 87
Goodman, Alan, 151–52, 177
Gophstein, Ben-Zion, 77, 96
Gordon, Baruch, 89
Gorelik, Alex, 156
Goren, Shlomo, 88
Great Arab Revolt (1936–1939), 13, 200n17
Great Revolt (66–73 C.E.), 4–8, 173
Greek Orthodox Monastery (Jerusalem), 140
Greenwald, Malchiel, 30
Greenzweig, Emil, 177
Gross, Aharon, 63
Gross, Matti, 15
Groupe Islamique Armé, 168
GSS. See General Security Service
Guinness, Walter Edward (Lord Moyne),
    18–22
Gush Emunim movement, 72, 171, 209n100;
    and Camp David Accords, 86; and
    Elon Moreh settlement, 219n42; goals,
    44; and Herut Movement, 44; ideology,
    42–44; and Kach movement, 75, 93–94;
    leadership, 44, 59
Gush Katif settlement, 127–29
Guzovsky, Mike, 89, 92, 96
Gvaot Olam farm, 115–16, 153

Haber, Eitan, 104
Haetzni, Elyakim, 100
Haganah organization, 10, 171, 213n58; and
    assassination of Lord Moyne, 22–23;
    ceasefire agreement with the British,
    25; and Etzel organization, 12–13

El Hai, Allah Abed, 118
Haifa: and Eliran Golan, 147–50; and Lehi organization, 26; terrorist attacks, 26, 133–34, 144–45, 147–51, 176, 179, 189–90
Ha'ivri, David, 77, 96, 131–33, 134
El Haj Abdallah mosque attack (2001), 148, 150, 190
Hakim, Eliahu, 19, 21–22
Halaf, Karim, 205n8
Halakha (Jewish law), 165, 171; and emergence of Brit Hakanaim organization, 35; and Gaza disengagement plan, 123; and hilltop youth, 114; and Oslo Accords, 100; proscriptions against violence, 8; and Rabin assassination, 106, 109; and Temple Mount operation, 59; and West Bank settlements, 43
Halevy, Benjamin, 30
Hamas, 98, 119, 164, 165–66, 168–70
Hamed, Mohammed, 152
Hamel, Gur, 153, 158, 188
Harel, Dan, 129
Harel, Isser, 29, 31
Har-Shefi, Margalit, 107–9
Hashomer organization, 10, 199n1
Hasmonean revolt, 1–4, 74; Yoel Lerner and the modern Hasmonean Revolt, 84–86
el Hatib, Ali, 95
Hatkhalata De'Guela, 42, 206n13
Hatzadik, Shimon, 126
Haus, Shlomo, 155
Haviv, Avshalom, 25
Hayishuv Hakhadash Yeshiva, 104
Hazan, Levi, 77, 89
Haze'ev, Eli, 77
Hebron, 69–74, 172; attack on the mayors (1980), 39–40; attacks on residents, 99, 183–89, 191; Avraham Avinu neighborhood, 89, 171, 184; and Bat Ayin group, 117; Beit Hadassah attack as precipitating event for Jewish

Underground, 50–55; chronology of terrorist acts, 180, 183–85, 187, 191; and Committee for the Safety of the Roads, 90–91; current conditions, 72–73; and Etzel organization, 12; first settlement in Park Hotel, 72; Hebron market attacks, 92, 177–78; Islamic College massacre (1983), 62–65, 178; and Jewish Underground, 47, 50–55, 62–67; and Kahane movement/Kach, 73–74, 92, 94; Sheikh El Rashad mosque attack (1983), 65; and TNT, 89. See also Bat Ayin group; Cave of the Patriarchs; Goldstein, Baruch; hilltop youth; Kiryat Arba
Heifetz, Jascha, 176
Hen, Elior, 126
Henman, Ben-Zion, 47, 53, 57
Henman, Bohaz, 47, 57, 66, 209n100
Henman, Ya'akov, 57, 58, 209n100
Herod, King of Judea, 6, 198n22
Hershkowitz, Abraham, 77, 78, 80–81
Hershkowitz, Gershon, 77, 96–97
Heruti, Ya'akov, 32–33
Herut movement, 42, 44, 75, 176
Herzog, Chaim, 152
Hezbollah, 164, 165, 170
Hillel, Michal, 143
hilltop youth: defined/described, 113–14; and Gush Katif settlement, 127, 129; Gvaot Olam farm, 115–16, 153; hostility toward Israeli government, 114, 116; ideology, 113–14; leaders, 114–15; names used by, 118, 120; negative interactions with neighboring Palestinians, 114–16; precautions taken to avoid detection, 120; radicalization, 114, 116; and recent counterculture collective, 136–37; and religious Zionists, 75; and Sa Nur settlement, 130; social distance from majority culture, 113–14, 116. See also Bat Ayin group
Hirbawi, Suleiman, 40–41

Hof Dkalim, 127
Hoffman, Bruce, 167
Homeland Front, 28
hooliganism, 78
Hunting Season, the, 23
Husan, 140

ideology, x, 160; Amir group, 104–5; Bat
    Ayin group, 116; Brit Hakanaim
    organization, 35; and comparison of
    Jewish and other religious terrorism,
    164–66; current trends, 170; Ein Kerem
    group, 141; Ein Vered Circle, 206n12;
    and Eldad's writings, 17; Etzel
    organization (Irgun), 11; Gal
    movement, 83; Gush Emunim
    movement, 42–44; Herut Movement,
    44; hilltop youth, 113–14; Kahane
    movement, 70, 73, 74, 131–32, 170;
    Kingdom of Israel organization, 32;
    lack of clear ideology in cases of
    spontaneous vengeance, 143–46; and
    leadership, xi; Lehi organization
    (Stern Gang), 11, 17, 29; Lifta Gang,
    142; modern Hasmonean Revolt, 85;
    and precipitating events, xi (see also
    catastrophic/precipitating events);
    Sicarians, 6–7. See also motives for
    terrorist acts
IDF. See Israel Defense Forces
immigrant countercultures, 76, 97, 138, 163.
    See also Kahane movement
India, 164
Indor, Yosef, 47, 52
Intifada, First (1987), 92
Intifada, Second (2000), 169; Palestinian
    violence, 111, 118, 144; as precipitating
    event, 111, 117–18, 144, 147–48;
    resistance to Gaza disengagement
    plan, 122–37. See also Bat Ayin group;
    hilltop youth
Iovi, Efraim, 184
Irgun. See Etzel organization (Irgun)

Ishah, Aharon, 144–45
Islam, significance of Temple Mount, 38
Islamic College massacre (1983), 62–65, 178
Islamic Jihad, 170
Islamic terrorism. See Salafi jihad
    networks; terrorism, Islamic; specific
    organizations
Israel, ancient, 197–98n14, 198n22; Great
    Revolt (66–73 C.E.), 4–8; Hasmonai
    revolt, 1–4; Sanhedrin, 49, 207n41;
    social networks, 5–6
Israel, early modern period, 10–37, 199nn1, 2;
    Black Sabbath (June 29, 1946), 23;
    British Mandate, 11–28; combat
    doctrine of political left, 10; defense of
    Jewish settlements by Bar-Giora and
    Hashomer militias, 10; Great Arab
    Revolt (1936–1939), 13, 200n17; the
    Hunting Season, 23; split between
    Etzel and Lehi, 15–18; United
    Resistance Movement, 23; UN
    Partition Plan, 25–28; War of
    Independence, 26–27; WWII, 15–16,
    30. See also Etzel organization (Irgun);
    Haganah organization; Lehi
    organization (Stern Gang); Yishuv
Israel, modern state of: amnesty for Lehi
    members, 28; Basic Law, 91, 214n93;
    Camp David Accords, 41–45, 74–75,
    85–88, 171, 205n8; change from
    paramilitary to social network
    structure of terrorist organizations, 33;
    chief rabbis, 214n75; chronology of
    events, 175–92; creation of, 25–28; First
    Intifada (1987), 92; founding myths,
    1–9; Oslo Accords, 70, 98–110, 166, 172;
    Prevention of Terrorism Ordinance,
    28, 71, 211n10; Second Intifada (2000),
    111–37, 147–48, 169; Six Day War (1967),
    42, 205n2; tension over secularization,
    33–36, 85; Yom Kippur War (1973), 38,
    82. See also catastrophic/precipitating
    events; countercultures; Gaza Strip;

Israel, modern state of (*continued*)
ideology; radicalization; settler
community; social networks; targets of
Jewish terrorism; West Bank; *specific
cities*
Israel Defense Forces (IDF): and
Committee for the Safety of the
Roads, 91; formation of, 26; and Gaza
disengagement plan, 122; ineligibility
to serve as contributing factor in
terrorism, 141, 147, 158; and recruitment
of girls, 35
Issa, Schada, 65

Jaber, Aziza, 94
Jabotinsky, Ze'ev, 11, 172
Japan, 164, 165, 166
JDL. *See* Jewish Defense League
Jerusalem: attacks on cars and buses,
66–67, 89–90, 143, 179; attacks on
Christian institutions, 82, 140–41;
attacks on commercial establishments,
154, 183; attacks on homes, 89, 179–80,
187; attacks on residents, 92, 96–97, 155,
179–92; attacks on schools, 111–13,
117–22; chronology of terrorist acts,
175–92; exceptional terrorist groups,
140–43; Israeli sovereignty in East
Jerusalem, 205n2; "Judea Police" in Old
City, 92; No. 18 bus attack (1984), 89;
settlement of Old Jerusalem, 213n58;
terrorism and political activism in
ancient Israel, 4–8; Western Wall, 42,
173. *See also* Temple Mount
Jewish Defense League (JDL), 70, 74–80;
activities of, 78–82; and Munich
Olympics massacre, 80; slogan, 78,
212n30; summer camps, 89; and Yamit
suicide pact, 87–88
Jewish law. *See* Halakha (Jewish law)
Jewish terrorism. *See* terrorism, Jewish
Jewish Underground: Ali Baka mosque
attack (1983), 65, 178; analysis/

conclusions about, 67–68, 164; attack
on the mayors (1980), 39–41, 50–55, 177;
bus attacks, 66; chronology of terrorist
acts, 178–79; disagreement over Temple
Mount operation, 55–56; emergence
following Camp David Accords, 41–45;
founding clique, 48–50; Islamic
College massacre (1983), 62–65, 178;
motives of actors, 46, 48, 63;
precipitating events, 50–55, 63, 65;
rabbinical endorsement for Temple
Mount operation sought but not given,
59–61; recruitment of members, 45,
52–53, 56–57; Sheikh El Rashad
mosque attack (1983), 65; social
networks, 45–50, 53–55, 64; Temple
Mount conspiracy, 46, 48–50, 55–62;
trial of members, 58–59
Jimjum, Nivin, 191
Jordan, and Temple Mount administration,
38, 205n2
Judea Police, 92
Juergensmeyer, Mark, 165

Kach movement, 69–97; avoided by hilltop
youth, 120; chronology of terrorist
acts, 177–78, 180, 184; and Committee
for the Safety of the Roads, 90–94;
declaration of the State of Judea, 93;
disqualified from Twelfth Knesset
elections, 93; and Goldstein, 71;
and Gush Emunim movement,
75; ideology, 74; and Kahane
assassination, 95–96; Kahane's
activities in the Knesset, 92–93;
Kahane's election to the Knesset, 88,
91; leadership, 72 (*see also* Kahane,
Meir); stolen weapons, 94; Yamit
suicide pact, 87–88, 177
Kaczynski, Theodore, 70
Kadosh, Avtalion and Akiva, 126
Kahalani, Eitan, 99, 186
Kahalani, Yehoyada, 99, 186

Kahane, Binyamin, 77, 96

Kahane, Meir, 69–97; arrests, 78, 81; assassination of, 95–97; charisma of, 81; and early JDL activities, 78–82; early years in Israel, 81; elected to Knesset, 88, 91; emigration to Israel, 78–79; founding of Jewish Defense League, 74; and Goldstein, 70–71; ideology, 73, 74, 75; Knesset activities, 92–93; and law enforcement agencies, 78, 212n30; and Libyan Embassy attack, 81, 177; and organized crime, 78, 212n36; reaction to Camp David Accords, 74–75; rebuffed by both mainstream and settlers/religious Zionists, 75; split with Dayan, 213n44; and Yamit suicide pact, 87–88

Kahane Chai, 71, 77, 96, 183

Kahane movement, 71, 164; activities of, 76, 86–88; and Begin, 74–75; and Ben-Horin, 129; Camp David Accords as precipitating event for radicalization, 74–75; and Cave of the Patriarchs massacre, 69–71; demographics, 75–76, 82; and the Disciples, 94–95; and God of Vengeance movement, 95–97; and Gush Katif settlement, 129; and hilltop youth, 114; ideology, 70, 73, 75, 131–32, 170; JDL's early activities, 78–82; leadership clique, 76–77, 81–82; origins, 70, 74–80; and recent counterculture collective, 136–37; and religious Zionists, 70, 75, 124; and Sa Nur settlement, 130; second generation, 77, 92; social networks, 76–77, 92, 97; and State of Judea movement, 93–94; and TNT, 89–90; and Yamit suicide pact, 86–88. *See also* Goldstein, Baruch; Kach movement; Kahane, Meir; Lerner, Yoel

Kanter, Issa, 119

Karamani, Eyal, 126

Karmani, Ronen, 94

Kashmir, 164, 165

Kastner, Israel, 28–31, 177

Kawasma, Fahed, 205n8

Kawasmeh, Faiz, 72

k-core analysis of Jewish Underground, 46–47

Keller, Elyashiv, 99

Kerem D'Yavne Yeshiva, 108

Kfar Tapuach settlement, 96, 131–35

Khalaf, Karim, 40

kiddush Hashem, 132–34, 171–72

King David Hotel attack (1946), 20

Kingdom of Israel organization (Tzrifin Underground), 31–33, 175, 176

Kiryat Arba, 211n13; and Committee for the Safety of the Roads, 90–91; founding of, 72; terrorist acts by settlers from, 177, 181, 183–86, 188; and Vengeance Underground, 99

Klandermans, Bert, 161

Kook, Zvi Yehuda Hacohen, 44, 61, 83, 94, 172, 207n29

Koren, Meir, 186

Laqueur, Walter, 157

leadership in terrorist groups, 161–62; Bat Ayin group, 117; contrast between exceptional terrorist groups and groups with established ideological bases, 146; Ein Kerem group, 141; and framing of precipitating events, xi, 44, 67, 138, 140, 146; Gush Emunim movement, 44, 59; hilltop youth, 114–15; Jewish Underground, 48–50; Kach movement, 72 (*see also* Kahane, Meir); Kahane movement, 76–77, 81–82; Lifta Gang, 142; Meshulam cult, 138–40. *See also* community/ religious leaders; social networks; *specific organizations*

Lebanon, 164

Lederman, Yisrael, 155, 158, 177

Lehi organization (Stern Gang), 11, 213n58; amnesty for members, 28; disarmed, 27; and the Hunting Season, 23; ideology, 11, 17, 29; origins and objectives, 11, 16; split with Etzel, 15–18; terrorist acts, 17–22, 26–27, 31, 175; and UN Partition Plan, 25–26

Leibovitch, Eliezer, 191

Leitner, Craig, 77, 89

Lekert, Hirsh, 9

Lerner, Yoel, 82–84; arrests and imprisonments, 84–85; and Dome of the Rock plot, 85–86; and Gal underground, 83–84; and modern Hasmonean Revolt, 84–86; and social network, 77

Levinger, Menachem, 190, 211n13

Levinger, Moshe, 51, 72–73, 211n14

Levinstein, Elitzur, 123–26, 192

Levinstein, Mordechai (Mordi), 123–26, 192

Levkowitz, Avraham (Mordechai), 123–26, 192

Levy, Moshe, 88

Levy, Ron, 154

Libyan Embassy attack (Rome), 80–81, 177

Liebowitz, Matt, 77, 89

Lifta Gang, 141–43, 146, 157, 178

Limaei, Yehuda, 142–43

Lithuania, 9

Livni, Menachem, 209n118; and attack on West Bank mayors, 51, 53, 54; on deterrence, 52; and Islamic College massacre, 63–64; recruitment of Jewish Underground members, 53; and Sheikh El Rashad mosque attack, 65; and social network structure of Jewish Underground, 47–49; and Temple Mount operation, 55–57, 59, 61

Livyatan, Shlomo, 47, 52, 53

Lorentz, Shlomo, 33

Maccabees. See Hasmonean revolt

MacMichael, Harold, 17–18

Magidish, Uri, 184

Mahmid, Yousef, 148

Mahsaya, Uzi, 142–43

al-Majaydeh, Hilal Ziad, 128

Makhoul, Issam, 149, 192

Makhoul, Suad, 149, 192

Maon Farm, 116, 117

Maoz Yam complex, 127–29

Martaga, Ibrahim, 156

martyrdom. See kiddush Hashem

Marzel, Baruch, 72–73, 77, 81, 92, 96

Masada, 4, 7

al-Matar, Jamal Ismail, 154, 179

Mattityahu (Mattathias), 1, 3

Meir, Kuzriel, 94–95

Meir, Uri, 47, 53, 209n100

Menkes, Joseph, 31

mental illness, 143, 147–53, 156–58

Meshbaum, Nehemia, 77, 96–97

Meshulam, Uzi: cult of, 138–40, 146, 185, 187, 221n8

Milner, Felix, 144–45, 158, 188

Mishkan, Misha, 84

mobilization potential, 161

monasteries, 140

Morag, Yarden, 111–13, 117, 120–22

Morali, Daniel, 186

Moro Islamic Liberation Front, 164, 166

mosques: Ali Baka mosque attack (1983), 65, 178; Al-Aqsa Mosque, 38, 170, 173; Beit Safafa mosque attack (1983), 140–41, 178; Dome of the Rock (see Temple Mount); El Haj Abdallah mosque attack (2001), 148, 150, 190; Sheikh El Rashad mosque attack (1983), 65

motives for terrorist acts, x; deterring Palestinian terrorism, 46, 51, 52, 70, 89–90, 120; disrupting evacuation of settlers from Gaza Strip, 122–37; disrupting evacuation of settlers from Sinai Peninsula, 52, 55, 86–87; disrupting Oslo Accords implementation, 70, 100, 101, 105–6; disrupting the peace process between Israel and Arab countries, 51–52; hostility toward Israeli government, 102, 109–10, 114, 116, 135, 160; maintaining relations among friends, 46; perception of ethnic discrimination, 138, 140; religious motives, 46, 48–50, 56, 74, 83, 100, 114, 142; revenge (*see* vengeance). *See also* ideology

Movement to Halt the Retreat in Sinai, 44, 86, 172

Moyne, Lord (Walter Edward Guinness), 18–22

Munich Olympics massacre (1972), 80

Muslim Brotherhood, 168

Nablus: attack on the mayors (1980), 39–40, 53–54

Nakar, Meir, 25

Nasser, Muhammad, 148

Natan-Zada, Eden, 134, 192

Natanzon, Natan, 45–46, 47, 52–54, 209n100

National Steering Committee (West Bank and Gaza Strip), 41, 205n8

Natshe, Ahmed Hamzi, 41

Neuberger, Menachem, 47, 53, 60, 209n100

New York City, and Kahane movement, 70

Nicholas II, Tsar of Russia, 8

Nir, Barak, 47, 63–64, 66

Nir, Shaul, 47, 63–67, 210n120

Norzich, Vadim, 144

Novik, Yitzhak, 47, 52

Odessa Group, 12

Oegema, Dirk, 161

Oklahoma City bombing, 164–65

Orthodox community. *See* ultra-Orthodox community

Oslo Accords, 98, 166, 172; Amir group and the assassination of Yitzhak

Rabin, 101–10; and Cave of the Patriarchs massacre, 70; resistance of religious Zionist community, 100–101, 104; and Vengeance Underground, 98–101

Palestine. *See* Israel, ancient; Israel, early modern period

Palestine Liberation Organization (PLO), 80, 166, 205n8. *See also* Oslo Accords

Palestinian Islamic Jihad, 164, 165, 166, 169

Palestinian National Authority (PNA), 70

Palestinians: and Camp David Accords, 42, 205n8; Kahanist ideas on, 73; National Steering Committee, 41, 205n8; negative interactions with settlers, 113, 114, 115–16, 128, 219n41; suicide bombers, 97, 111, 148. *See also* Intifada, First; Intifada, Second; targets of Jewish terrorism; vengeance; *specific cities*

Paley, Gil'ad, 47, 49, 54, 59, 60, 209n100

Palmach, 10–11, 23, 172

Pantik, Yitzhak, 67

Park Hotel settlement, 72

Partition Plan, 25–28

Pass, Shalhevet, 117–18

Pass, Yitzhak, 117–18, 122

Pawacha, Moussa, 119

Peres, Shimon, 103

Pharisees, 4, 198n14

Philippines, 164, 166

Pinkas, David, 34, 175

Pinner, Daniel, 94

PLO. *See* Palestine Liberation Organization

PNA. *See* Palestinian National Authority

Polak, Tiran, 77, 92, 96

political activism: in ancient Israel, 1–8; 19th and early 20th century, 8–9. *See also* Gush Emunim movement; settler community political parties: and Basic Law, 91, 214n93; Bund, 9; Herut, 42, 44, 75, 176; Kahane Chai, 71, 77, 96; and Prevention of Terrorism Ordinance, 28, 71, 211n10; Tzomet, 220n56. *See also* Kach movement

Popper, Ami, 150–51, 158, 182–83

Porat Yosef yeshiva, 33

Portugaly, Mendel, 199n2

Prevention of Terrorism Ordinance, 28, 71, 211n10

primordial (cultural) approach to the study of terrorism, ix

public opinion, 17, 55–56, 167

Al-Qaeda, 164, 166, 170

Rabin, Yitzhak: assassination of, 101–6, 187 (*see also* Amir, Yigal and Hagai); on Goldstein and Cave of the Patriarchs massacre, 71; and Halakha (Jewish law), 106, 109; and religious Zionists' reactions to Oslo Accords, 100

Rabinovitch, Alexander, 148–49

Rabo, Asher, 153, 177

radicalization, xi–xii, 118, 163; and Amir group, 105, 110; and Brit Hakanaim, 36; circular response process, 161; and Ein Kemem group, 141; and Etzel organization, 12; and hilltop youth/Bat Ayin group, 114, 116, 118; and Jewish Underground, 67–68; and Kingdom of Israel, 33; and Meshulam cult, 140; and Orthodox community, 126; and Vengeance Underground, 99. *See also* catastrophic/precipitating events

Raful-Rafael, Eliyahu, 36

Ramallah: lynching incident, 144–45; terrorist attacks, 39–40, 54, 64, 90, 118, 186, 188–89

Ran, Avri, 114–15

Rapaport, Ira, 47, 52, 54

Rashid, Miriam Salman, 95

rational choice theory, ix

Raziel, David, 15–16

religion. *See* community/religious leaders; Halakha (Jewish law); ideology; motives for terrorist acts; Temple Mount; ultra-Orthodox community; Zionists, religious

research methodology, xii–xiv, 46, 196–97nn29–31

Revava movement, 134

Revenge of the Infants, 120, 190

Revisionist movement, 11, 172

Richter, Yehuda, 77, 81, 87–88

Rieder, Yehuda, 36

Roman Empire, 3–8, 198n22

Rome. *See* Libyan Embassy attack

Royal Broadcasting House attack (1939), 14

Rubin, Yoram, 103

av-Rumeilah, Riad, 152

Russian Revolution, 8–9

Sabbath, as polarizing issue, 34–35

Sabha, Musa Abu, 156

Sadducees, 4, 197–98n14

Sa'id, Avner, 139, 186

Salafi jihad networks, 76, 97, 163, 165, 169

Salakh, Bassam, 189

Salim, Issa Mahmoud, 118

Sanhedrin, 49, 207n41

Sa Nur settlement, 129–31

Sayeret Hanekama (Vengeance Patrol), 97

Schneerson, Menachem Mendel, 142, 220n50

Schneider, Joseph, 80–81

schools, as terrorist targets, 111–12, 117, 119–22, 169

Schwartz, Eric, 107–8

Season, the. *See* Hunting Season, the

Second Intifada. *See* Intifada, Second

Second Temple era, 1–8, 172–73, 197–98n14

Segal, Hagai, 47, 52, 61

Segal, Moshe Zvi, 77, 84–85, 213n58

Segev, Barak, 111

Seleucid dynasty, 2–3
September 11, 2001, 169
Seri, Revital, 154
"serial stabber," 187–88
settler community: Adei Ad farm, 116, 117; Amona settlement, 135–37; authority in law enforcement, 43; Bat Ayin settlement, 113; chronology of terrorist acts by settlers, 177–91; Ein Vered Circle, 42, 206n12; Elon Moreh settlement, 219n42; frontier culture, 43; Gush Katif settlement, 127; Gvaot Olam farm, 115–16, 153; Kfar Tapuach settlement, 131–35; Kiryat Arba settlement (see Kiryat Arba); Maon Farm, 116, 117; Maoz Yam complex, 127; Meshulam cult, 138–40; negative interactions with neighboring Palestinians, 113, 114, 115–16, 128, 219n41; permission to carry weapons, 108, 217n44; resistance to Gaza disengagement plan, 122–37; resistance to Oslo Accords, 100–101; resistance to Sinai Peninsula evacuation, 52, 55, 86–87; Sa Nur settlement, 129–31; secular support for, 42, 43; Yitzhar settlement, 124, 219n41. See also Gaza Strip; Gush Emunim movement; hilltop youth; Sinai Peninsula; West Bank; specific cities
Shabaz, Gil, 112
Shabo, Matityahu, 122
Shabo, Yoav, 139
Shahar, Tal, 77, 96–97
Shaka, Bassam, 40, 53, 54, 205n8
Shamgar, Meir, 70
Shami, Ziad, 99
Shamir, Yitzhak, 16, 21
Shapira, Avraham, 94
Sharabaf, Uzi, 47, 64, 65
Shar'abi, Yeshayahu, 32
Sharon, Ariel, 122–23
Sheikh El Rashad mosque attack (1983), 65

Shevi, Yoav, 186
Shilansky, Dov, 31, 176
Shin Bet, 31, 36. See also General Security Service
Shkolnik, Yoram, 155–56, 184
Shohat, Israel, 199n1
Sicarians, 6–7
Sicarii movement, 93, 182
Silva, Flavius, 7
Sinai Peninsula: and Gush Emunim movement, 43–44, 86; and Jewish Underground, 52, 55; and Kahane movement, 86–88; Movement to Halt the Retreat in Sinai, 44, 86, 172
Sitner, Yosef, 21
Six Day War (1967), 42, 205n2
Skornik, Ohad, 107–9
Smirnov, David, 156, 192
socialization, x–xii; secondary mechanisms (media etc.), 158; social distance of terrorists from majority culture, xii, 76, 110, 113–14, 116, 162, 163. See also countercultures; ideology; radicalization; social networks
social networks, xii–xiii, 160–63; all-channel networks, 76, 211n21; and Amir group, 107–8; in ancient Israel, 5–6; and Bat Ayin group/hilltop youth, 113; and Brit Hakanaim organization, 33, 35–36; central figures/hubs, 45, 48, 54, 68, 161, 207n31 (see also leadership in terrorist groups); circular response process, 161; and Ein Kemem group, 141; and Etzel organization, 12; and exceptional terrorist groups, 140–41, 144, 147, 157–58; and Jewish Underground, 45–50, 53–57; and Kahane movement, 76–77, 92, 93, 97; and Kingdom of Israel organization, 33; and lone avengers, 157–58; overlap in network membership, 93; peripheral collaborators, 162; similarity to Salafi jihad networks, 76, 97; and terrorist

social networks (*continued*)
  acts in Israel's early statehood period,
    29; and Vengeance Underground, 99.
  See also radicalization; terrorist cells
Sons of Judah cult, 142
Soufir, Julian, 192
Soviet Embassy attack (1953), 31
Soviet targets in the U.S., 78–79
Srour, Eliahu, 142–43
Srour, Nissim, 143
Starashnatzev, Irena, 155–56, 158
State of Judea movement, 93–94
Stern, Avraham (Yair), 16, 19–20, 84
Stern Gang. *See* Lehi organization (Stern
    Gang)
Stolypin, Pyotr, 8
street gangs, 161
subcultures, x, 160. *See also* countercultures;
    Gush Emunim movement; hilltop
    youth; immigrant countercultures;
    Kahane movement; settler community;
    ultra-Orthodox community; Zionists,
    religious
suicide: of Eliran Golan, 150; Masada
    fortress mass suicide, 7; Yamit suicide
    pact, 87–88, 177
suicide bombers, 97, 111, 148, 167
Sword of Gideon, 120

Takhan, Khalil Ben Saud, 155
Tamir, Shmuel, 30
targets of Jewish terrorism: Bedouins, 181,
    185; Cave of the Patriarchs, 69–70, 185;
    Christian institutions, 82, 140–41, 178;
    chronology of events, 175–92;
    commercial establishments, 36, 89,
    144–45, 154, 177–79, 183; Czech targets,
    176; Deheishe refugee camp, 91;
    doctors, 153; Dome of the Rock (*see*
    Temple Mount); farmers and villagers,
    153, 181, 182, 185–88, 191; foreign
    diplomats, 175–76; Islamic College
    students, 62–65, 178; Israeli

government officials, 28–31, 36, 98–110,
    149, 175, 177, 187; Israeli law
    enforcement personnel, 135–36, 139, 185,
    186; Jewish-Arab couples, 148–50, 189;
    Libyan Embassy (Rome), 80–81, 177;
    and mass casualties, 167–69; monks
    and nuns, 140–41, 153, 178; mosques,
    65–68, 140–43, 148, 150, 178, 190 (*see also*
    Temple Mount); musicians, 176;
    Palestinian citizens (*see specific city*);
    pilgrims, 153; schools, 111–13, 117–22,
    169, 190, 191; secular society, 168, 175;
    Soviet targets, 31, 78–79, 176. *See also*
    Gaza Strip; Haifa; Hebron; Jerusalem;
    Ramallah; Tel Aviv; West Bank
Tawil, Ibrahim, 40
Tears of the Widows and the Orphans, 118,
    120
Tehomi, Avraham, 12
Tel Aviv: and *Altalena* incident, 27; Ayalon
    Highway plot (2005), 123–25, 192;
    Kastner assassination, 28–29; and Lehi
    organization, 17–18, 20, 24, 31–32;
    Rabin assassination, 101–6, 187;
    terrorist attacks, 17–18, 24, 31, 123–26,
    175–76, 179, 186
Temple Mount: administration by
    Jordanian Waqf, 38, 205n2; Brit
    Hashmonaim sabotage plot, 85–86;
    current security measures, 38;
    described, 173; Etzion's sabotage plot,
    38, 39, 55–62; Goodman's shooting
    spree, 152, 177; Kadosh brothers'
    anti-tank missile plot, 126; Lifta Gang
    sabotage plot, 141–42, 178; potential
    consequences of a successful strike,
    170; rabbinical endorsement for
    Temple Mount operation sought but
    not given, 59–61; and religious goals of
    terrorists, 39, 46, 48–50, 83, 141, 170;
    significance in Islamic and Jewish
    traditions, 38–39
Terra Sancta (Jerusalem), 140

terrorism, approaches to study of, ix–xii; *k*-core analysis of networks, 46–47; primordial (cultural) approach, ix; problems with organizational assumption, 159–60; and rational choice theory, ix; research methodology, xii–xiv, 196–97nn29–31. *See also* catastrophic/precipitating events; countercultures; ideology; leadership in terrorist groups; motives for terrorist acts; radicalization; social networks

terrorism, Islamic, 163–69. *See also* Palestinians; Salafi jihad networks; vengeance; *specific groups*

terrorism, Jewish: chronology of events, 175–92; compared to other manifestations of religious terrorism, 162–69; current trends, 164, 169–70; defined, xii–xiii; demographics, 75–76, 82, 162; lack of institutional structure in many Jewish terrorist groups, 45, 92, 113, 159–60; and public opinion, 17, 55–56, 167; recruitment of members, 168–69 (*see also* social networks); terrorism and political activism in ancient Israel, 1–8. *See also* Amir, Yigal and Hagai; Bat Ayin group; Brit Hakanaim (Covenant of the Zealots); catastrophic/precipitating events; Committee for the Safety of the Roads; Dov movement; Elnakam Underground; Etzel organization (Irgun); Gal underground; God of Vengeance movement; Hasmonean revolt: modern Hasmonean revolt; hilltop youth; Jewish Underground; Kach movement; Kahane movement; Kingdom of Israel organization; Lehi organization (Stern Gang); motives for terrorist acts; radicalization; Sicarii movement; social networks; targets of Jewish terrorism; terrorist cells;

terrorist groups, exceptional cases; terrorists, characteristics of; TNT

terrorist cells: Amir group, 108; Bat Ayin group, 113, 118–22; Gal network, 83; hilltop youth, 120; Jewish Underground, 45–46, 54–55; Kadosh brothers cell, 126; Kahanist networks, 93; Levinstein brothers cell, 123–26; and socialization processes among peers, x. *See also* social networks

terrorist groups, exceptional cases, 138–58; analysis of exceptional groups, 145–47; Ein Kerem group, 140–41, 146; Lifta Gang, 141–43, 146, 157; lone avengers, 153–58; and mental illness, 143, 147–53, 156–58; Meshulam cult, 138–40, 146; "serial stabber," 187–88; spontaneous vengeance, 143–46

terrorists, characteristics of: biographical availability of terrorists, xii, 158, 162; demographics, 75–76, 82, 162; ineligibility for IDF as contributing factor in terrorism, 141, 147, 158; and mental illness, 143, 147–53, 156–58; social distance from majority culture, xii, 76, 110, 113–14, 116, 162, 163. *See also* ideology; motives for terrorist acts; radicalization; social networks

Thassi, Shimon (Simon), 3–4

Third Temple, 11, 83, 142, 165, 204n1, 205n3

Tibi, Avraham, 99

Tikman, Danny, 144–45, 158, 188

TNT (Terrorism Against Terrorism), 89–90, 178–79

Tor, Sela, 116

Tor, Yehoshafat, 114–15, 116

Tsfati, Avraham, 175

Tubol, Lior, 94

Tutanji, Hamis, 143–44, 179

Tzomet, 220n56

Tzrifin Underground, 31–33, 176

Tzur Baher boys' school attack, 119–20

Tzuria, Yosef, 47

ultra-Orthodox community: contrast to Kahane movement, 74; objections to establishment of secular state and its policies, 34–36; radicalization, 126; and recent counterculture collective, 136–37; and Sa Nur settlement, 130. *See also* Brit Hakanaim (Covenant of the Zealots)

unemployment, 162

United Resistance Movement, 22–25

United States: Christian fundamentalism, 165, 167, 168; and Kahane movement's origins in JDL, 70, 74–80; Soviet targets in, 78–79; Weatherman underground movement, 8–9

UN Partition Plan, 25–28

Vanunu, Eli, 179

Vargas, Danny, 188

vengeance, 94, 98, 101, 144, 154; for Beit Hadassah attack, 50–55; for "blood bus" attack, 151; for Kahane assassination, 95–97; mindset of lone wolf avengers, 156–58; for Munich Olympics massacre, 80; for No. 18 bus attack, 89; for personal losses, 63, 68, 117–18, 153–56; for Second Intifada violence, 117–20, 144; spontaneous vengeance, 143–45

Vengeance Patrol (Sayeret Hanekama), 97

Vengeance Underground, 98–101

Verthaim, Moshe, 77

Vespasianus, Emperor of Rome, 5

Vietnam War, 9

Vilna, Lithuania, 9

Visoli, Aviad, 150

Waldeman, Rabbi, 51, 53

Wallerstein, Pinchas, 181

Walls, Nachshon (Wolf), 94–95, 183

Waqf, 38, 205n2

Weatherman underground movement, 8–9

Weinberg, Avishalom, 107–8

Weisenberg, May, 14

Weiss, Yaakov, 25

Wermesser, Noah, 36

West Bank: Amir's student trips to, 105; Amona settlement, 135–37; attack on the mayors (1980), 39–41, 51–55, 177; consequences of settlers' authority in law enforcement, 43; difficulty of travel, 129, 131; Elon Moreh settlement, 219n42; first settlement in Park Hotel, 72; frontier culture of settlers, 43; Kfar Tapuach settlement, 131–35; Kiryat Arba settlement (*see* Kiryat Arba); National Steering Committee, 41, 205n8; political activism of settlers, 42–43; removal of settlements in northern Samaria, 123, 129–31; Sa Nur settlement, 129–31; Yitzhar settlement, 124, 219n41. *See also* Cave of the Patriarchs; Hebron; hilltop youth; Jewish Underground; Oslo Accords; *other cities*

Western Wall (Jerusalem), 42, 173

White, Jonathan, 157

Wolf, Nachshon. *See* Walls, Nachshon (Wolf)

Wolf, Ze'ev, 77, 96–97

World War II, 15–16, 30

Yadin, Yigal, 27

Yad L'akhim, 178, 179

Yamit, 44, 86–88, 177

Yatta schoolyard attack (2002), 119, 191

Yehudah (Judah), son of Matityahu, 3

Yellin-Mor, Natan, 16, 21

Yemen: and Meshulam cult, 138

Yenon, Noam, 47

Yeshiva, Mercaz Harav, 94

Yeshiva of the Jewish Idea, 94, 96

Yeshivat Hesder, 173

Yishuv, 11, 13, 15, 25, 173. *See also* British Mandate; Israel, early modern period

Yisraeli, Tikvah, 15
Yitzhar settlement, 124, 219n41
yochanan, 5
Yom Kippur War (1973), 37, 82
Yonatan (High Priest assassinated by
    Sicarians), 7
Yosef, Yonatan, 94
young people, as dominant demographic
    group involved in terrorism, 162. *See
    also* hilltop youth; social networks
Yousef, Ramzi, 95

Zada, Eden Natan. *See* Nata-Zada, Eden
Zalman, Schneur, 220n50
Zar, Moshe, 47, 51, 54
Zeevi, Rehavam, 190
Zfati, Avraham, 28
El Zid, Suliman, 65

Zionists, religious, 213n58; Amir group,
    101–10; and assassination of Yitzhak
    Rabin, 98–110; and Brit Hashmonaim
    movement, 84; community leaders,
    100–101, 213n58; contrast to Kahane
    movement, 74; and Gush Katif
    settlement, 129; and Hatkhalata
    De'Guela, 42, 206n13; and hilltop
    youth, 75, 115; and Kahane movement,
    70, 75, 124; political activism of West
    Bank settlers, 42–43; and recent
    counterculture collective, 136–37;
    resistance to Gaza disengagement
    plan, 123–37; resistance to Oslo
    Accords, 100–101, 104; Revisionist
    movement, 172. *See also* community/
    religious leaders; Gush Emunim
    movement